THE MAGIC MIRROR

General Editors
David Bordwell, Vance Kepley, Jr.
Supervising Editor
Kristin Thompson

THE MAGIC MIRROR

Moviemaking in Russia 1908–1918

DENISE J. YOUNGBLOOD

THE UNIVERSITY OF WISCONSIN PRESS

The University of Wisconsin Press
2537 Daniels Street
Madison, Wisconsin 53718

3 Henrietta Street
London WC2E 8LU, England

1   3   5   4   2

Printed in the United States of America

Library of Congress Cataloging-in-Publication Data
Youngblood, Denise J. (Denise Jeanne), 1952–
The magic mirror : Moviemaking in Russia, 1908–1918 /
Denise J. Youngblood.
232 pp.   cm. — (Wisconsin studies in film)
Filmography: p.
Includes bibliographical references and index.
ISBN 0-299-16230-3 (cloth: alk. paper).
ISBN 0-299-16234-6 (pbk: alk. paper).
1. Motion pictures — Russia — History.   2. Motion pictures — Soviet
Union — History.   I. Title.   II. Series.
PN1993.5.R9Y59   1999
791.43′0947′09041 — dc21   98-48706

In the hands of man, the screen is a magic mirror in which . . . life in all its variety is reflected.

Pegasus, 1915

CONTENTS

ILLUSTRATIONS

ix

Costume Dramas

Frame enlargement from Petr Chardynin's *The Boyar's Daughter* (1911)
Frame enlargement from André Maître and Kai Hansen's
  Princess Tarakanova (1910)

Literary Adaptions

Frame enlargement from Petr Chardynin's *The Idiot* (1910)
Still from Iakov Protazanov's *The Queen of Spades* (1916)

PREFACE

THIS IS THE STORY OF HOW THE CINEMA, A COMMERCIAL, TECHNOLOGI-
cal, and therefore thoroughly Western art form, developed in Russia, a
newly urbanizing and Westernizing society. A "local history" of the movies
in Russia, *The Magic Mirror* provides a window into middle-class city life
in Russia. It is an album full of snapshots of life as it was dreamed, not by
Romanovs or revolutionaries, but by some of those ordinary, anonymous,
and not very glamorous Russians who passed through history leaving
scarcely a trace behind. Like all local histories, this one deals with large
issues — the social, economic, and cultural implications of urbanization
and modernization — on a small scale, the more precisely to see them.

It is a work that grew out of my previous studies of early Soviet cinema,
and the questions I could not answer about the extent of the relationship
between Soviet cinema in the 1920s and its Russian parent. The chapters
that follow negate a number of my earlier conclusions about the novelty
and uniqueness of early Soviet cinema, especially those in my first book,
Soviet Cinema in the Silent Era. As we shall see by the end, few of the
concerns — or solutions — of Soviet cinema were new at all, most having
deep roots in the Russian past.

When the movies came to Russia in the spring and summer of 1896,
only a few months after the first screenings in Paris in December 1895,
the empire was in the first stages of a rapid, if highly uneven, process of
industrialization and urbanization. Although Russia's social and political
instability had long-standing and complicated causes that were quite independent of its late surge toward "modernization," this instability was

exacerbated by the pressures of industrialization, which brought an increased push for adoption of Western mores and values.

Western European influences profoundly affected the film industry's evolution, and we shall see that in most important respects, Russian cinema follows European patterns with only the most minor variations. Given the pioneering role of the French in the development of the movie industry in Europe, their early technical superiority over Edison, and the heavy investment of French capital in Russian markets by the 1890s, it was only natural that the French should introduce cinema to Russia. French companies — first Lumière, and then Pathé and Gaumont after the turn of the century — dominated the fledgling Russian market until 1908. (Indeed, the French dominated the European market until World War I.)

The movies shown in Russia in these early days were the same as those screened in other European countries: the highly popular *tableaux vivants*, "events" of the day, comic sketches, exotica, and a few short melodramas. French filmmakers also began to make movies on Russian themes, notably historical costume extravaganzas (although on a small scale) to cater not only to Russian audiences, but also to the European desire to learn more about Russian culture and experience vicariously "exotic" Russian life.[1]

The native industry (that is, Russian films made by Russian producers and directors) had its uncertain beginnings about a decade later, in 1907–8. With many of the early entrepreneurs having learned the trade at Pathé and Gaumont in Moscow — and a few in Paris itself — it is not surprising that it took time for a distinctive Russian style to emerge. But the first Russian filmmakers recognized that they would have to compete with the technically superior and better financed European productions for a long time. Their best hope, therefore, would be to develop a niche market for authentic Russian films that would also serve as an export cinema for the rest of Europe. From 1908 to the end of 1914, when war began to impede the importation of foreign films into the country, Russian filmmakers specialized in literary and historical melodramas with a Russian flavor. (As we shall see, making inroads into French and then American domination of the comedy market proved almost impossible.)

By 1914, then, there was a small but established and sophisticated filmmaking community centered in Moscow, ready to take advantage of the remarkable opportunity the war offered to dominate the domestic market. This market was small and decidedly urban, but not inconsiderable given that the urban elite had the most discretionary income. Russian city dwellers had already developed a taste for the movies, and the market was ripe for expansion. At this time, all cities of any size in European Russia had at least one movie theater, and major cities like St. Petersburg, Moscow, Kiev, and Odessa had many theaters ranging from the grand "palace" to the modest "storefront" operation at a railroad station. In addition, the Russian audience was early characterized by its class differentiation, with audiences drawn from among the skilled workers, the professional classes, and the artistic elite, and, paradoxically, by a markedly "bourgeois" orientation.

As admittedly localized and marginalized as it was in the context of late imperial history, cinema nonetheless holds great potential to enlighten us about urban life, reactions to modernization, and the creation of a new public cultural arena. We can also learn much about culture and society in the cities by examining the reasons Russian urbanites were attracted to the movies. As in every other country in Europe and North America, the cinema's initial appeal was its novelty. In an era of fads, movies were the most amazing fad of all. But unlike the crazes for roller skating or the tango, movie madness did not fade away to become a historical curiosity. Endlessly adaptable, the moving picture epitomized modernity by capturing the ephemera of modern life on screen. Like the "magic mirror" of my epigraph, the movies reflected and validated the passions of the moment: the books people read (or always meant to read), the plays they attended (or wanted to attend), their idols (from Lev Tolstoi to Max Linder), their entertainments (the newer and stranger, the better), their hunger for sensation, particularly of the catastrophic variety.

But in Russia, the cinema was more than commodified entertainment. It was also commodified culture, available to anyone who had forty kopeks. Early filmmakers, often drawn from the Westernized younger generation of the merchant caste (*kupechestvo*), were self-conscious promoters of their perceived "civilizing" mission. The movies, through the high life shown in increasingly popular contemporary melodramas, could serve as a "guide to life," much as novels had served the reading public in the nineteenth century. Better than any etiquette book, films could show those aspiring to improve themselves how to behave graciously, how to dress beautifully, how to eat elegantly, how to dance gracefully—how to live.

Closely connected to this, and certainly inextricably linked to the self-interest of the producers, was that the dream world shown on screen demonstrated how social status could be obtained through the consumption and display of material goods, rather than by birthright. Not coincidentally (though probably unconsciously), the goods consumed on screen were the very same soft goods (clothing, jewelry, furniture, fine foods and wine) that were central to the business concerns of the merchantry. The same is true of the modes of entertainment seen on screen: fashionable shops, food emporia, shopping arcades, cafes, restaurants, cabarets, theaters, dance halls, amusement parks, roller rinks, and public stables.

The pages that follow seek to describe cinema in Russia from its origins in 1896 to the end of its first Russian phase in 1918, focusing mainly on the decade 1908–18. By so doing, I hope to provide another angle on an era most often viewed through the revolutionary lens. As we shall see, early Russian cinema provides a parallel history of the nation on the eve of revolution. Through an analysis of the industry, its producers, its films, its audiences, we can see how "modernity" was constructed in a Russian context. Far from the intellectual abstractions in the pages of the nineteenth century's "thick" journals like *European Herald* (*Vestnik Evropy*) or *Russian Wealth* (*Russkoe bogatstvo*), movies illuminate, reflect, capture, and mediate the popular attitudes of the times—what *was*, rather than what *should be*.

Like most scholarly endeavors, this one could not exist without the foundations laid by its predecessors. I consulted numerous books and articles on the Russian, European, and American cultural, social, and cinematic fin de siècle, but I owe particular intellectual debts to the writings of Edith Clowes, Samuel Kassow, Thomas Owen, JoAnn Ruckman, and James L. West on the *kupechestvo*; Jeffrey Brooks, Louise McReynolds, and Richard Stites on Russian popular culture; James Bater, Joseph Bradley, Michael Hamm, and Daniel Brower on urbanization; Laurie Bernstein, Laura Engelstein, and Joan Neuberger on Russian urban culture.

I am especially indebted to Yuri Tsivian, whose pathbreaking works on early Russian cinema sparked my own interest in the subject—and whose sustained efforts to preserve the extant body of work made this research possible. This book should, therefore, be regarded as a companion, not a competitor, to Tsivian's *Early Cinema in Russia and Its Cultural Reception* (English ed., 1994). His focus is on the relationship of cinema to the aesthetics of Russian high culture; mine is on the same story from the "bottom up." That two such different books can be written about the same subject is testament, I think, to the richness and timelessness of the material.

The research for this book was funded in part by grants from a number of sources, for whose aid I am grateful. The International Research and Exchanges Board sponsored my trip to Moscow to work with the extensive runs of trade journals housed in the Russian State Library and with the remnants of studio archives in the Russian State Archive of Literature and Art. The Kennan Institute for Advanced Russian Studies supported my viewing of the extensive video collection at the Motion Picture Division of the Library of Congress. The University of Illinois Russian Research Center sponsored me for three summers as a research fellow at the university's library, where I did most of my reading of the Russian popular press and revisited the "thick" journals in the library's impressive late imperial periodical collection. The staffs of these institutions deserve thanks for their generous assistance, which enabled me to use my limited research time efficiently. This was especially true at the Library of Congress, where I watched movies for hours on end.

My home institution, the University of Vermont, has also supported this work in a number of ways. The College of Arts and Sciences provided a sabbatical leave in spring 1995 for research in Moscow and the United States; the Graduate College supported research trips to Urbana, Ill., and Washington, D.C.; and the International Studies Program provided the services of two research assistants, Allan Nafte and Richard G. Snyder.

As always, it gives me pleasure to acknowledge the generosity of my colleagues in film, history, and Slavic studies. Lois Becker, Peter Kenez, Frank Manchel, and Josephine Woll read and reread this book in various drafts. Their knowledge and encouragement, suggestions and criticisms, queries and quips were vital. Robert Rosenstone provided much-needed encouragement for experimentation at the beginning of the writing, and Richard Taylor at the end (along with many valuable corrections). For the University of Wisconsin Press, Vance Kepley and Yuri Tsivian offered close readings and challenging critiques at a point when I had convinced myself that I was "done." I also benefited from the careful editing and sharp questioning of Kevos Spartalian. For the illustrations, I am grateful for the generosity of Paolo Cherchi Usai, Dennis Doros (of Milestone Film & Video, New York, which owns U.S. distribution rights to many of the films discussed herein), and especially, Yuri Tsivian, who provided a number of rare promotional postcards from his private collection.

On a purely personal note, I would like to thank my family and friends: my parents, James and Laurette Young; my brother and sister-in-law, Jim and Lisa Young; my sister, Arlette Boehning; my son, Ethan Youngblood;

and my friends, Ernestine Abel and Shirley Gedeon. This project was born at a difficult moment in my life, and I would not have been able to continue it without their help.

This book is dedicated to Frank Manchel, who despite his own time of troubles has been unstinting with his support and assistance.

ABBREVIATIONS & TRANSLITERATION

KZh   *Kine-zhurnal* (*Cinema Journal*)
RS   *Russkoe slovo* (*Russian Word*)
SF   *Sine-fono* (*Cine-phono*)
VK   *Vestnik kinematografii* (*Cinematographic Herald*)

Transliteration of Russian is according to the Library of Congress system, with the exception that the soft sign (') and hard sign (″) have been omitted. I have also rendered the *ie* of the old orthography as *e* and *ago* as *ogo*, so that, for example, *viestnik* becomes the more recognizable *vestnik* of contemporary Russian and *starago* becomes *starogo*.

It is also important to note that there was no standardized spelling, or indeed, words, at the time for cinema, cinematography, and the like. These appear variously as *kinematografiia*, *sinematografiia*, and so forth, and are not, therefore, transliteration errors.

Titles in the text are given in English, followed by the Russian on first mention. Titles in the notes are in Russian only. All translations from the Russian are mine unless otherwise indicated. Details from films are based on my screening notes.

THE MAGIC MIRROR

INTRODUCTION

History and Film History

RUSSIAN CINEMA DEVELOPED RAPIDLY, DESPITE CONDITIONS THAT DID not appear conducive to the flourishing of a lively new cultural industry. The decade 1908–18 was among the most unstable and violent in the saga of Russian imperial history. It is also a decade whose legacy is hotly disputed, now more than ever, given the final failure at the end of the 1980s of the socialist experiment that began in 1917. These days, both Russian and Western historians look back to what was *not*, to the social groups that were not revolutionary and therefore not victorious — and to the "roads not taken," especially when they provide free market and entrepreneurial models.

This important transitional period in Russian history has provided the subject matter for literally hundreds of books and articles and much historiographical debate, particularly over the true extent of the crisis that eventually led to revolution. The historical sketch that follows undoubtedly paints a picture too dark, in strokes too broad to satisfy specialists in the era's political nuances, but that is beside the point. We are interested here in perceptions, attitudes, stereotypes, and values. Even a cursory glance at the sources reveals the uncertainty and pessimism of the city dwellers who formed the bulk of movie audiences as to their future prospects in a Russia of out-of-touch royals, intransigent bureaucrats, professional revolutionaries, and an overwhelming majority of the poor and disenfranchised. For many, it was a time to live every day as it came, for reasons that are not hard to understand in retrospect.

HISTORY

Indeed, with every year since the accession of Nicholas II to the throne in 1894, thinking Russians understood more and more clearly that their country needed significant change. Disaffection with the government in

3

the countryside after the terrible famines of the early 1890s contributed to continuing unrest in the form of riots and "incidents" of peasant insubordination. These, coupled with deteriorating economic conditions in some areas, spurred a peasant exodus from the countryside to the major industrial centers. There, although they lived and worked in horrific conditions, they were at least able to earn cash wages to send home to the family members remaining behind, a situation described not only by early sociologists and later historians, but more vividly by writers like Anton Chekhov and Maksim Gorkii. Revolutionaries, driven underground by the counterrevolutionary "reforms" of Nicholas's father, Alexander III, resurfaced in the late 1890s to exploit rising "class consciousness" of the new urban proletariat as well as of the poor peasantry. By the turn of the century, the two major revolutionary groups, the Socialist Revolutionaries (SRs) and the Social Democrats (SDs, better known by their later sobriquets of "Bolsheviks" and "Mensheviks") had organized.

Nicholas's paternalism and near-total isolation from reality, coupled with his obtuse conservatism and his tendency to surround himself (probably unwittingly) with unsavory reactionaries, exacerbated rising tides of resentment and eroded what little support the regime continued to enjoy. Russia's disastrous engagement and humiliating defeat in the Russo-Japanese War of 1904–5 only confirmed what many Russians already suspected—that their government was incapable of leading Russia into the twentieth century.

The anger and anxiety found expression in a major social revolution, the Revolution of 1905, which brought mutinies, strikes, peasant riots, and street skirmishes to the beleaguered nation. The issuance of the October [1905] Manifesto, promising the country a bill of rights and a constitution, and the arrest of the members of the St. Petersburg Soviet in December 1905, essentially ended the revolution in urban Russia, but the troubles continued in the countryside. Fueled by a wave of assassinations orchestrated by the terrorist wing of the SR party and the government's counterattacks, revolutionary unrest was not fully contained until 1907.

The promises of the October Manifesto quickly faded, as it became obvious that Nicholas intended to subvert the constitution whenever and wherever possible. He usually succeeded in doing so, especially when aided by the country's energetic, controversial, and aggressively conservative new prime minister Peter Stolypin, who served until his assassination in 1911. Stolypin altered the electoral laws effectively to ensure a conservative and monarchist parliament (called the Duma) and sought an end to centuries of communal social organization in the countryside by forcefully encouraging the separation of the peasantry from the commune. This policy, which Stolypin called his "wager on the strong," favored the peasant entrepreneurs known as "kulaks."

In the short term, Stolypin's policies bought the tsarist regime a little more time. In the long run, however, these policies exacerbated existing tensions, led to endless confrontations, contributed to an aura of continuous crisis, and thereby completed the disaffection of most of the elite from the government and its empty promises. The uneven performance (or more bluntly, scandalous ineptitude) of the Russian high command during World War I was responsible, in the minds of many, for the high toll in human misery: nearly two million Russian soldiers died. The equally scandalous political machinations of the Empress Alexandra and her "spiritual advisor" Grigorii Rasputin served as the proverbial straw that brought the three-hundred-year-old dynasty to its ignominious end in early 1917. Collapse was total, and the Bolshevik wing of the SD party was able to take advantage of the continuing chaos by autumn.

There were, however, two constructive counterpoints to this striking narrative of misery, conflict, and disintegration that indicate that revolution might not have been the only road to modernity. The most obvious is Russia's sparkling "high culture" from the 1890s through the 1910s, its "Silver Age." As was the case in imperial Vienna, and arguably in fin de siècle Paris, cultural glory provided a sharp contrast to the state's economic and political decline. More than ever before in Russia, art served as a substitute for political power. Given the long-standing prejudices of the elite against commercial activity (they were interested in spending money, not in making it), the best and brightest were drawn to careers in the arts if they had not already found the revolutionary road. Theater, opera, ballet, belles lettres (especially poetry and the short story) flourished, stimulated after 1905 by radical curbing of the censorship, one of the few areas in which the tsar did not subvert the liberalizing promises of the October 1905 Manifesto. With few exceptions (Gorkii and Tolstoi being chief among them), the great artists of the day were almost defiantly apolitical. Art for art's sake reigned.

The second positive counterpoint is the emergence of various middling social groups connected with the breakdown of the old caste (*soslovie*) system, the increase in literacy, the beginnings of industrial revolution, and the growth of urbanization. At the time of the empire's first general census in 1897, about 12.2 million out of a population of 125.6 million lived in cities, a small percentage compared to the West, but still more than double what it had been at the time of Alexander II's accession to the throne in

1855.[1] Population growth and urbanization were so rapid that by 1913 the urban population had doubled to 25 million (out of about 140 million).[2] Because of the size of the country, the inefficiency of the bureaucracy, and the intricate complexities of the *soslovie* system, it is very difficult to translate the census results into modern class terms.

We do know, however, that these urbanites, who formed the potential movie audience, were concentrated in five very large cities (though Russia's urbanization was slow, its cities were large, just as its industry was concentrated). In 1914 St. Petersburg had 2.2 million inhabitants; Moscow, 1.5 million; Warsaw, 885,000; Odessa 655,000; and Kiev, 600,000.[3] The ten next largest cities in the empire, with populations ranging from 184,000 to 416,000, were also home to many movie theaters, as were the two dozen other cities with populations near the 100,000 mark.[4]

Most city and town dwellers belonged to the caste (*soslovie*) known as the *meshchanstvo* (petty bourgeoisie), of whom there were 13.4 million in the country at large in 1897, on the eve of the movie era.[5] (Obviously many in this group lived in villages as well). The numbers for other urban middling groups are much harder to determine because the composition of the *kupechestvo* (merchants) depended on a number of factors. (Lenin, for example, calculated a figure of some 3 million for what he called the *haute bourgeoisie* in his 1899 scholarly study *The Development of Capitalism in Russia*, not an unreasonable number.)[6] In part because of such uncertain and constantly changing data, at this point there is general agreement among the social historians working on class and caste definitions in late imperial Russia that these "middle classes" were not yet truly a bourgeoisie in the Western (and Marxist) sense of the word, although they were probably on the way to becoming so. These people, as best we understand them, were educated and entrepreneurial, Western oriented in their tastes, and came not only from the merchant caste (*kupechestvo*) but also from the upper ranks of the petty bourgeoisie (*meshchanstvo*), as well as from the poor aristocracy and the declassed intelligentsia and professionals usually labeled *raznochintsy*.

FILM HISTORY AS PARALLEL HISTORY

Where do the movies fit into this picture of Russia on the eve of revolution? They certainly shed little light on the rise of the socialist movement or the death throes of tsarism, the traditional focal points of political history. With the advent of various "new" histories over the past twenty years, and especially since the fall of the Soviet Union, the late imperial period has provided fertile ground for revisionist evaluation. Studying the movies puts another face on "revolutionary Russia" and expands our notions of what Russia's fabled "Silver Age" looked like.[7] It also sheds light on what we know about Russia's "forgotten classes," to paraphrase Valentin Bill, since the movies were, without question, an urban phenomenon at this time.[8] Cinema provides, therefore, not so much a counterhistory of the period as a *parallel* history. This parallel history of "the road not taken" to cultural modernization is not only a portrait of one aspect of modernity. It is, furthermore, a story that is curiously postmodern in its fragmentation and resistance to narrativization.

As Soviet film historian Semën Ginzburg perceptively noted in his important 1963 history of Russian silent cinema, the empire's last decade was indeed the time of

> Gorkii and Andreev, Bunin and Kuprin, Blok and Maiakovskii, Rimskii-Korsakov and Scriabin, Rakhmaninov and Stravinskii, Stanislavskii and Meierkhold, Repin and Surikov, the World of Art and the Jack of Diamonds group.[9]

But why, Ginzburg asked, when the era is defined, should these artists and arts automatically be privileged over commercial entertainments and artists like Verbitskaia, Artsybashev, Severianin, Bem, Klever, pseudo-gypsy romances, farce — or, I would add, the movies?[10] Part of the answer to Ginzburg's question lies in the persistent high culture biases in the academy, and indeed, the restrictive definitions of high culture, long the bane of cultural historians seeking the middle ground. The other part has to do with the fragmentation of the sources. Much in the film world was ephemeral to start with, and much has been lost forever. Without sources, there is no history, or at least not the familiar and comfortable kind of history that relies on massive data collection, or at least, seamless narration.

What we *will* be able to see from the (re)assembled mosaic that follows is this: the movies were much more than a popular upstart. They were, in fact, an intrinsic part of Silver Age culture, expanding the possibilities of "high art" by providing a much-needed synthesis of high culture, entertainment, and technology as well as drawing on Russian folk motifs. The development of the cinema in Russia followed patterns so remarkably similar to those in Western Europe that they will be immediately clear to readers familiar with cinema's origins elsewhere and therefore will rarely be belabored here. Given the supposed "backwardness" of Russia, this high degree of adaptability is noteworthy. The replications of these patterns indicate the extent of the Westernization of the Russian middle classes and cultural entrepreneurs—and the willingess of city dwellers readily to adopt Western novelties, and to adapt them to their own cultural motifs and traditions.

As already noted in the preface, the first films were shown in Russia fewer than five months after the moving pictures appeared in France, a sign of the speed at which fads traveled in the modern age, not to mention the close cultural and economic ties between France and Russia. The film age began in Russia on May 4, 1896, in the capital city of St. Petersburg at the Aquarium (Akvarium) summer amusement park, later the site of the Lenfilm movie studio. Some three weeks later, on May 26, the movies debuted in Russia's second largest city, Moscow, at the Hermitage (Ermitazh) Operetta Theater.[11] For the first decade (twelve years, to be precise), films shown in Russia were entirely foreign, mainly of the "attraction" (rather than narrative) variety, with programs designed to last under an hour, the belief being that audience attention spans were too short for more.[12]

In fall 1907, the French faced their first native competition. Aleksandr Drankov announced that he was establishing a production studio in St. Petersburg on Kazan Boulevard, next to the Moderne movie theater.[13] The honor of "first Russian movie" usually goes to the Drankov studio's costume picture *Stenka Razin* (1908), which exploited the colorful legend of the seventeenth-century peasant rebel. Although we shall see that Drankov was a man whose contemporaries held him in scant regard, he understood the historic importance of this moment and how to dramatize it. He commissioned I. M. Ippolitov-Ivanov to compose a special score for the movie that could be "sung, played on the grammophone, piano, or orchestra."[14]

Native film production increased rapidly, as indicated by table I.1. It is important to keep in mind, however, that only 85 of the Russian movies made from 1908 to 1912 were acted films (about one-third of the total); the rest were newsreels or otherwise based on factual material. Fifty-three percent of these "art" films were screen adaptations (of belles lettres, plays, and songs), undoubtedly prompted by the success of the French Film d'art series. Of the remaining acted films, 26 percent were historical dramas; 13 percent, contemporary melodramas; 8 percent, comedies.[15] The 1913

Table I.1.   Native film production, 1909–13

Year	Number of films
1909	19
1910	32
1911	73
1912	102
1913	129

Source: N. A. Lebedev, *Ocherk istorii kino SSSR*, vol. 1,
Nemoe kino (Moscow, 1947), p. 15.

figure nonetheless represents impressive growth, especially considering the increasing length of films.

As in other countries, the length and number of films gradually increased, with a move away from the "attraction" type of nonnarrative film, toward stories constructed along more conventional narrative lines. The first full-length feature film made in Russia is usually considered the Khanzhonkov studio's *Defense of Sevastopol* (*Oborona Sevastopolia*, 1912, directed by Vasilii Goncharov). This film, which Ginzburg counts as the first Russian "hit" (*boevik*), was 2,000 meters long with a running time of more than an hour and a half, give or a take a minute or two.[16] By 1913, the year of the 5,000-meter box office sensation *The Keys to Happiness* (*Kliuchi schastia*), which was shown in two parts, about 25 percent of Russian films could be considered full-length (that is, films of more than 1,000 meters, with a running time of just under an hour).[17]

With the rapid increase in film production, it was clear that new ideas for story lines needed to be readily available, and Russia's high culture provided a rich and extensive source for cinema to synthesize. Screen adaptations of plays, novels, stories, poems, and operas became key to the industry's success. Adaptations from classic Russian and Ukrainian writers like Pushkin, Lermontov, Gogol, Tolstoi, Dostoevskii, Goncharov, Chekhov, Nekrasov, and Shevchenko were common (see table I.2).[18] Most of these were what might be called "cinema illustrations" that assumed some knowledge of the original, rather than full-fledged narrative adaptations.[19]

Yet there were limits to how many films on themes by Pushkin, Gogol, and Chekhov could be made. By 1912, it had become apparent to studio heads that the works of "sensational" living writers like Andreev, Kuprin, and Verbitskaia could attract even larger audiences than those for the classics. (Soviet scholars, like Nikolai Lebedev, typically designated these

Table I.2. Number of adaptations by author, 1907–12

Author	Films
Pushkin	21
Gogol	17
Chekhov	13
Krylov	7
Lermontov	7
L. Tolstoi	7
Ostrovskii	6
Nekrasov	4
Dostoevskii	2
A. Tolstoi	2
Shevchenko	2
Sukhov-Kobylin	1

Source: S. Ginzburg, *Kinematografiia dorevoliutsionnoi Rossii* (Moscow, 1963), p. 10.

pictures "boulevard" melodramas, popular with the "petty-bourgeois" [*meshchanskii*] public.)[20] Historical themes provided another important source for story lines, especially after the acclaim *The Defense of Sevastopol* enjoyed. Romanticized peasant stories enjoyed ephemeral vogues, as did ethnic films.[21] Melodramas of Jewish life, like their counterparts in early American cinema, were mainly intended for Jewish audiences but occasionally played major cities and attracted sympathetic attention from liberal critics who were opposed to official anti-Semitism.

The network of movie theaters grew apace. By 1913, there were 1,400 movie theaters in Russia, with St. Petersburg leading at 130 theaters for its population of just over two million. (Moscow, the major movie-*producing* city, had about half that number, 67, for a population about half the size.) Theaters ranged in capacity from a few dozen seats to 2,000, with the typical range being 300 to 800 seats.[22]

On the eve of war in summer 1914, the infrastructure for the native film industry was solidly in place. Foreign pictures still overwhelmingly dominated the market, with Italian costume dramas, the French Film d'art series, and Pathé's Max Linder comedies preferred by many viewers.[23] Nonetheless, there was a clear and growing niche market for Russian movies produced and directed by Russian talent. Russian personnel gradually supplanted foreign production staff in most areas of film work, though the influence of foreign cameramen—Forestier, Toppi, Meier

(French); Vitrozzi (Italian); Serrano (Spanish); Siversen (Swedish) — remained strong.[24]

World War I stimulated the growth of the native Russian movie industry, in part because the closing of the nation's borders made trade contact much more difficult, even with Russia's allies. (At least one film critic believes that the prohibition of vodka also had a positive impact on the industry, drawing a new audience, the lumpenproletariat or "dark masses," to the movies.)[25] The very popular German films (and essential German film stock, projectors, and other supplies) were entirely cut off. American companies and American films replaced them in part (Kodak became a major supplier of celluloid and chemicals for Russian cinema),[26] but Russian studios saw the opportunity to increase their market share and took it. For example, in the first months of the war, the Khanzhonkov studio, Russia's largest, more than doubled its working capital, to 1.25 million rubles.[27] Russian production figures during the war (as seen in table I.3) also reflect this dramatic growth. More films required more studios to produce them, as shown in table I.4. Russian directors made movies so rapidly now that a studio could produce a new title in a couple of days, sacrificing quality to quantity. Although audiences came to resent such pap, during the war they did not have much choice.[28]

The Russian army more often than not faltered at the front, but the Russian cinematic juggernaut during the Great War was so effective that the long-established Pathé closed down its Russian operations in 1915, after concluding a deal with the Ermolev studio to distribute its French-made films.[29] The number of theaters grew as well, from about 1,500 in 1913 to 4,000 by 1916, serving two million viewers daily (or about 10 percent of the urban population). Petrograd (as the capital was renamed in

Table I.3.   Native film production, 1913–16

Year	Number of films
1913	129 (majority shorts)
1914	230 (majority full-length)
1915	370
1916	500

Sources: N. A. Lebedev, *Ocherk istorii kino SSSR*, vol. 1, *Nemoe kino* (Moscow, 1947), p. 35; S. Ginzburg, *Kinematografiia dorevoliutsionnoi Rossii* (Moscow, 1963), p. 157.

Table I.4.   Native film studios, 1913–16

Year	Number of studios
1913	18
1914	31
1915/16	47

Source: S. Ginzburg, *Kinematografiia dorevoliutsionnoi Rossii* (Moscow, 1963), p. 159.

1914) now had 229 theaters, 15 on Nevskii Prospect alone![30] For comparison with the commercial popularity of the "legitimate" stage, Semën Ginzburg claims that by 1916 there were ten times more movie than theater tickets sold in the empire.[31] One must keep well in mind, however, that film audiences were still small and localized by the standards of France or the United States, where cinema was already more of a "mass" entertainment (though not compared with what it would become in the 1920s).

Nonetheless, there were serious problems facing the studios despite the unflagging demand from the public for more films to distract them from Russia's pressing problems. The shortages in film stock were continuous, and a black market, with black market prices, sprang up. The smaller studios found it virtually impossible to compete, and when a big shipment of Kodak film arrived in 1916, a cabal of the major studios essentially confiscated the entire stock, leaving nothing for the minor players.[32]

This boom in production expanded opportunities for Russian actors, and a Russian star system developed (even if they were stars who succeeded in part because they "looked" European). Popular movie stars Vladimir Maksimov, Vitold Polonskii, and Ivan Mozzhukhin were joined by Osip Runich, Vladimir Gaidarov, Oleg Freilikh, Amo Bek-Nazarov, and Vladimir Strizhevskii. We likewise see expansion in the ranks of female stars: although Nataliia Lisenko, Vera Kholodnaia, Vera Karalli, and Olga Gzovskaia remained in the top tier, Zoia Barantsevich, Mariia Gorcheva, Z. Karabanova, A. Rebikova, and N. Rutkovskaia were also worthy of note.[33]

Historical films lost their cachet during the Great War, being seen as too sedate. Literary adaptations remained popular, but there was a strong movement away from the classics and toward contemporary writers and contemporary themes. This shift appears to reflect public tastes as much as it did the tastes of producers, if we compare the movies with other forms of cultural production at the time. There was a synergistic relationship among the Russian arts, which cinema was particularly suited to taking advantage of. Lighthearted adventure serials like *Sonka the "Golden Hand"* (*Sonka zolotaia ruchka*), *Anton Krechet*, and *Sashka the Seminary Student* (*Sashka seminarist*) attracted large audiences in the movies, just as serialized novels attracted large readerships in the penny press. Increasingly "decadent" erotic melodramas with mystical or "satanic" overtones also attracted a great deal of attention, just as they sold many books, making authors like Mikhail Artsybashev rich and famous.[34]

In terms of genre development, comedy continued to lag behind, which was not surprising considering the grip Max Linder had on the imaginations of the Russian public. During the war, however, the comedians "Antosha" (Anton Fertner) and "Arkasha" (Arkadii Boitler) — reputed to model themselves, respectively, after Charlie Chaplin and the American comic John Bunny (known in Russia as "Fat Man Pokson") — became popular with the fans. There were few prominent comediennes, but one notable name from this period was director Evgenii Bauer's wife "Lina" Bauer (as a dramatic actress, she called herself "Emma" Bauer).[35]

One of the more curious characteristics of Russian cinema during the war was the fate of the war film. Initially, as may be expected, studios vied with each other to prove how patriotic they were. From August 1, 1914, to December 31, 1914, nearly 50 percent of Russian fiction film production concerned the war (50 pictures out of 103). But audience interest quickly faded, due in large part to the rapid collapse of nationalistic fervor and declining support for the tsarist regime. In 1915, only 21 fiction films concerned the war; in 1916, 13; in 1917 — none.[36]

Despite the strength and relative independence of Russian cinema during the war, it would be a mistake to underestimate the profound influence Western European filmmaking had overall on Russian filmmakers and audiences. In the three-year period from 1912 to 1914, for example, more than a thousand French, Italian, Danish, and German films were shown in Russia.[37] The extraordinary popularity of the French comic Max Linder will be discussed in some detail in chapter 3, but other French phenomena, like the stylish *Fantomas* detective-adventure serials, spawned Russian imitators. The Italian costume dramas from the life of ancient Rome were considered the height of good taste and elegance, and certainly the dark "psychologism" of Danish cinema had an important impact on Russian style.[38]

The influence of American cinema at this time is much harder to gauge, although the well-known Russian director Iakov Protazanov was familiar with some of D. W. Griffith's work, and Russian directors generally admired American editing styles.[39] For example, Charlie Chaplin's films were not imported until late in the war; his decade of Russian popularity was the 1920s, not the 1910s. The two major companies importing American films during the war were Trans-Atlantic (run by the confidence artist Cibrario de Goden, who earned his curious place in history by cheating the Soviet government out of one million dollars)[40] and the Khokhlovkin company. Khokhlovkin introduced Russian audiences to the (Anglo-)American comics Chaplin, Monty Banks, Fatty Arbuckle, and Billy Richie.[41] In addition, according to B. S. Likhachev (who emphasizes the impact of American filmmakers on Russian cinema to a greater extent than do other Soviet film historians), Tom Mix westerns, Pearl White serials, and the films of Cleo Madison and Caitlin Williams were wartime hits.[42]

By 1917, the economic and political crisis was crippling the film industry just as it was crippling the country as a whole, and the revolution of February/March had no positive impact on this crisis. Studios began to fail, and American films secured a corner on the market, with "escapist" fare like *Secrets of New York* and *King of the Circus* especially popular.[43] Studio heads began to organize a producers' union (ONO), which met at the Arts (Ars) theater in Moscow on March 3, 1917, with 300 in attendance—and again on March 6, at the Khanzhonkov theater. Some 2,500 film and theater workers attended that meeting. Throughout the spring and summer of that fateful year, 1917, numerous unions were founded: the Union of Workers in Art Cinema (SRKhK), the Union of Film Publishing Societies (OKO), the All-Russian Society of Owners of Electric Theaters (VOVET), the All-Russian Society of Owners of Distribution Companies (VSVPK), the Professional Union of Filmworkers (PSK). These were all branded "reactionary," "counterrevolutionary," and "politically illiterate" when the Bolsheviks came to power in October/November 1917.[44]

Only a few studios remained operative in 1917: Khanzhonkov, Ermolev, Era (formerly Thiemann & Reinhardt), Libken, Rus (formerly Trofimov), Vekshtein, Biofilm (formerly Biokhron), Taldykin, and Vengerov.[45] The Bolsheviks temporarily closed movie theaters in November and December 1917, following the October Revolution, and the exodus of film companies south, primarily to the Crimea where the "White" forces dominated, began in 1918. Nonetheless the box office take in 1917 broke previous records. Even reckoning the skyrocketing inflation that led to a

50 percent increase in ticket prices, the box office improved by 33 percent over 1916, which was itself also a banner year.[46] The movies were in Russia to stay.

ENDS AND MEANS

This book is intended first and foremost as a description and celebration of early Russian cinema. It is constructed as an experiment in historical narration — kaleidoscopic rather than encyclopedic, which seems to me to reflect the excitement of the times best. My approach is unapologetically that of the sociocultural historian; fact and context, not theory and aesthetics, are my areas of expertise.

Situating Russian cinema as a cultural and social institution in the space of Russian history is my second major project here, and the leitmotif of the book is the interrelationship between class and culture. As I have already suggested, early Russian film history sheds little light on the rising tide of revolution, except as it tangentially reflects on class conflict. It rarely intersects the major political developments of the period, except when the Great War's tax and supply exigencies forced confrontation. The information it provides on Russian business history or the rise of capitalism in the country is also fragmentary.

The cinema does intersect Russian high culture quite often. It may be considered a variant of it, which is a position that Yuri Tsivian implicitly takes in his work, especially *Early Cinema in Russia and Its Cultural Reception*, with interesting results. Or — as I think more valid in the context of cultural studies — early Russian cinema may be considered as a *synthesis* of Russian high culture with Western and native popular cultural traditions. Through its borrowing of literary themes and theatrical personalities, early Russian cinema attempted to bask in reflected glory before creating its own paradigm in the years of the Great War. Still, cinema's commercial aspects and technical concerns are so integral that it seems to me that we must admit that we are dealing with quite a different kind of cultural phenomenon. Cinema should not be considered only as a corollary to, or bastardization of, high culture — nor as a particularly pretentious form of popular culture. During the Great War, Russian cinema underwent a Kuhnian paradigm shift, creating its own energy and its own aesthetic system.[47]

We can also find common ground between cinema history and "history" when we look at cinema's social aspects, which help us understand the dynamics of the development of the middling classes in Russia. Cinema represents an important aspect of the birth of a middle culture in Russia connected to urbanization and social change at the turn of the century. This importance is apparent when we compare Russian cinematic developments with the commercial, "bourgeois" culture of Western Europe in the period 1890–1918. Ben Singer, drawing from Georg Simmel's 1903 analysis of modernity, adopts Michael Davis's term "hyperstimulus" to describe the hunger for sensation in prewar Western cultures.[48] We see this hyperstimulus in Russian urban culture as well.

Scanning the pages of the Russian popular press of the period—publications like the *Kopek Gazette* (*Gazeta kopeika*), the *Russian Word* (*Russkoe slovo*), the *Sun of Russia* (*Solntse Rossii*), *The Field* (*Niva*), and even the glossy and elegant *Capital and Country Estate* (*Stolitsa i usadba*)—provides independent verification of the movie-made images of Russia. Here is the Russia of the movies, the Russia that people lived in, even if it is not the Russia that most historians have written about previously.

This "middle world" was a place of burgeoning opportunities. The novelties of the day, especially technological marvels like airplanes, cars, zeppelins and dirigibles, hot air balloons, and the telephone, attracted people's attention and pocketbooks. The Russian petty bourgeoisie wanted *things*, lots of them, with Western brand names, the more "modern" the better—Swift bicycles, Michelin tires (the Michelin man wore a Russian fur cap)—or for children, popguns. The middling classes wanted to be entertained, at air shows, amusement parks, roller-skating rinks, cabarets, horse races, boxing matches, and the movies. They were avidly concerned with disasters, especially if they occurred elsewhere (like earthquakes in Italy) and could be measured by a new invention (the seismograph). Local fires, explosions, murders, and suicides were also good for many columns of news. These city folk had heroes, both past (Pushkin and Herzen) and present (Lev Tolstoi, Valentin Serov, Robert Peary, and the aviator B. V. Matevich-Matsevich, who died in a plane crash in Sevastopol on April 18, 1911). European royalty were especially popular. Heroes could even be fictitious, like Nat Pinkerton, or quite ordinary folk, like the latest high stakes lottery winner.[49]

People wanted to look good—hence, the many advertisements for ladies' creams, perfumes and cosmetics, corsets, and exercise devices guaranteed to enlarge the bosom. Men were not exempt; they, too, could have well-developed chests like the musclemen in the photographs. Russians wanted to be healthy as well, and new medical and hygiene products abounded — toothpastes, especially, but also cures for hair loss, eczema, alcoholism, smoking addiction, venereal disease, and sexual impotence. They were hungry for information — about the medical applications of radium, the invention of the parachute, the hows and whys of hypnotism, whether it was proper to wear the new, radically short skirt styles that appeared late in the war. They were interested in other forms of self-improvement, too, such as increasing "personal magnetism" and memory, and learning to play the piano.[50] The true historical context of early Russian cinema is situated, therefore, as much in the tabloids as in Silver Age high culture.

The book is divided into two parts, which examine institutions and production thematically rather than chronologically. First we will look at the organization and operation of the industry. This section, which should be considered "scenes from a film history" rather than a metanarrative, includes a discussion of business practices, audience behaviors, the construction of celebrity, and finally, cultural politics. The purpose is to determine the attitudes and mores of the people who were involved in the business — both as consumers and as producers.

The second part, labeled "fragments from a film program," is less straightforward than the first. This section focuses on the film texts themselves, primarily the melodramas which were the mainstay of the industry. The organization of the "programs" is arbitrary (as all such schemata are in the end), and the chapter titles ironic, but both are intended to establish dominant themes and styles as well as mood. Russian cinema may have been art, but it was also high-style entertainment, and the "magic mirror" through which Russian middle culture was reflected.

PART I

Scenes from a Film History

1

In the Movies

Studios and Producers

THE HISTORY OF EARLY RUSSIAN CINEMA MAY BE BEST TRACKED IN
Moscow. Moscow was the center of the Russian empire's cinema production world, with approximately twenty firms in the 1910s, which includes
distributors as well as studios. They were clustered along Tverskaia Street
and Petrovskii Passage. Other film production centers were, in order of
importance, St. Petersburg/Petrograd, Kiev, and Odessa.[1]

Few studio archives from the prerevolutionary period have survived, so
we must reconstruct studio operations mainly through examination of the
trade press and memoirs. In 1912, the independent trade journal *Cine-
phono* (*Sine-fono*) provided a capsule history of the industry in honor of
the fifth anniversary of Russian production. Given the highly fragmentary
nature of the extant documentation, the *Cine-phono* account is an important source of information with which to reconstruct the origins of the
industry. It clarifies the degree to which foreign firms, especially Pathé and
Gaumont, contributed to Russian expertise and also gives us a good idea
of the fluidity of the industry, its relationship to class change in Russian
society, and its potential for growth.

PRODUCERS AND DISTRIBUTORS

The French companies Pathé and Gaumont, which had been distributing
their French films in Russia since the turn of the century, opened their
Russian production studios in 1907. This was in response to Russian competition from Aleksandr Drankov, a commercial photographer who announced his intentions to establish a studio that same year.[2]

Another important producer joined the Pathé, Gaumont, and Drankov companies in 1907: Aleksandr Khanzhonkov, who opened the soon to be famous Khanzhonkov studio, with his wife as partner. Most Russian and Soviet film historians consider Khanzhonkov a more respectable figure than Drankov, the founder of the Russian cinema industry.[3] Khanzhonkov definitely exemplified the most up-to-date business practices of Russia's early cinema entrepreneurs. In 1910, he began to expand, buying Globus and Kinerus. This was the earliest sign of the monopolistic practices that made him a giant in the business — and more comparable than any of his Russian counterparts to an American producer.

Two years after the formation of the first production studios in Russia, another major native producer entered the arena, Pavel Thiemann. The French company Gaumont unwittingly served as a farm team for Russian talent on a number of occasions. As one prominent example, in 1909 Thiemann, who had headed Gaumont's Russian operation, defected to found the Thiemann & Reinhardt studio with Friedrich Reinhardt. The wealthy tobacco merchant Reinhardt provided the capital; Thiemann, the expertise.[4] Like many later studios, Thiemann & Reinhardt began as a distributor — of Nordisk, Ambrosio, and Vitagraph films, an important step in diversifying the repertory. As distributors, Thiemann & Reinhardt helped break the French hold on the infant Russian movie industry by introducing the distinctive artistic styles of American, Italian, and Danish filmmakers to Russian audiences. The studio's own Russian-produced films also bore the signs of this cosmopolitanism.

From 1911 to 1913, a few other studios with staying power appeared on the scene. (Many Russian film companies were fly-by-night operations, disappearing from view as quickly as they had appeared, which again was a characteristic of the business everywhere in Europe and America.) The Perskii studio, which opened in 1911, was an example of this second stage of studio building. An engineer named Robert Davidovich Perskii, like Thiemann a defector from Gaumont, initially called his small enterprise "Dukes." As "Dukes," Perskii imported mainly German films and published *Cine Journal* (*Kine-zhurnal*), an important trade journal that was less biased than most. When the production side of his business blossomed after 1914, during the war boom that will be discussed shortly, the studio became known by his surname, Perskii, the typical practice.

Also worth noting, if only as historical curiosities, were Variag and Gloria. Variag, founded in 1911, was headed by two women, a Mme. Elizariants and a Mme. Shtern, making it a rarity in the world of Russian private enterprise, but not unheard of.[5] The Russian Gloria studio (always spelled with Roman characters rather than Cyrillic) produced few titles but must be remembered for giving a start to the prominent Russian (and then Soviet) director Iakov Protazanov. Gloria soon stopped making movies in favor of providing film-developing and title production services and was eventually purchased by Thiemann.[6] (It should not be confused, as it often has been, with the Italian Gloria studio, whose distributor in Russia was Paganelli.)[7]

Two other major film-producing enterprises, Ermolev and Kharitonov, emerged from what we might call the third, wartime stage of studio building, when the native industry exploded. Founded in 1914, the Ermolev studio became an extraordinary success story that will be discussed in some detail below.[8] Kharitonov's production enterprise had an impressive start, though it was begun too late (1916) to make a lasting artistic or commercial impact before the revolution brought an abrupt end to private enterprise. Given Kharitonov's entrenched role in film distribution, the studio doubtless would have continued to be a success had it not been for the events of 1917.

Distributors played an important role in the development of the industry. Thiemann & Reinhardt, Perskii, Kharitonov, and Libken (the movie theater mogul) were leading importers and distributors as well as producers. Foreign companies also operated successfully in the Russian market, although often in collaboration with Russian firms. In 1909 K. Paganelli established a Russian section of the prominent Italian studio Cinès, and the following year K. M. Brenner left Paganelli to open his own firm in Moscow. G. Mark, Downey & Co. (later known as Downey & Co.), a London company, started a Moscow office in 1910.

"Musical chairs" continued as entrepreneurs struggled to find the formula for success. In 1911, P. L. Pendrier, who had replaced Thiemann as head of Gaumont, Moscow, fled the unlucky French firm to establish his own distribution company, which handled Éclair, Film d'art, and Savoy productions. In 1912, Gaumont suffered yet another defection as N. Torporkov left to join A. Vinkler and M. Bystritskii at the Swedish concern Tanagra. (Tanagra also imported German films, featuring those of the silent cinema diva Asta Nielsen.) Bystritskii later decamped from Tanagra to start his own production studio. And in 1914, S. V. Lure, who had proudly touted the complete independence of his *Cine-phono* journal from any cinema enterprise, opened his own distributorship, taking over Éclair from Pendrier and adding Kai Hansen and Danmark films to his list.[9] By the time war broke out in July 1914, therefore, Russian audiences had a complete menu of European films from which to choose and were nearly as au courant with the latest stars and fads as their counterparts in Paris or Berlin.

By 1916, however, on the eve of the Revolution, we can see the way the distribution problems related to the war (discussed in the introduction) had benefited native producers, greatly reducing the cosmopolitanism of the repertory. That year the top ten studios (according to the number of titles released in the Russian empire) were all Russian, as shown in table 1.1.

The capital required to start the firms, often organized as joint stock companies, was significant. For example, Semën Andreevich Frenkel's company, which never became a major player, was reportedly capitalized at one million rubles; the Khanzhonkov company at 500,000 rubles.[10] (At this time, the ruble was valued at half a U.S. dollar.) As a result, the generally anticapitalist Russian cultural critics expressed the fear, in part well-founded, that "cinema has fallen into the hands of people who are more concerned with the interests of the ruble than with the tasks of art, science, society. . . ."[11] This kind of antagonism to the supposedly crass values of the Russian bourgeoisie was common.

Table 1.1. Top ten studios in 1916

Studio	Number of films produced
Khanzhonkov	93
Drankov	85
Perskii	42
Ermolev	40
Vengerov & Gardin/Vengerov[a]	35
Thiemann, Reinhardt & Osipov	24
Kharitonov	24
Skobolev Committee	22
Taldykin	17
Trofimov	10

Source: VK, no. 123 (January 1917), pp. 39–42.

[a] Vengerov announced that as of October 14, 1916, Vladimir Gardin was no longer with the company and had been replaced by Semën Frenkel as director (advertisement, Proektor, no. 21 [November 1, 1916], p. xxiii).

The early studio heads and major distributors were, for the most part, solidly "bourgeois," at least on the surface. The majority came from backgrounds that passed for the middle classes in Russia (the lower ranks of gentry families or from the merchantry).[12] They were reasonably well educated, through the secondary school level, although a few had technical or university-level higher educations. Despite persistent rumors to the contrary, they appear to have cared about art as well as commerce. Financial rewards were important to them, but in Russia, art and culture were so value-laden that it was impossible to achieve higher social status merely on the basis of money or birth, alone or together. Nonetheless, as we shall see from examining their biographies, many early producers were, somewhat paradoxically, refugees from respectability, the proverbial black sheep of their families.

THE CAPTAINS OF INDUSTRY

A look at the captains of the industry enables us to see quite a gallery of middle-class "types." Russian cinema's pioneer, Aleksandr Osipovich Drankov (1880–?), is also the industry's most colorful figure. He was an unscrupulous Petersburg entrepreneur and self-annointed court photographer, who had been "in and out" of the business since 1902. Commentary on Drankov has until recently been invariably critical.[13] Soviet film historian Rashit Yangirov, for example, describes him as a

> repellent caricature of a plump but extraordinarily familiar and restless character with red hair, always dressed in pretentious lack of taste, a vainglorious man of considerable ambition always involved in various dubious schemes.[14]

Another Soviet film scholar, Romil Sobolev, described Drankov as a "typical" figure in early Russian cinema: energetic, but uncultured, poorly educated, and unprincipled, like the obnoxious character Nozdrev in Gogol's *Dead Souls*.[15]

But it was not only Soviet scholars who despised Drankov. In his own time, Drankov was usually made the whipping boy for the supposed unbridled sins and sensationalism of Russian cinema. The ditty entitled "To A. O. Drankov" that appeared in *Cine Journal* in 1915 provides an amusing example of the attitude toward him, using language remarkably similar to the conservative cultural rhetoric attacking the film and television of our own times:

> Awful lives,
> Terrible excesses,
> Various murders,
> Loud trials.
> For you all this is the best,
> A gift from heaven.
> Every new event
> Is bread in your mouth.[16]

In 1913, Drankov recapitalized his studio and renamed it Drankov & Taldykin. In so doing, he joined his film experience with the business acumen and financial resources of A. G. Taldykin, a "solid businessman" and "famous major Moscow capitalist," with long-established businesses providing costumes and props to the legitimate stage. Taldykin was seen as someone who might be a steadying influence on Drankov, although this did not prove to be true in the end.[17]

Despite all this negative publicity, an examination of Drankov's extant oeuvre reveals that he was neither more nor less exploitative than anyone else. Not as artistically "sensitive" as the other "big names" in the business, Drankov nonetheless (or for those very reasons) showed remarkable instincts for what would sell to audiences. His series of lighthearted crime films (*Sonka the "Golden Hand"* and *The Robber Vaska Churkin*) proved that Drankov understood the public's desire to thumb their noses at authority and enjoy themselves at the same time. There is art to entertainment, and Drankov understood that well.

Drankov was creative in other ways, too, launching an innovation in the relentless search for good scripts: the screenplay contest (which would become a regular feature in the early Soviet era). Drankov advertised his 1,000-ruble first prize on the front page of the mass circulation daily *Russian Word* (*Russkoe slovo*); the only stipulation was that the studio would not accept historical themes, which Drankov considered overworked and boring.[18] By way of comparison, professional movie scenarists received only 100 to 200 rubles per script.[19]

After the Bolshevik Revolution, Drankov emigrated to Istanbul, where he continued making movies for a while. He was last heard of running a photography studio in San Francisco, a center of the "first wave" of postrevolutionary Russian emigration. The date and circumstances of his death, however, are unknown.[20]

Another allegedly unsavory type among the leading producers was G. I. Libken, the immensely wealthy and "colossally" energetic owner of a sausage factory and three large houses in the central Russian town of Iaroslavl. Libken began his cinematic business ventures in exhibition, rather than distribution or production. His first theater was the Magical Dreams (Volshebnye grezy) in Iaroslavl, and later he was among the first to develop and own a chain of movie theaters. In addition to his lucrative exhibition business, Libken was the major film distributor in central Russia. Among his ventures as a producer were the sensational "blackmail" melodramas *The Sons of Peter Smirnov* (*Petra Smirnova synovia*), to prevent the showing of which the vodka producer paid 18,000 rubles, and *Merchant Bashkirov's Daughter* (*Doch kuptsa Bashkirova*).[21] (The latter film, which Libken guaranteed to be a "colossal success," will be discussed in chapter 6.)[22] Actor and director Amo Bek-Nazarov described Libken as no more than a crook, who in addition to having a demonstrated flair for extortion, cheated Khanzhonkov out of a large sum of money.[23] To be fair, however, Libken proved himself an unusually civic-minded producer during the war, closing one of his Iaroslavl theaters shortly after the conflict began, turning it over to the government for use as a hospital for war wounded.[24]

If most producers had been Drankovs or Libkens, Russian cinema could never have achieved the artistic legitimacy for which it fervently hoped. Dmitrii Ivanovich Kharitonov, who opened his first theater, the Apollo, in Kharkov in 1906, was another successful exhibitor and distributor from a prosperous provincial merchant family, but there his resemblance to Libken ends. By 1913, Kharitonov's distribution empire included offices in Kiev, Ekaterindar, Odessa, Petersburg, Ufa, Simferopol, and other locations. His palatial residence was located near his grandest theater, the Empire (Ampir), proclaimed "one of the finest in Russia."[25] As noted above, Kharitonov opened a studio during the war and became a successful producer as well. The most telling tribute paid his business skills, and a sign of the reputation of U.S. business practices in turn-of-the-century Russia, was that he was known as the "Russian American."[26]

The three leading "captains of industry," in terms of the high artistic quality of their films, were A. A. Khanzhonkov, P. G. Thiemann, and I. N. Ermolev. All three are exceptionally interesting figures. Thiemann and

Khanzhonkov in particular were men who did not quite fit into the old, deteriorating caste system, thereby signifying the birth of new social orders that was characteristic of this period in Russian history.

Aleksandr Alekseevich Khanzhonkov (1877–1945), the oldest of the three, was born to a Don Cossack "gentry" family. He served as an officer in the imperial army for a decade before he turned to film. Why he would leave the army for a "disreputable" field like cinema must be left to our imaginations, but he became such a renowned producer that for early Soviet film critics, Khanzhonkov epitomized Russian commercial cinema. The term "khanzhonkovism" (*khanzhonkovshchina*), used as an epithet for cinematic decadence in the 1920s, was coined after him.

Khanzhonkov & Co. was far and away the leading studio in Russia before the Revolution. By 1915, Khanzhonkov employed a staff trumpeted as "colossal" (probably the most commonly used word in early Russian film publications): two directors (Petr Chardynin and Evgenii Bauer), fifty actors, and five cameramen were on regular contract.[27] On the eve of revolution, Khanzhonkov's cinematic empire was far-flung. He had offices in Moscow, Petrograd, Rostov, Samara, and Saratov and had affiliated with six subsidiary companies: A. G. Sazonovskii (Urals-Siberia); Hit (Boevik) (Kiev, Odessa, Ekaterinoslav); S. G. Mintus (Riga); Alekseev, Donotello & Co. (Irkutsk); M. Litsanskii & I. Shvarts (Kharkov); and Film (Filma) (Baku).[28] Khanzhonkov received a minor imperial decoration, the St. Stanislav Cross, 2d degree, for his "cultural services" to the nation after Nicholas II honored the studio by asking Khanzhonkov for a private showing of the patriotic film *The Defense of Sevastopol* (*Oborona Sevastopolia*).[29]

Khanzhonkov was among the first Russian studio heads to recognize the importance of star promotion. When the charismatic prima ballerina Vera Karalli joined the firm, Khanzhonkov announced it in a two-page advertising spread at the beginning of *Cinematographic Herald* (*Vestnik kinematografii*), with Karalli's name appearing in bold red letters over three inches high.[30] Khanzhonkov also recognized the drawing power of well-known writers and signed one of the most popular (and sensational) of the day, Mikhail Artsybashev, author of *Sanin*, to an exclusive contract.[31] In addition, Khanzhonkov heavily promoted Evgenii Bauer as his "lead" director, going so far as to put Bauer on the front cover of an issue of *Cinematographic Herald*, a singular honor for a director at this time, when all but a few were laboring in obscurity.[32] (It is amusing to note that Khanzhonkov was not averse to "borrowing" ideas from his archrival, Drankov.

For example, he copied Drankov's screenplay competition in 1917, offering a 1,500-ruble first prize.)[33]

The second leading producer of high-quality motion pictures was Pavel Gustavovich Thiemann (1881–?, "Timan" in Russian). The head of Thiemann & Reinhardt (later Thiemann, Reinhardt & Osipov), Thiemann was born in Iurev, Livland province (now in Estonia), to a wealthy Baltic German family of indeterminate caste. Thiemann was noted as a polyglot, having mastered French, German, and English as well as Russian. He doubtless found his language skills useful in establishing contacts in the industry throughout Europe, but he also used them to impress his Russian peers (who, unlike members of the intelligentsia and nobility, were rarely proficient in foreign languages). Unlike Khanzhonkov, Thiemann early embarked on a career in the movies and traveled to Paris in 1902 to learn the business. The "Golden Series" of full-length feature films based on popular or classic literary works cemented Thiemann's position as a leading producer; by 1913, he was among the top three. With the outbreak of war in 1914, however, he faced difficulties beyond his control due to his Germanic surname.

Thiemann struggled unsuccessfully with anti-German sentiment and was forced to remind audiences, distributors, and theater owners that he was as authentic and patriotic a Russian as anyone else. Indeed, in fall 1914, his studio was attacked by a mob as part of an anti-German pogrom.[34] The 1915 defection of the studio's star directors, Vladimir Gardin and Iakov Protazanov, was a blow from which Thiemann, Reinhardt & Osipov never completely recovered. Thiemann did not lose heart, however, and the studio immediately hired Viacheslav Viskovskii and Aleksandr Uralskii to replace Gardin and Protazanov. Thiemann also scored a coup by signing Vsevolod Meierkhold to direct and star in an adaptation of Oscar Wilde's *The Picture of Dorian Gray*, and announced plans for a new series of films based on Turgenev's novels.

But despite his herculean efforts to save his business during the war, Thiemann was eventually exiled to the town of Ufa in the Urals, not returning to Moscow until after the February Revolution.[35] During his exile, his Russian wife, Elizaveta Vladimirovna—who had played key roles in casting, script supervision, and occasional directing from the beginning—ran the firm alone.[36] Despite Mrs. Thiemann's considerable talents, wartime suspicions prevented her from maintaining the studio's production at its prewar levels.[37]

The third member of the triumvirate of leading producers, Iosif Niko-laevich Ermolev (1889–?), was thoroughly Russian, a Muscovite from a wealthy and distinguished merchant family. Like many others of his generation in the *haute bourgeoisie* of the merchantry, he had a good classical education. Not only did he attend a gymnasium, he also studied at Moscow University (although graduation seems doubtful since he joined Pathé at the age of eighteen). But unlike others of his generation and milieu, Ermolev eschewed a career as a patron of the legitimate arts and accepted a post in the financial division of Pathé.[38] From there, he began his meteoric rise in the film industry, the most dramatic success story in Russian cinema.

From 1907 to 1911, Ermolev worked for Pathé, learning the trade. He did this so well that the firm sent him to Baku, then an oil boomtown, to open a new Pathé office there. In 1911, only twenty-two years old (if 1889 is an accurate birthdate), the wunderkind left Pathé to start his own film distributorship in Rostov-on-the-Don: Ermolev, Zarkhin & Segel.[39] By 1912, he had returned to Moscow, planning to found his own production company, capitalized with family money as well as his own profits. Fewer than five years later, he was Russia's fourth-leading producer in terms of numbers, and during the war, second only to Khanzhonkov in prominence and artistic achievement. The methods that Ermolev employed to achieve his startling success are instructive, for by studying the trade journals we can see that he devised an impressive and stunningly modern campaign strategy.

In February 1914, before his first picture was released, Ermolev began heavily advertising the company's new trademark (an elephant) with the slogan "A picture with this trademark will give the theater colossal box office [*sbory*]."[40] (Trademark identification in early Russian cinema was strong; Drankov films were instantly recognized by the peacock; Khanzhonkov's, by Pegasus.)

Ermolev's timing was uncanny. By late 1914, it had become clear that the war would not soon end. It was also obvious that the difficulty of obtaining films from abroad had created a vastly expanded domestic demand for the native product. (In 1914, 90 percent of the films shown in Russia were foreign; the next year only 10 percent were.)[41] By early spring 1915, *Cine Journal* noted, correctly, that of all the new firms that had sprung up to take advantage of this demand, Ermolev's was the one to watch, noting that "I. N. Ermolev's high level of culture can be seen in all his affairs."[42]

Shortly thereafter, Ermolev began his incursions into competing firms to raid them of their star talents in both directing and acting. In April and May 1915, he took out full-page advertisements in *Cine Journal* to announce that he had signed the "best director in Russia," Iakov Protazanov (ironically twice misspelled in the ads as "Protozanov") to an exclusive contract of 20,000 rubles a year, a significant sum for a director. (Protazanov had left Thiemann, Reinhardt & Osipov in a dispute over salary.) *Cine Journal* noted with approval that Protazanov's "great talent will be well used at Ermolev"[43] —and this time spelled his name correctly.

Ermolev also lured a popular Moscow Dramatic Theater actor, Ivan Mozzhukhin, away from the "legitimate" stage in 1915.[44] No figures are available for Mozzhukhin's contract, but he was doubtless offered even more than Protazanov, given that established stars always earned the highest salaries in the movies.[45] The following year, when Ermolev signed the Moscow Art Theater star Olga Gzovskaia, he published a full-page announcement accompanied by a very flattering full-page publicity photograph of the actress.[46] (Studio raids then became fairly common, as when Kharitonov copied Ermolev's tactics in 1916 by stealing director Petr Chardynin from the Khanzhonkov studio.)[47]

By fall 1915, Ermolev was in the process of building a new, technically up-to-date studio, "in the American style" (*po Amerikanskii*), a studio that was admiringly described as "an entire cinema city."[48] He also recognized the importance of publishing his own journal, especially since Khanzhonkov had *two*, the glossy *Pegasus* (*Pegas*, a reference to his trademark) and the trade-oriented *Cinematographic Herald* (*Vestnik kinematografii*). Ermolev's *Projector* (*Proektor*) launched its first number at the beginning of October 1915, and it was as professionally polished as all his other endeavors. (*Projector's* capable editor, M. N. Aleinikov, became the head of the Soviet Mezhrabpom studio in the 1920s.)[49] In the pages of *Projector*, Ermolev elaborated his advertising campaigns and began to copy the "forthcoming" format foreign companies had used to such effect before the war. Among the earliest of these "teaser" promotions were the full-page advertisements for Protazanov's *Queen of Spades* (*Pikovaia dama*), where the director's name appeared more prominently than usual (but, of course, in letters considerably smaller than those used for Pushkin's).[50] During the revolutionary year of 1917, Ermolev was a leader in an effort to organize a producers' union, a subject to be discussed in chapter 4. Capable to the end, he organized the full-scale evacuation of his company, first from

Moscow to Yalta and then from Yalta to Paris, probably in late 1918. In the 1920s, Ermolev reemerged in France as "Joseph Ermolieff," owner of a studio first called Films Ermolieff and later Films Albatros.[51]

As important as the producers, studios, and distributors were to the formation of the industry and to the formulation of its strong class component, they were only one part of the equation. The next chapter explores the world of theaters, owners, and audiences. This was a chaotic universe that delighted and alarmed in equal measure and again provides a vivid picture of a society in flux and demonstrates the values of the new middle and entrepreneurial classes.

2

At the Movies

Theaters, Owners, Audiences

BY THE 1910–11 SEASON, WHEN THE FIRST TRADE JOURNALS WERE WELL under way, a Wild West atmosphere of energy, entrepreneurship, and a dash of danger prevailed in the Russian film industry. We have seen in the previous chapter the extent to which the production side of the business was in flux, a typical feature of early industrial development. But even more than in the production side of the business, the "local color" in exhibition was so vivid that it supported the fears of many in the intelligentsia about the corrupting effects of cinema (and by implication, of cultural commercialization) on Russian life.

Despite the continued trumpeting of the "brilliant" and "gigantic" economic potential of the industry, the frequent openings and closings of theaters attested to the fundamental instability of the business. In 1911, according to one report, there were 1,500 theaters nationwide, with 45 million rubles in annual revenue, but these figures are impossible to confirm and tend to fluctuate undoubtedly on the side of exaggeration.[1] In the early years, the prevalence of fly-by-night theater operators with un(der)developed business ethics did not help redeem cinema's troubled (and to a certain extent, undeserved) reputation for vulgarity, triviality, and trickery.[2] Nor did the hasty conversion of a large number of substandard buildings into theaters (at least one a former brothel) bolster the movies' reputation.[3] The concerns of the genteel about the possibilities of rubbing shoulders with the *hoi polloi* in the relatively democratic public space of the movie theater were minor compared with the real physical dangers. Theater fires were frequent, especially in the provinces, destroying the often ramshackle wooden structures that served as cinemas.

33

THE PROBLEMS OF THEATER OWNERSHIP

Unlike the producers we have discussed, who tended to come from established "middling" families or respectable professions, most theater owners were small-scale entrepreneurs. They usually had little previous business experience and relatively little capital and operated the "storefront" type of theater that dominated everywhere at this stage of cinema history, not just in Russia. In 1909, for example, a movie theater in Kursk was advertised for sale in the petty-bourgeois daily *Russian Word* (*Russkoe slovo*) for 4,000 rubles (as opposed to the 500,000 rubles needed to capitalize a studio).[4] Early movie theater operators faced many problems, not the least of which was the difficulty in ensuring a constant and adequate supply of electricity, a significant worry in the empire's provincial towns, though not so much in Moscow and St. Petersburg.[5]

Not surprisingly, personnel issues ranked high among theater owners' concerns. Finding qualified staff, especially projectionists and pianists, was difficult given the rapid and uncontrolled expansion of the industry and the undereducated population. As in every other aspect of the business, personnel turnover was high, 50 to 60 percent annually according to one source.[6] It was, furthermore, difficult to assess the qualifications of potential replacements, not surprising considering the lack of industry standards and the general predilection within the industry for grandiose overstatement of credentials and experience. Sometimes one can find a relatively straightforward notice in the "positions wanted" section of a trade journal, like that for Konstantin Leonidovich Shur of Kiev, an experienced movie theater manager, who sought 200 rubles a month and 8 percent of net profit for his services.[7]

Usually, however, hyperbole reigned. The "first-class, famous lady pianist [*pianistka*]" with "first-class references" who played the "first-class cinemas in Moscow and Petersburg" might well be worth the 125 to 150 rubles a month she was asking in salary.[8] But on the other hand, she might turn into a "Baroness von Disterlo" (as her name was rendered in the Cyrillic alphabet), whom the owner of the Progress theater in Omsk reported to the readers of *Cine Journal* (*Kine-zhurnal*) as a swindler. (The baroness had charged him a 25-ruble booking fee to engage her services but did not show up to play.)[9] Naturally, this meant the Progress's owner had to deal with angry audiences as well as financial loss, since movie performances without musical accompaniment were unheard of, apparently even in Omsk.[10] (Comically, *Cine Journal* was still running advertisements from the selfsame Baroness Alisa Ivanovna von Düsterlow as late as 1914, four years after the initial complaint.)[11]

Exploitation worked the other way as well. It was naturally much more common to hear sad stories about employers mistreating employees than the reverse. Although an experienced projectionist might earn 120 to 130 rubles a month in Petersburg or Moscow, 30 to 40 rubles was typical outside the capitals.[12] Belying this small salary, a projectionist, however, had to have considerable training in order to minimize the risk of fire and maximize the general enjoyment of the show by running the film at a reasonably correct and consistent speed.[13]

Mistreatment of theater workers, especially the pianists, frequently made the news, usually in a sensational way. In one of the earliest reported cases, Olga Bezpalova, a *pianistka* in a Petersburg movie theater, died from a heart attack brought on by exhaustion after several weeks of playing seven hours on weekdays, without a rest break (ten hours a day on holidays). On the day of her death, according to one account of the incident, she had played for twelve hours straight.[14]

Unscrupulous distributors sometimes tricked theater owners into booking nonexistent films falsely advertised as "sensational hits."[15] Extravagant advertising was the norm, even when the film was "real," and the theater owners themselves were often guilty of exaggerated promotions of their films. Dissatisfied customers, especially those misled by extravagant advertising claims, demanded redress. The Triumph (Triumf) theater in Samara drew large crowds in 1911 for the "scientific-educational" film *The Operations of Doctor Modlinskii (Operatsii d-ra Modlinskago)* because it promised quite a graphic depiction of the amputation of frozen fingers and the removal of a cancerous breast. Gory photos from this Khanzhonkov film, showing "before and after" shots of the diseased breast, had already appeared in the firm's journal, *Cinematographic Herald (Vestnik Kinematografii)*.[16] But apparently the film was not sickening enough for the audience. Disappointed spectators clamored for their money and demanded that the film be withdrawn from circulation.[17]

Such questionable or unethical practices were believed to be a common failing of private enterprise in Russia at this time, but the movie business seemed to be particularly susceptible to them. Other examples are less dramatic, though of more practical concern to patrons. Some theater owners sought to economize by turning the electric lights off in the foyers, leaving their prospective audiences waiting in the dark. Patrons found this especially troublesome if the show were not started on time, another problem commonly encountered in theaters where the program did not run continuously.[18]

Codes of "proper" conduct were well established in the legitimate theaters in Petersburg and Moscow, but discourtesy often prevailed at the movies and sometimes provoked disputes. (A drive for "passive politeness" in U.S. theaters and movie houses indicates that such discourtesy was also an issue in the United States at this time.)[19] These stories were rarely related to friction caused by the unfamiliar mixing of social classes, and more often sound more like the material for many of the period's farcical comedies. For example, the Moderne theater in Vladimir (the French *moderne* was a popular name for theaters) was the site of a "scandal" that provoked the audience enough to be reported in the press. "Mme. E." refused to remove her enormously large hat during the show and declined to accede to the vociferous demands of her fellow spectators that she take it off.[20] Failure to doff coats in the movie theater was also seen as a gross breach of etiquette that never would have been tolerated in "higher-class" urban entertainments.[21] Loving couples also took advantage of the darkness and "privacy" of movie theaters to hug and kiss during the shows.[22] (Vladimir Nabokov and his first love, Tamara, used to settle in "the last row of seats" for just this purpose.)[23] Finally, the etiquette mavens frequently cited loud coughing and inappropriate chatter and laughter as irritants encountered in the movies (a complaint that sounds all too familiar to the present-day moviegoer).[24]

The bad manners of movie reviewers also angered theater owners. To cite but one case, the editor of *Cinematographic Herald* told an owner after a preview (presumably gratis) that the film was not only good but "better than many of the other pictures of Russian production" — then had the nerve to turn around and write in his published review that it was "boring."[25] The idea that a film review should reflect independent critical judgment had not taken hold, the more commonly held belief being that unqualified admiration of films was essential for attracting audiences to the theaters and building the reputation of the industry.

ACCIDENTS AND FIRES

Much more serious, of course, than kissing, coughing, hats, and bad reviews were the accidents that occurred in theaters due to shoddy construction or poor maintenance. For example, at the Grand Hotel (Grand otel) theater in Lodz, Russian Poland, the upper balcony balustrade broke, sending several dozen people crashing down to the main floor. According to the dramatic account of the accident, "the whole hall rang with the cries of the wounded."[26]

Theater fires, sparked by the highly flammable nitrate film stock, poorly maintained equipment, and improperly trained projectionists, were, however, the most frequent and serious cause of injury. These conflagrations usually occurred at makeshift theaters, often with disastrous results. As Boris Pasternak's younger brother Aleksandr, the Soviet architect, recalled in his memoirs, his local cinematograph, located next to Erman's Emporium in Moscow, "would have appalled any fireman chancing to glance inside."[27] Soviet novelist Konstantin Paustovskii described the sound in the theater as one of terrific sizzling, "as if they were roasting a wild boar behind our backs."[28]

In 1909, to name only one of many examples, 14 people died in a theater fire in Tula.[29] But it was not until the Bologoe disaster in 1910 that the authorities and the industry were forced to take notice and enact serious preventive measures. The Bologoe fire broke out at a social club theater at the village railroad station, on the Nicholas (Nikolaevskii) line, midway between Moscow and Petersburg. Nearly 150 people (300 according to another account) were crammed into a long rectangular room with only one exit from the room and only one exit from the wooden building.[30] The theater quickly burned to the ground. Although precise figures of the dead and injured are hard to come by, two years after the accident it was reported that "dozens" (desiatki) perished.[31] The one specific casualty count in the cinema press claimed that 93 people died, mainly women and children, with 45 seriously injured.[32] This extraordinarily high casualty figure is quite believable considering the layout of the auditorium and the building, making the toll comparable to the Bazar de la Charité cinema fire in Paris in 1897.[33]

The response to the Bologoe tragedy was quick and uncompromising. One of the most blistering attacks appeared on the pages of Cine-phono (Sine-fono), the industry's only independent magazine (edited by Samuel Viktorovich Lure, who as we have seen later became a distributor). In the words of critic D. Kumanov, "the tragedy is the result of our lack of culture [nekulturnost], our lackadaisicalness [khalatnost], our ho-hum attitude toward everyone and everything."[34] Other articles called for an investigation in order to determine responsibility for the fire and demanded anti-fire ordinances.[35] Within the next few weeks, Cine-phono reported the government-ordered inspection and closing of unsafe theaters and the establishment of the first safety regulations.[36] These theater inspections continued throughout the year.

SUICIDES

A very peculiar source of negative publicity for theater owners stemmed from suicides in movie theaters, the apparent result of the emotions engendered by watching a movie. This bizarre phenomenon involved both staff and patrons and added even more melodrama to the sensational and violent ambiance of early moviegoing. Suicide was a fashionable preoccupation of European fin de siècle culture, and this was especially true in Russia, which underwent a suicide "epidemic" in the period 1906–14.[37] The press was filled with suicide stories, and suicides, especially youth suicides, were often connected to the rise of Westernized commercial culture and its deleterious moral effects. As an example, a cartoon in the popular illustrated magazine *Niva*, entitled "The Soul of the Times," showed a little boy holding a popgun to his head, a *Nat Pinkerton* novella at his feet.[38] As we shall see in chapter 5, suicide was also a major leitmotif in Russian films, and so there was concern about the influence of these particular films on audiences.

One of many examples reported in the press was the unexplained suicide of the anonymous "quiet and reserved" ticket taker at the Michel (Mishel) theater in Saratov, who "never drank vodka" (as the reporter took pains to note). The sad young man nevertheless killed himself right in the theater.[39] Another touching story was that of the suicide of the "talented youth" Nikolai Petrovich Melioranskii, a twenty-two-year-old student who moonlighted as a projectionist at merely eight rubles a month in the hopes of saving enough money to further his education.[40] At the Don theater in Novocherkassk, the seventeen-year-old pianist, T. Fakerot, shot himself at the stroke of midnight while playing for the show. His suicide letter said that he would need neither "laughter nor tears" at his future destination.[41]

Even more tragic was the suicide of Ekaterina Iakovlevna Mitina, the "young and beautiful" twenty-four-year-old cashier of the Mirage (Mirazh) theater in the town of Arzamas (Novgorod province). She killed herself after a quarrel with the Mirage's owner, her elderly (sixtyish) common-law husband, identified only by his initials "A. P. R-z-S-skii," described as "old, jealous, and not very attractive." The opprobrium unleashed by the scandal, which included charges that he had regularly battered Mitina, eventually forced "R-z-S-skii" to sell his business and leave town.[42]

Another particularly sensational suicide was that of Sh. Belokhovskii, the manager of a movie theater in Odessa, who hanged himself on the stage behind the screen. His body was discovered near the end of the evening's last show by the projectionist, Golovatiuk, who had gone to check the lighting in the wings when he noticed Belokhovskii's dangling legs. He ran back into the hall shrieking, "Stop the film! A person has hanged himself!" The reasons for this suicide, which occurred shortly after the outbreak of the war, were unknown.[43]

From reading Russian history and especially Russian literature, one can easily imagine the poverty and sense of marginalization that may have attended these foreshortened lives in provincial backwaters. The most prominent person to commit suicide in a movie theater was I. M. Timonin, member of a well-to-do Moscow merchant family and owner of the elegant Coliseum (Kolizei) theater. Coincidentally, the week of Timonin's death *Cine Journal* published a feature article on the Coliseum, which described the theater as "one of the best cinema palaces in Moscow." Its reputation for mounting a consistently excellent program of films drew moviegoers even from outside the city environs. According to *Cine Journal*, the Coliseum's profitability could reliably be expected to increase even further.[44] On the day of his death, Timonin, ever attentive to detail, made certain that everything was set for the evening's show, discussed new bookings with one of his employees, then went to his office and shot himself. His enigmatic suicide note read: "Dying, I beg forgiveness. I'm tired of fighting with failure."[45]

Moviegoers also found the movie theater a satisfactory public setting for the usually private act of suicide. In the town of Pskov, at yet another Moderne (Modern) theater, a man identified as the "petty-bourgeois [*meshchanin*] M. V. Bykhovskii" shot himself with a bulldog revolver at the moment that a suicide was taking place on screen. His suicide note said that he was unable to live without Lev Tolstoi (who had died some two months before this incident). The audience initially thought the shot was a sound effect added for their enjoyment.[46]

In Krasnovodsk, a twenty-four-year-old man identified only by his surname, Koshelev, killed himself in the theater before the show started, at the end of a musical piece ("Longing" [Toska]) that was playing on the gramophone for the audience's enjoyment.[47] And at the cinema at the Constantine (Konstantinovskii) railroad station (Donskoi district), a young man became very agitated during the film, identified in the newspaper account as *The Last Hour* (*Poslednyi chas*), which according to the reporter depicted an unhappy love affair. The young man abruptly left the theater before the film had finished, went home, and shot himself.[48]

These unfortunate incidents continued to plague theater owners in the provincial towns right up to the time of the Revolution. Nonetheless, by the eve of the First World War, in major cities the movie exhibition business had become reasonably legitimate and definitely profitable as business practices were regularized. Given Russia's economic and political instability, this was no mean achievement. The requirements for running a successful movie theater in Moscow or Petersburg demonstrate that the standards of the major urban areas were quite sophisticated, on a "European" level (as satisfied or dissatisfied critics always phrased the comparisons). Certainly, the discrepancies in exhibition standards between the city and the country provide yet another illustration of the vast chasm between urban and rural life in Russia at that time.

AUDIENCES

It is difficult to determine audience composition and audience preferences in Russia during the early years of cinema, except through fairly indirect means. No equivalents to the helpful Soviet audience surveys of the 1920s exist for the prerevolutionary period. It is also hard to calculate the numbers of spectators precisely, because box office receipts, potentially a useful indicator, are unreliable owing to widely varying ticket prices. One 1914 report, however, put attendance in 1913 at 108 million.[49] Regular patrons were numbered at 12 million, less than 10 percent of the population of about 140 million. These numbers are, however, fairly impressive given that cinema was then an almost exclusively urban phenomenon in a nation that was overwhelmingly rural, and represent half the urban population.[50]

The Russian haute bourgeoisie and cultural intelligentsia did not recoil from the cinema to the extent their Western counterparts did; they quickly reconciled themselves to it, and even, we dare imagine, enjoyed themselves. Nonetheless cinema going was a pastime primarily identified with the "middling classes" in the cities, including the literate proletariat. This was especially true in the provinces, where there was little to do at a reasonable cost (despite the increase of "people's theater" and other populist cultural efforts).[51] At least one budding Marxist believed that there was enough working-class identification among movie audiences to warrant passing out Social Democratic leaflets as people left the theater. In Letichev (Podolsk province), a seventeen-year-old Jewish youth named Meier Tenenbaum was arrested and sentenced to eight months in prison for this crime.[52] A very different kind of theater-related crime, that shows the unsavory elements one might find at the movies, was committed by the three "hooligans" in Izmailovo who beat up the ticket taker at the Beau Monde (Bomond) theater because he wouldn't let them in for free.[53]

Much of the early criticism of cinema was frankly elitist, focusing on the fearful fact that the movies appeared to hold special appeal for those who had to work for a living. G. Tsyperovich, a critic writing in *Contemporary World* (*Sovremennyi mir*), asserted that the typical cinema audience consisted of proletarians and "Gorkii character types" (from *The Lower Depths*, perhaps) who possessed the moral values of "hottentot philistines." Tsyperovich also complained that the arbitrary tsarist censorship was more concerned with preventing Tolstoi's funeral from being shown on the screen than with inhibiting the infiltration of the "bourgeois capitalist" values that predominated in melodrama and comedy.[54]

Regardless of all the talk about the supposedly democratic nature of cinema and the viewing experience, class consciousness was strong, reflecting the difficulties in defining the new public space of the movie theater. Theater owners catered to specific social groups (although there is no evidence that they showed movies specifically intended to attract them). The cinema press was quite concerned with discussions of social class and with identifying which class(es) attended which theaters, probably to inform potential spectators, helping them to avoid an unpleasant surprise. *Cine-phono*, for example, reported that the "so-called middle class" attended the Grand Moscow Electric (Bolshoi moskovskii elektricheskii) theater, specifying that this consisted of salespeople from the fashionable shops, clerks, and the petty bourgeoisie (*meshchane*).[55] Baku's five theaters were categorized as follows: the aristocracy and the intelligentsia attended the Odeon, the middle classes and lower intelligentsia went to the Phenomenon (Fenomen). The French Electric-Biograph (Frantsuzkii elektrichesko-biograf) and the Express (Ekspress) catered exclusively to the middle classes, and the Moderne (Modern), to "simple people."[56]

Writers for trade journals were under the impression that for the first decade of film exhibition in Russia, people mainly went to the movies to "kill time," not caring what the show was.[57] Young people went to the pictures specifically to meet friends and generally to be seen.[58] And Aleksandr Pasternak's vivid recollections of the "hot, excited children" who packed his favorite cinema and were transfixed by whatever happened to be showing seem quite believable.[59]

The fact that audiences would "drop in" on impulse, and regardless of whether or not the program had started, was reported early.[60] By late 1911, it was occasionally the case that a film like Goncharov's *Defense of Sevastopol* (*Oborona Sevastopolia*), with its "noisy" publicity campaign and patriotic theme, would attract audiences regardless of critical merit.[61] Movie reviews had little apparent influence on potential audiences at this time and were generally extensions of advertising campaigns.

EXHIBITION PRACTICES

One of the most important ways to increase the status of cinema going as a leisure practice was to upgrade theaters. Aleksandr Pasternak, who was born in 1893, describes the typical storefront theater in the days when cinema was still an "illusion":

> Everything from projector to auditorium was ludicrously home-made and primitive. Quite obviously an ordinary, rather low-ceilinged first-floor apartment had been gutted to create a little hall, reached directly from the main house-stair. Perhaps as a precaution against fire, the door had been lifted off its hinges and replaced by a heavy red-plush curtain, which was drawn tight during performances, to block out the light from the stairwell. Ordinary Viennese chairs were set out in two or three rows and, in contradistinction to all later cinemas, the Pathé projector . . . stood in *front* of the audience reminding me of the old magic-lantern shows at home. It was set up on a primitive trestle stand, and in front of it hung the screen — if not a sheet like ours, then some equally makeshift substitute, which used to billow in mid-performance.[62]

Certainly, adults would quickly tire of such discomfort. Owners of the deluxe movie theaters had to figure out how to attract the elite without alienating the urban middle classes who were the mainstay of the movie business. An appeal to the Russian love for European-style luxury was a logical answer.

As was the case in Western Europe and the United States, the size of the auditorium and lobbies mattered a great deal to the "better" clients.[63]

First-class urban theaters needed to be large enough (usually 900 to 1,000 seats) to enable separation of spectators of varying socio-economic backgrounds. Prices for seats on the main floor ranged from 20 to 50 kopeks, loge boxes from 4 to 6 rubles, a very considerable amount of money, even taking into account that the boxes could seat up to six people. Because of the fear of fires, deluxe theaters advertised their ample number of fire exits, eight to ten in buildings of the type described, and touted the care they took to ensure patron safety and comfort.

When rating movie establishments, overall grandeur came next to size in importance. Amenities, heating (essential in Russian winters), and the luxury of their appointments were all key factors. (The decoration of the foyer was of special importance in Russian cinemas, perhaps because of the inclement Russian climate which encouraged people to use the foyer as refuge from the elements.) Next came the quality of the music, with live music, piano and violin, preferred over the gramophone. During intermissions in the "best" Moscow theaters, a "small" orchestra of 36 to 40 pieces would play selections from the "classics," enhancing the cultural experience.[64]

Only then were the movies themselves considered as evaluative criteria, not as individual titles, but as repertory. Trade journals instructed owners on how many pictures constituted a standard program and how often the program should change, based on European and American models. Before the war, a first-rate theater had four to five pictures on its program, including at least one comedy, and changed the program more than twice a week, as often as *five* times a week.[65] Programs with "Parisian flavor" commanded the highest prices, according to the recollections of Thiemann & Reinhardt cameraman Aleksandr Levitskii.[66]

Clearly, variety mattered a great deal to early audiences. Not until later, as we shall see in the next chapter, were owners drawn to book the much longer, more expensive, "exclusive hits" like *The Keys to Happiness*.[67] In 1911, the ideal program was described as being 1,240 meters in length (about ninety minutes, allowing for variations in projection speeds). According to this particular recommendation, an exemplary program should consist of five films: one "sensational" (erotic and/or violent) melodrama (600 meters), one "long" comedy (300 meters), one short documentary (100 meters), two short comedies (120 meters each).[68] (In the very earliest years, programs lasted fifteen to twenty minutes, at least according to Aleksandr Pasternak. He recalled the reason being the projector's propensity to overheat very quickly and start smoking.)[69]

Not surprisingly, given the nature of capitalist expansion and the Russian penchant for grandiosity, as time went on, bigger became better, and entrepreneurs vied with each other to open the best and most lavish "palaces to the god cinema."[70] The first-class, first-run theaters were believed to be the most profitable, attracting ever larger audiences, especially during the war, when movie attendance skyrocketed.[71] A theater like the Artistic (Khudozhestvennyi), on Arbat Square in Moscow, which opened in 1909 and has been a movie theater ever since, had to be continuously remodeled and expanded in order to keep its "first-class" status.[72] In 1911, the Saturn theater in St. Petersburg was renovated to become what we now call a multiplex, with *three* screening halls, a spacious entryway and foyer, and wide stairs.[73] The Soleil (Solel) theater, also in St. Petersburg, located on Nevskii Prospect, featured ten thousand watts of lighting in the main foyer, an electrical ventilation system, and a twenty-five-piece orchestra to accompany the program.[74] But even a less grandiose theater like the Forum in Moscow, with a mere 1,018 seats, still counted as a true cinema palace, noted as much for its great pianist, A. Levin (who excited applause after each show) as for its movies.[75]

Most movie theaters were independently owned and operated, but as we have seen in the previous chapter, a few owners like Libken and Kharitonov eventually became producers, too. The reverse was also true. Studio head Aleksandr Khanzhonkov, a very clever businessman who early developed distribution monopolies of his films, saw the advantage of building his own theaters in Moscow to show his movies. The Pegasus theater, named after his studio trademark, opened in late 1913 with two thousand seats, an orchestra in the lobby and a pianist for the films.[76] (This theater, located on Maiakovskii Square in Moscow, is still in operation.)

With the outbreak of war and the cinema boom it engendered, the trend toward ever larger and grander theaters accelerated, especially in Moscow, now entrenched as the empire's moviemaking capital. The Empire (Ampir), with its interior gardens and its masses of brilliant electrical lights, immediately attracted overflow crowds. The Arts (Ars) featured two foyers; the large one on the main floor offered a cafe with seating (rather than a stand-up buffet) and a lobby orchestra in addition to the orchestra playing for the film. Of course, such luxury came at a high cost (even factoring in the inflation that accompanied the war). A third-balcony seat at the Arts cost a hefty sixty-five kopeks, with a loge box bringing in *ten* rubles.[77]

By 1915, competition among the big city theaters for audiences was stiff, especially in Moscow and Petrograd (as St. Petersburg was patriotically renamed). As a result, advertising claimed a significant proportion of theater operating budgets. Continuous, elaborate advertising was especially important because it was believed that although working-class moviegoers attended only theaters in their own neighborhoods, the "middling classes" that were the mainstay of the business attended whichever theaters in town attracted their attention.[78] As a result, advertising budgets in Moscow and Petrograd for the "palaces" supposedly averaged an astonishing 2,000 to 3,000 rubles a month; advertising for an exceptional film might cost that much a week, for posters, flyers, brochures, and other gimmicks. (One Petrograd theater regularly mailed 32,000 programs *weekly* to its regular customers.)[79]

Theater advertisements began to extol not only their film programs, but also their accoutrements. Petrograd's Parisian theater, for example, claimed it was the "most comfortable" in the capital and promised a biweekly change in its repertory of "sensational" pictures. According to one ad: "Our three interests are: (1) the interests of our clients; (2) the best films; (3) accuracy" (the last point presumably referring to the industry's well-known proclivity for rather extreme exaggeration).[80]

That these grand theaters became the shabby, bullet-pocked halls of the 1920s, with dirty torn screens, where audiences were treated to the doleful music of a single broken-down piano was but one sign of how the Revolution had changed the urban landscape and popular culture.[81] Another sign was the emigration (or, in a few cases, the deaths) of the stars of the Russian cinematic firmament. These stars, who launched Russian cinema to a higher plane, are the subject of the next chapter.

3

Sensation!

Stars and Hits

NOT UNTIL THE EARLY 1910S, WHEN THE NOVELTY FACTOR OF CINEMA
had worn off and producers learned more savvy business practices, did
Russian moviegoers become starstruck. We have seen in the previous
chapter that at first people tended to drop in at the movies, not caring what
film was showing or even if it had already begun. Audiences gradually
began demanding more, and producers and directors were now ready to
give it to them. Two key factors in the further commercialization of the
industry were the development of a rudimentary star system, building on
the public's lust for heroes, and the production and promotion of specific films as hits, usually featuring recognizable "names" who epitomized
urban glamour and style.

THE ALLURE OF FOREIGN STARS

The long-standing glamour of the foreign in Russian elite culture, which
was pronounced in urban culture as well, proved a serious impediment to
building a native star system. Among all the actresses whose films were
shown in Russia, whether Russian or foreign, Asta Nielsen (1883–1972),
the world-famous Danish star of German cinema, reigned supreme in
Russia as she did elsewhere. After the legendary, European-wide success
of her first film, The Abyss (Afgründen [Danish]; Bezdna [Russian]), her
name appeared over and over again in the Russian press.[1] Initially, Nielsen's training at the Royal Copenhagen Theater was an important selling
point in Russian promotion of her work, another sign of the way the film
industry attempted to link itself to an already well established art like the
theater.

The Tanagra company, which distributed Nielsen's films in Russia, advertised her as the "[Eleonora] Duse of the Cinema," thereby connecting her to yet another much-admired foreign star.[2] Tanagra's promotion of Nielsen was extravagant, even by the hyperbolic standards of the time. One typical Nielsen advertisement read: "the brightest star in the international heavens of cinema."[3] Or more simply and effectively:

TWO magical WORDS:

ASTA NIELSEN![4]

Mintus, which distributed Nielsen's films in the empire's Baltic provinces, promoted her much the same way.[5]

Among actors, the undisputed king of the screen was also a foreigner: the French comic sensation Max Linder, whom the Pathé studio advertised in Russia as the "king of laughter."[6] Linder (after whom Charlie Chaplin modeled himself) was truly a continental phenomenon. His popularity in the prewar period crossed all national boundaries in Europe. Touted as the highest-paid movie star of his time, he was reputed to receive an annual salary of one million francs.[7] Vladimir Nabokov used him as a mnemonic device in his memoirs, dubbing one of his tutors "Max" owing to his resemblance to Linder.[8]

In December 1913, Max, as he was familiarly known, came to Russia on a publicity tour sponsored by Pathé. (Negotiations for this visit had begun more than a year earlier, in May 1912, when Charles Pathé himself visited Russia.)[9] Linder's popularity had reached "epidemic" proportions among the entire urban population of European Russia: "everyone loves him—men, women, children. . . ."[10] Newspapers publicized his itinerary in advance so that "every move" of the "hero of the screen" could be followed in the press.[11] Russian entrepreneurs were understandably frantic to derive some advantage or, at least, bask in a little reflected glory from the charismatic French comic.[12]

Linder's first stop was St. Petersburg, where "'Max' came, he was seen, and he conquered."[13] Large crowds braved the cold to greet him at the station, and the scene was repeated outside the Astoria Hotel, where he was staying while in Petersburg.[14] Next "King Max I" went to Moscow, to be met with the same levels of crowd enthusiasm.[15] He stayed in Moscow for one dazzling week, and *Cine Journal* (*Kine-zhurnal*) printed his entire itinerary *day by day*.[16] A highlight of his tour was a banquet in his honor attended by six hundred local luminaries.[17] Linder visited not only Petersburg and Moscow, but also Odessa, where his welcome was as tumultuous as it had been everywhere else.[18]

Linder's fans were known as the "Maxists" (*Maksistki*) prompting the feuilletonist "Vorwarts" to quip (with a political aside):

Who is more popular?
—Marx or Max?
—Max.
He's the most popular man on earth!
Everybody knows him . . . everybody loves him.[19]

Linder's fame and fan following inspired the ever-enterprising producer A. O. Drankov to find a Russian double for the Frenchman, A. P. Kozlov, who acted under the name "Maxi."[20]

Linder volunteered for service in the French army as soon as war broke out,[21] and on August 30, 1914, the movie fan's worst nightmare appeared to have come true. Russian newspapers (the general press as well as the cinema press) reported that Linder had been killed in battle, based on information from the "special correspondent" of the *Russian Word* (*Russkoe slovo*) in Bordeaux. The press was filled with page after page of lamentations and tributes, before the happy news came three weeks later: "LINDER LIVES!"[22] Apart from worries over the effect the new entertainment taxes levied to help finance the war would have on ticket prices, Linder's rumored demise was the chief concern the war seems to have engendered in the rather apolitical film community.

The evidence that Linder and Nielsen were truly international movie stars is unambiguous and overwhelming. The other major European star popular in the empire was the handsome Danish actor Valdemar Psilander, renamed "Garrison" for Russian consumption. Ivan Perestiani, actor and director in both the Russian and Soviet periods, recalled in his memoirs that "Garrison" was guaranteed to fill theaters. Soviet director Fridrikh Ermler also remembered the Dane fondly as one of his favorite actors, when Ermler was a young movie "maniac" growing up in a provincial town in Latvia.[23] And in 1911, an industry survey of the most popular movie stars in Russia came up with only three names: "Garrison," Linder, Nielsen.[24]

Distributors attempted to capitalize on the authentic fame of these European actors by fabricating fame through advertising. Other Westerners trumpeted in a similar manner in the Russian press—like Liza Nebushka, Tanagra's "new star from Lisbon," or Vitascope's Toni Silva, the "tsaritsa of the screen"—probably did not deserve the accolades they received.[25]

Tanagra, for example, launched an advertising campaign intended to persuade Russian audiences that the versatile French movie actress Suzanne Grandais was a movie star à la Nielsen:

SUZANNE GRANDAIS
A sorceress [*volshebnitsa*] of the screen!!!
A star of cinematography!!! [26]

Robert Perskii likewise promoted the German actress Henny Porten tirelessly. Grandais and Porten were undeniably major film stars in their respective homelands, but whether they appealed to Russian audiences in the same way they did to French and German audiences is an open question.[27] The same is true for the Italian stars Lyda Borelli and Francesca Bertini, both glamorous actresses who were prominently featured in promotions for their films, which were imported in large numbers. (Bertini, however, could count a few "independent admirers," like Perestiani and Ermler.)[28] In Russia, therefore, film stardom often became as much a matter of advertising as of credible talent or proven box office drawing power. *Saying* someone was a star tended to make it (as good as) true.

THE CONSTRUCTION OF RUSSIAN FAME

Could Russians ever be seen as attractive as these European stars? Not surprisingly, given the status of the "legitimate" theater in Russia and Russia's rich theatrical tradition, one of the very first Russian actresses to be featured in a movie advertisement came from the stage: the Malyi Theater's E. N. Roshchina-Insarova. Thiemann & Reinhardt, which soon excelled in star building, bought a full page in *Cinematographic Herald* (*Vestnik kinematografii*), most of it for a portrait photograph of Roshchina-Insarova.[29]

But Russian theater actors and actresses initially proved even more reluctant than their Western counterparts to act in the movies, a fact often lamented in the cinema press. It was noted, for example, in *Cinematographic Herald* that the great French dramatic actress Sarah Bernhardt could appear on the screen in France and draw praise rather than criticism, whereas in Russia Roshchina-Insarova was, at that point, one of very few daring enough dare to make the transition.[30] (In an interview, Roshchina-Insarova noted that her chief incentive for film acting was her desire to preserve her work for posterity, a statement that provides evidence of her historical consciousness as well as of her ego.)[31]

Disingenuous promotion seemed to be the answer. One blatant example came from the Bystritskii studio in Petrograd. Bystritskii promoted his new "star," opera singer Nataliia Ivanovna Tamara, dubbed "the Famous," by purchasing a *six*-page, red-tinted, glossy photo insert to *Cinephono (Sine-fono)* to advertise her first film. This included a full-page soft-focus photo portrait of the singer and a two-page layout of all the other actors in the film, their photos inset in stars. Tamara can be found center stage, located inside the biggest star, since she was the major star in this "pléiade." [32] There is, however, no credible evidence that Tamara actually occupied a position of any importance in early Russian cinema.

Although critics had recognized as early as 1908 that Russian cinema would benefit from a native movie star system modeled after the theater's, efforts to promote local talent were halfhearted until the outbreak of the war. [33] As the demand for "stars" grew, especially for native Russian stars, few theater actors and actresses could resist the temptation to work in the movies. First, the cinema had the power to reach much wider audiences; which actress would not want to be as internationally famous as Asta Nielsen? Furthermore, its large salaries (paid for by the wartime boom in the industry) were an added attraction. By 1915, doubts seem to have vanished and "everybody" of note in the theater world was trying out movie acting. [34]

Movie studios vied for the biggest names, and salaries rose astronomically (at least by Russian standards). In 1916, for example, the Kharitonov studio signed Vladimir Vasilevich Maksimov (1880–1937) for a reputed 48,000 rubles a year, a sum ironically referred to as "small change" by the reporter. [35] Maksimov was the son of a singing teacher at the Petersburg conservatory and had begun his acting career at the Malyi and Moscow Art Theaters. Wooed away from R. D. Perskii, where he had had a ten-picture contract, Maksimov was widely recognized as one of the Russian screen's finest actors (Jay Leyda, however, believed that Maksimov's resemblance to Danish matinée idol Valdemar Psilander was the chief source of his appeal). [36] Maksimov was one of the first Russian film stars invited to make a picture abroad, and he continued working in the early Soviet period. Sadly, he suffered a severe nervous breakdown in 1926, after watching one of his old movies, where he had costarred with the luminous Vera Kholodnaia. No one in the audience recognized him, which was apparently too painful for him to bear. [37]

Ivan Mozzhukhin (1889/90?–1939), who earned an international reputation for his work as an emigré in French cinema after the Revolution (as "Mosjoukine"), was undeniably an authentic Russian star. Mozzhukhin — who according to Neia Zorkaia came from a Penza peasant family, and to Romil Sobolev, from an intelligentsia family! — invariably ranked after Maksimov in terms of acting ability, screen presence, and drawing power in the opinion of his peers.[38] (Vladimir Nabokov, however, remembered him as the "favorite actor of the day" and admired his "steely eye" and the "celebrated little muscle [that] twitched under the tight skin of his jaw.")[39] As a sign of the stature of European stars, and the persistent Russian national inferiority complex, the highest compliment paid to Mozzhukhin and Maksimov was that they were as "good on the screen as any Westerners."[40]

Just as it proved impossible to find a Russian Linder, so it was hard for native studios to "discover" Russian actresses with the same charisma and screen-acting ability as an Asta Nielsen. (Critics already understood that actors who were brilliant on the stage could not necessarily transfer their genius to the screen.) So high was Nielsen's position in the firmament that it was rare for an actress even to be compared to her (although as we have seen Russian producers never feared hyperbole). One exception, from the studio of the unflappable Iosif Ermolev, was Apollonia Chalupiec (1894–1987), known in the West as "Pola Negri," the "vamp" who became a major Hollywood star in the 1920s. Negri, whom Ermolev touted as the "Russian Asta Nielsen" though she was in fact Polish, did not make much of a splash in early Russian cinema. She emigrated before the Revolution, first to Germany and then to the United States.[41]

Olga Preobrazhenskaia (1881/84?–1971), a former stage actress from a respectable gentry family, was poised to become a major movie star after her leading role as Mania in Thiemann & Reinhardt's record-breaking blockbuster *The Keys to Happiness* (*Kliuchi schastia*).[42] Although the cultivated Preobrazhenskaia continued to land leading parts, she was much less successful in subsequent screen roles, and indeed was often criticized for her lack of screen presence. In her early thirties, Preobrazhenskaia was seen as too old for the parts of Liza in *Nest of Gentlefolk* (*Dvorianskoe gnezdo*) and Natasha in *War and Peace* (*Voina i mir*). By 1916, she had turned to directing, mainly in partnership with Vladimir Gardin (her director in *The Keys to Happiness, Nest of Gentlefolk,* and *War and Peace*), and became an important Soviet director in the 1920s, best known for *Peasant Women of Riazan* (*Baby riazanskie*).

The most lucrative contract for an actress (insofar as there is available evidence) was Olga Gzovskaia's three-picture deal with Robert Perskii, for a very handsome 20,000 rubles.[43] Gzovskaia (1889–1962), like Preobrazhenskaia a classically trained actress from a minor gentry family, received critical praise for her "musical" movements and "splendid" screen presence. She brought genuine personality to her roles, a quality rightly prized but hard to find.[44]

Among those other, very rare Russian actresses whose work received both critical praise and (apparent) popular acclaim was former Bolshoi ballerina Vera Karalli (1888/89?–1972), who turned to movie acting following a dancing injury that ended her balletic career. Her portrayal of the eponymous Natasha Rostova in the Khanzhonkov studio's version of *War and Peace* (*Natasha Rostova*, directed by Chardynin) was described as "enchanting" in a *Cine Journal* review. *Cine Journal* proclaimed Karalli (with justice) as "a true artist of the screen."[45] She made even lesser pictures tolerable by virtue of her ethereal beauty and exquisite grace.[46]

And finally, but most importantly, there was Vera Kholodnaia, in B. S. Likhachev's glowing words "the first and only true Russian cinema actress."[47] Kholodnaia (1893–1919) was born in Poltava as Vera Levchenko, the daughter of a teacher. After her father's death, relatives sent her to Moscow to study ballet at the Bolshoi, but she married a lawyer (or military officer, according to some accounts) at the age of seventeen.[48] Kholodnaia, the only major early Russian movie star to have gone straight to cinema, began her dazzling career at the Khanzhonkov studio with the great director Evgenii Bauer. According to Vladimir Gardin, he "discovered" her and very generously introduced her to Bauer.[49]

However it happened, Kholodnaia's name was first featured in summer 1915 and her photo in the fall of that year. For a star of such legendary status, there is surprisingly little contemporary evidence with which to support that legend, although I combed the trade journals assiduously. Indeed her contemporary, Ivan Perestiani, "broke his head" trying to understand her posthumous popularity.[50] But Perestiani's views aside, those few performances still extant, some of which will be examined in part 2, indicate that Kholodnaia was an actress of extraordinary luminosity, a star who prefigured the style (and cult) of Louise Brooks a decade later. However trite the vehicle, Vera Kholodnaia lit up the screen.[51]

Alive, Kholodnaia was honored with a ditty in *Cine Journal* that offers a wordplay on her surname, which means "cold" in Russian. Loosely translated, it goes like this:

Here's an artist of the first rank,
In a Muscovite's opinion.
Her name is "cold,"
But her acting is hot.[52]

Even in death, her public adored her, and the stir caused by her untimely death in Odessa from the Spanish influenza, at the age of only twenty-six, has been captured in a fragment of the newsreel of her funeral.[53]

With a clear sense that an era had ended, an accounting of the "kings and queens" of the screen appeared in the final issue of *Cine Journal* (dated December 30, 1917). The "queens" so honored were listed as Vera Karalli, Nataliia Lisenko (russifying the spelling of her name from the Ukrainian "Lysenko"), Vera Kholodnaia, and Vera Iureneva. The "kings" were proclaimed to be Ivan Mozzhukhin (who was Lisenko's husband), Vladimir Maksimov, Vitold Polonskii (1879–1919), Osip Runich, and Ivan Khudoleev.[54] This article proved to be an epitaph to the stars of Russian cinema, since the industry began to disband and flee the country the following year.

DIRECTORS AND WRITERS

Although by the time of the Revolution studio heads had definitely decided that the most effective way to "sell" pictures was through the stars, directors and writers were often promoted as well. While most Russian directors of this era worked in virtual anonymity, there were four whose names were invariably featured with their films as a hallmark of artistic excellence: Evgenii Bauer, Petr Chardynin, Vladimir Gardin, and Iakov Protazanov.

Evgenii Frantsevich Bauer (1865–1917) was arguably the best director among the four and certainly the most creative and original talent of early Russian cinema. A painter, photographer, and set designer before he became a film director, Bauer came from an artistically inclined family of Czech origins. Bauer's father, Franz, was a musician and composer, and his sister, Zinaida, known as the "Beloved of the Public," starred in operettas.[55] Bauer worked briefly for Pathé as an art director before joining Khanzhonkov, reputedly for a salary of forty thousand rubles a year, which would have made him Russia's highest paid director.[56] Bauer "carried" the Khanzhonkov studio alone after the defection of Chardynin to Kharitonov, and his death in summer 1917 was a serious blow to the artistic aspirations of the Russian film industry.[57] Bauer's aestheticized visual style was so distinctive that the term "Bauer film" was used by his contemporaries. At the time of his death, he was considered "highly talented and popular" as well as "one of the best Russian and even, *European* directors [emphasis added]."[58] There could be no higher praise.

Petr Ivanovich Chardynin, born Krasavchikov (1873/77?–1934) was perhaps the most prolific of the early Russian directors and continued to direct in Soviet cinema. By 1917, he had more than two hundred films to his credit, most of them commercial successes, though few are artistically memorable, certainly not by comparison to Bauer's.[59] An actor who had played with the Moscow City People's Theater, Chardynin began working in film as a narrator, offering his services for "artistic cinema declamations."[60] He continued to act after he became a director, even in his own films. His work, as we shall see in part 2, was characterized by its range and eclecticism.

Like Chardynin, Iakov Protazanov and Vladimir Gardin became important directors in the early Soviet period, providing interesting continuities between Soviet cinema and its lively Russian predecessor. Gardin and Protazanov, who quickly went their separate ways, first came to fame in 1913 at the Thiemann & Reinhardt studio (soon Thiemann, Reinhardt & Osipov) as the co-directors of the major hit of Russian cinema, *The Keys to Happiness*, discussed below. Which of them was the "lead" director on this extraordinarily successful film became a matter of bitter debate between the two men. In his garrulous account, the egocentric Gardin claimed virtually all the credit: he wrote the script, he cast Preobrazhenskaia as the lead; the only time the "quiet and reserved" Protazanov did anything (according to Gardin) was when Gardin, who played the role of Svirskii in the film, was in front of the camera.[61] (Anastasiia Verbitskaia, author of the novel on which the movie was based, neatly sidestepped the issue by praising both.)[62] Protazanov and Gardin left Thiemann at the same time, in 1915, under rancorous circumstances. The beleaguered, Baltic-born Thiemann, struggling against the anti-German backlash that erupted during the war, felt that his star directors had betrayed him.[63]

Vladimir Rostislavovich Gardin (1877–1965) wrote three vivid, entertaining, and often rather suspect volumes of memoirs, so we have much more information about him than we do about other figures of early Russian cinema. Gardin's mother abandoned the family when he was a baby, leaving his sister Margo and himself in the care of his father, an army officer, and his mother's sister (whose relationship with his father was, as Gardin slyly noted, "not entirely clear"). Gardin's father forced him into a military career, which the self-described young scamp found "as boring as school"; to divert himself Gardin became involved in amateur theater. He left the army to work as a theater director and joined Khanzhonkov as an actor in 1912, quickly moving on to the Thiemann studio, where he became a director.[64]

Gardin claims he left Thiemann in 1915 over a contract dispute, not because of the "German" problem; Gardin wanted 30 percent of the net profits on his films, which Thiemann not surprisingly refused. Gardin then became a co-owner of Vengerov & Gardin, part of the wartime boom in new studios, and worked as the studio's chief director, with Vengerov handling the business end of the operation.[65] Gardin took Thiemann's leading lady Olga Preobrazhenskaia with him to Vengerov & Gardin and staged another coup by signing the well-known "gypsy" singer Nadezhda Plevitskaia as an actress.[66] The partnership between Vengerov and Gardin lasted only a year, however, and in 1916 Gardin was on his own, with Vengerov continuing to run the studio they had founded.

Iakov Aleksandrovich Protazanov (1881–1945) was the well-educated grandson of a rich Moscow merchant and abandoned the family business to go abroad in 1905.[67] He became acquainted with the Pathé studio while in France and in 1908 entered the business as an interpreter for the short-lived Gloria studio (to translate for the cinematographer). He worked briefly and with little success as a film actor and scriptwriter before coming into his own as a director for Thiemann. The first time his name appeared in print in connection with a Thiemann film was in 1912, when he co-directed a picture with Elizaveta Thiemann, Thiemann's capable wife. This film, *The Passing of the Great Old Man* (*Ukhod velikogo startsa*), about the last days of Lev Tolstoi, cost a phenomenal forty thousand rubles. It was advertised by the studio before its limited release due to a lawsuit from the Tolstoi family as a "sensation" and, redundantly, as a "chef d'oeuvre of art" (*shedevr iskusstva*).[68] Despite Protazanov's fame as a director, the spelling of his name proved confusing, as we have already noted. If his surname did not appear as "Protozanov," then his initials were reversed, as in "the famous director A. Ia. Protazanov."[69]

One other director of note must be mentioned, Vasilii Goncharov (1861–1915). Goncharov died just as the industry was poised for takeoff; had he lived, he would doubtless have joined the ranks of Protazanov et al. in making better and more ambitious feature-length films. Goncharov, a longtime civil servant in the imperial Transportation Ministry, suffered a personal crisis after the death of his wife and left the bureaucracy to become a writer. Discovering that he had no talent for writing, he went on to the movies, then often seen as a dumping ground for people with artistic aspirations but no apparent talent. Goncharov first directed films for Pathé and Gaumont in 1909 and 1910, before joining Khanzhonkov as a historical director par excellence, earning fame for *The Defense of Sevastopol* (*Oborona Sevastopolia*).[70]

Along with actors and directors, writers found that cinema could bring them a new measure of acclaim, and the public seemed to be especially interested in movies scripted by well-known writers. At least, producers hoped to entice new audiences to the movies by showing the works of their favorite authors. As we shall see in the next chapter, early support for the new art came from prominent writers like Leonid Andreev and Lev Tolstoi, who were instrumental in earning "respectability" for the movies. Given the centrality of writers in Russian culture, it is not surprising that scenarists were singled out from among other film workers for special praise. Among writers, Al. Voznesenskii, a playwright and scenarist who continued to work in the Soviet period, was frequently featured as a drawing card for the films he wrote. Though he is little remembered today, Voznesenskii was a very prominent writer in his time. His name often appeared in the favored position, above that of the director and the actors, and in larger letters, even when the director was as prominent as Evgenii Bauer and the actress as famous as Vera Iureneva, one of the "queens" of the screen.[71]

Certainly, novelist Mikhail Artsybashev was a major asset to the business, even though Thiemann was unable to obtain censorship approval to film a screen adaptation of Artsybashev's notorious Nietzschean novel *Sanin* (which would have been a great period relic).[72] And the equally popular Anastasiia Verbitskaia, delighted with the "colossal" success of the screen version of her novel *The Keys to Happiness*, enthusiastically began to work in film as a scenarist, adapting her own work.[73] Indeed, when Artsybashev's and Verbitskaia's scripts or novels were filmed, their names were always featured much more prominently than those of the actors or the director.[74]

Leonid Andreev's name likewise appeared very prominently when his "special screenplay" became the movie *Days of Our Lives* (*Dni nashei zhizni*).[75] Anatolii Kamenskii, identified in the press as the "famous artistic Russian writer" (for the apparent edification of any readers who were unaware of this), frequently wrote for film. His screen adaptation of his novel

The Tragedy of Leda (*Tragediia Ledi*) provoked great interest because of the censorship trouble it ran into and because of the daring advertising campaign featuring the sorrowful, bare-breasted Leda.[76] Finally, it is important to note that authors' works were sometimes appropriated without their permission for screen adaptations, a problem Lev Tolstoi's family often faced after his death. His eldest daughter, Aleksandra Tolstaia, took a prominent role in attempting to defend his literary estate from the depredations of unscrupulous filmmakers.[77]

HITS

As the viewing public grew more sophisticated, producers and distributors found it easier to capitalize on people than on genres. Emphasizing the human component in films was just as much a factor in enhancing and broadening cinema's appeal in Russia as it was elsewhere. In relatively few cases, the film itself was presented as the star, irrespective of its personnel, and was promoted accordingly.

Most of the time, the rhetoric used was as exaggerated for the films as it was for some of the stars, and by 1915 hyperbolic promotion was so common that it had become an industry-wide "insider's joke," as the following only slightly absurd example shows:

Sensation! Sensation! Sensation!
Attention! Attention! Attention!
Hit! Hit! Hit!
Monopoly! Monopoly! Monopoly![78]

The problem that this kind of hyperbole created for the moviegoer is obvious: lacking independent critiques of the films (since most reviews appeared in studio journals), unable to trust the advertisements, how could one decide which films to choose? The researcher also faces this problem of authenticity: if almost every picture was labeled a "chef d'oeuvre," how are we to know which films were truly commercial or artistic successes?[79] We certainly cannot trust the advertisements as evidence.

The Keys to Happiness

The one indisputable "blockbuster" of Russian cinema was Protazanov and Gardin's 1913 adaptation of Verbitskaia's best-selling novel *The Keys to Happiness* (*Kliuchi schastia*). The long melodrama, shown in two parts, told a story full of human interest, following the picaresque romantic adventures of Mania, a bold, young, and indisputably "new" woman who attempts to navigate the treacherous new world of changing social and sexual mores, and having done so, commits suicide. The "keys to happiness" of the title are the precepts of Nietzsche, whose work was, as already noted, enormously popular in Russia.[80] This film, no print of which has survived, was one of the Thiemann, Reinhardt & Osipov studio's innovative "Golden Series" of handsomely produced, feature-length films based on famous works in Russian classical and popular literature.

The importance of *The Keys to Happiness* to Russian cinema cannot be overemphasized. It literally revolutionized Russian filmmaking, since it showed that audiences would watch long Russian-made movies — even longer than *The Defense of Sevastopol* — and would pay handsomely for the privilege. (As noted in the previous chapter, prior to this point producers and theater managers believed that audiences could not stay focused on a single storyline for more than about thirty minutes; hence the popularity of the multifilm program.)[81]

Keys also showed skeptical theater owners that one feature-length film could earn even more than the traditional four- to five-picture program. Downey & Co., the British distribution company, had tried for a while to convince Russian theater owners of this ("Why do theaters in America earn more than those in Europe? . . . The reason is! Longer pictures!"). But it took the "insane" box office success of *Keys* to persuade them.[82] Of course, the length and complexity of the film forced a change in viewing patterns; now theaters began to advertise specific showtimes for specific film titles (not just when they opened their doors, as had been the case in the past). Presumably, spectators learned that it was preferable to see a film from the beginning, rather than walking in and "catching" it at a random point, which Yuri Tsivian says the surrealists found a particularly chic aesthetic practice.[83]

The Thiemann studio advertised the film extensively but in an innovative and effective way, eschewing hyperbole for simplicity (undoubtedly because the sensationalism of the story was already so well-known). The starkness of the advertising campaign came as welcome relief. In one four-page layout, for example, the film's title appeared solo on pages 1 and 4; the centerfold pages (2 and 3) contained only the studio's name and Anastasiia Verbitskaia's, certainly a sign of her name recognition.[84] This name recognition extended to the borderlands of the Russian empire as well; K. Stefan, the picture's distributor in Riga and Tiflis (Tbilisi), featured *only* Verbitskaia's name in his promotions for the picture.[85] Color was low-key but striking — yellow used in one ad, orange in another —

markedly different from the black and red (for dripping blood) that usually predominated in two-color promotions.[86] The co-directors' names were absent; Protazanov told Gardin that Thiemann wanted to hide their identities so that other studios wouldn't steal them away.[87]

The film was printed in twenty-seven copies, an unusually large number, and each sold for 35,000 rubles, with the studio also getting a percentage of the box office.[88] Co-director Vladimir Gardin reported that Thiemann earned a net profit of 200,000 rubles, while Gardin himself received "only" 2,500 rubles, even though he had written the script, too.[89] Although the film was costly, the studio quickly recouped expenses, and the record profits enabled it to embark on a major remodeling project.[90]

Critical acclaim for the film, which Gardin sardonically described as a "series of suicides" carried out by "crazy" and "hysterical" characters, was unanimous in the film press.[91] *Cine Journal* proclaimed that "one could wish for nothing better" and that "if this film had appeared on the European market, its appearance would have been noted not only by the specialized [that is, trade] journals but by the entire press."[92] *Cine-phono* concurred, noting that the film marked a "new era" in Russian cinema by taking a "record-breaking" best-seller and turning it into a record-breaking film characterized by its good taste, energy, and careful production values.[93]

The first part of *Keys*, more than an hour in running time, enjoyed "colossal" success, to continue to employ the overheated terminology of the critics. The early Soviet film historian B. S. Likhachev, writing in the 1920s, described it as a "megahit" (*sverkh-boevik*) and reported that tickets were sold in advance (an unusual practice), for *standing* room as well as for seats.[94] In St. Petersburg, it played two weeks in the Giant (Gigant) theater. The audience numbered 24,622, bringing in a gross box office listed as precisely 22,699.20 rubles, a "grandiose" figure for a single film in a single theater.[95] The Thiemann studio began quoting these figures in their subsequent advertisements for *Keys*, and the film's distributors all listed it as their top-billed picture.[96] Distributor D. I. Kharitonov, for example, told theater owners in an advertisement:

> If you want more RUBLES in the cash register of your theater than there are meters in the film, then hurry to order *The Keys to Happiness*. Length 5,000 meters.[97]

The second part of the film, released three weeks after the first, continued to draw audiences in record numbers. Theater owners explained this unusual enthusiasm by the fact that this was a *Russian* film made according to *European* standards.[98] Pavel Thiemann concurred, promising that his goal was to put Russian film production on a par with European.[99] *Keys* continued to be available for booking as late as April 1914, more than six months after it had opened, very unusual in the "easy come, easy go" world of early Russian cinema.[100]

It is worth noting that Anastasiia Verbitskaia, arguably the best-selling Russian novelist of her day, remained loyal to Thiemann, Reinhardt & Osipov, even after the chief players in *Keys* had defected in the wake of the Great War. Despite the departure of directors Gardin and Protazanov and the film's star, Olga Preobrazhenskaia, in June 1915 Verbitskaia sold the exclusive film rights to all her work to Thiemann, in order to guarantee (in her own words) the "quality" of the screen adaptations.[101] Nonetheless, R. D. Perskii announced at the end of 1916 that he was producing a "sequel" to *Keys* to be called *The Victors and the Vanquished* (*Pobediteli i pobezhdennye*), noting: "Who doesn't remember what a golden fleece for theater owners *The Keys to Happiness* was?" This happy reminder was framed on all sides by the words "Profits! Profits!"[102]

After *Keys*

Thereafter any film's potential for success was measured by that of *Keys*. *Cine Journal* believed that the new Ermolev studio would have a similar hit in *In the Maelstrom of Moscow* (*V omute Moskvy*) since Ermolev had reportedly paid an astonishing four thousand rubles for the scenario.[103] There is no evidence, however, that this was more than wishful thinking. The enormous profits generated by *Keys* also made it clear to producers that the classics were not the only surefire source for quality storylines.

Alexander Drankov began a series of feature-length films based on the legends of "the famous Russian adventuress" and thief Sonia Bliuvshtein, entitled *Sonka the "Golden Hand"* (*Sonka zolotaia ruchka*). These were heavily advertised in the popular general daily newspaper the *Russian Word* (*Russkoe slovo*). As an unmistakable sign of its box office appeal, *Sonka* was playing at eleven theaters simultaneously in Moscow, a veritable "who's who" of the Western-style movie palaces, with fantastical names like Luxe, Moderne, Union, Empire, Vulcan, Uranus, Odeon, Napoleon, Tango, Orion, and Hermes.[104] Part 3 of *Sonka the "Golden Hand,"* the most successful of the lot, was shown at twelve theaters simultaneously, a sure sign of its continued box office appeal and testimony to Drankov's mastery of "sensation for the sake of sensation." [105] Worried critics also believed *Sonka* promoted a "lighthearted" attitude toward crime.[106] Encouraged by this success, and apparently without any qualms about promoting lighthearted attitudes toward crime, Drankov went on to celebrate another criminal in *The Robber Vaska Churkin* (*Razboinik Vaska Churkin*), advertised as "the noisiest hit of the season." [107]

Iosif Ermolev's first major hit was a series launched in direct competition to *Sonka*: the serial adventures of *Sashka the Seminary Student* (*Sashka seminarist*).[108] Though *Sashka* was playing Moscow's Vulcan, Uranus, and Empire theaters simultaneously, a segment of the *Sonka* series ousted it a week later.[109] The Ermolev studio's biggest hit was probably Iakov Protazanov's 1916 screen adaptation of Pushkin's beloved story *The Queen of Spades* (*Pikovaia dama*).

Pushkin was a favorite author for adaptation to the screen; unlike living writers, he could not sue a studio for infringement of author's rights, and his stature in the Russian literary pantheon was unsurpassed. *The Queen of Spades* was produced by the high-powered Ermolev studio, known for the artistic and technical quality of its productions. Its director, Protazanov, was one of Russia's most capable, and the film starred the charismatic and popular actor Ivan Mozzhukhin. The names of both director and star figured prominently in the advertisements. The independent Odessa weekly *Theater and Cinema* (*Teatr i kino*) described *The Queen of Spades* as an "event" and the best picture of the 1916 season, lamenting that it would not appear in Odessa for four or five more months.[110] *Cine Journal* (*Kine-zhurnal*) confirmed that the "brilliant" film was a hit, although it found Mozzhukhin's portrayal of the antihero German (as "Herman" is pronounced and spelled in Russian) too reserved.[111]

Evidence for "hits" is sketchy, but by looking at which films were most widely distributed, it is possible to infer other box office successes. Two films based on the works of Mikhail Artsybashev, *Jealousy* (*Revnost*) and *The Husband* (*Muzh*), were also trumpeted in the pages of the daily press and playing multiple venues simultaneously. The same was true of two movies based on historical themes, Khanzhonkov's *Stenka Razin* and the very timely *War and Peace* (*Voina i mir*), released less than six months after the outbreak of World War I.[112] (Actually, at least three versions of *War and Peace* appeared after the war began.)

Two other feature-length films attracted much attention and appear to have been major and influential hits in Russia, as they were elsewhere in Europe. These were the well-known Italian pictures *Quo Vadis?* and

Cabiria. Italian historical melodramas of ancient Rome were renowned for their artistry (developing parallel to, but independent of, similar innovations by D. W. Griffith in the United States), and they enjoyed great popularity in Russia during the war. The "brilliant success" of *Quo Vadis?* in St. Petersburg, Moscow, and major provincial cities launched the "craze" for films of the swords-and-sandals type, and it was followed by Italian imports like *Nero, Cleopatra, Spartacus,* and *Julius Caesar.*[113] *Cine Journal* considered *Quo Vadis?* to be a leading moneymaker, vying with *The Keys to Happiness,* despite the acknowledged difficulties of verifying box office receipts.[114] Indeed, *Quo Vadis?,* not *Keys,* should properly be considered the "turning point" from short program to feature film, but it is typical of the Russocentrism of film critics that this point was conveniently ignored.[115]

Cabiria made even more of an impression than *Quo Vadis?*. A stately film of impressive and tasteful beauty, it was discussed at length in the general press as well as in the film journals.[116] The heavily illustrated and stuffy middlebrow culture magazine the *Sun of Russia (Solntse Rossii),* which never deigned to review films although it sometimes condescended to carry advertisements for a few "quality" pictures, made an exception for *Cabiria.* The pseudonymous critic "Um-skii" praised *Cabiria's* high artistic level and noted, pointedly and approvingly, that *this* film attracted an elite audience of government ministers and members of the intelligentsia at its opening. "No one who sees [*Cabiria*]," he concluded dramatically, "will ever forget it."[117]

Comparing *Cabiria* and *The Keys to Happiness* is instructive because the two pictures sent very different messages to producers. *The Keys to Happiness* promised a surefire recipe for box office rewards, high on any studio executive's wish list. But the elegant, pompous *Cabiria* (or a Russian version thereof) offered something else the middle-class producers wanted very badly: *respect,* the subject of the next chapter.

4

Respect and Respectability

Russian cinema entrepreneurs yearned not only for riches but also for artistic respectability. Russia, unlike the United States, was a nation that prized its artists, and its artists, like artists everywhere, scorned riches. Another problem that producers faced were the various stereotypes about and prejudices against "merchants." As part of a social group in the process of self-definition, producers quickly learned that cultural acclaim was much harder to come by than money. Their efforts to achieve respect and respectability were erratic and inhibited by the country's chaotic political and economic conditions in the decade 1908–18.

Despite marked cultural differences between Russia and, say, France, cinema pioneers everywhere faced remarkably similar problems, although the intensity of these issues naturally varied according to local and national cultures. The possible physical effects of the new cinematic technology were one major source of concern. For example, the medical profession, especially in Germany, raised repeated alarms about the dangers cinema posed to the general health of viewers (especially to their eyes), from the "rays" emanating from the screen.[1]

Cinema also engendered the fear of widespread moral deterioriation. In the United States, with its puritanical moral environment, the notion that cinema promoted violence and corrupted youth and women was especially pronounced and had great staying power. (Indeed, these attitudes are still with us, especially since the advent of television.)

A third major issue was whether the democratization of culture that cinema represented was a positive or negative force in society. In other early film-producing nations with entrenched "high culture," like France or Germany, we see that the literati feared the effects competition with not only movies, but all forms of commercial, commodified, or just plain low-brow entertainment would have on "respectable" and "artistic" forms like the play, the opera, or the novel. (That these art forms had not always been

so admired was conveniently overlooked.) Even the comparatively plebe-
ian United States resisted the blurring of the lines between highbrow and
lowbrow culture.[2]

THE CASE AGAINST CINEMA

All these concerns existed in Russia, though sometimes in surprising variations. Although the Russian Orthodox Church strenuously opposed the
more "sensational" films, censorship on religious and moral grounds was
rare enough not to be a matter of pressing concern to producers. Russian
culture had never been particularly puritanical or "Victorian." With regard to the dangers of technology, Russia was so underindustrialized by
comparison with the other Great Powers that the evil eye was more to be
feared than "rays" from a movie projector.

The Russian industry worried most about establishing cordial relations
with the powerful members of "high culture" circles—novelists, critics,
theater actors. As we have seen in the previous chapter, prominent Russian
writers, especially modernists, were enthusiastic about the possibilities of
cinema.[3] The relationship between the "legitimate" stage and the movies
in Russia was, however, particularly uneasy—as it was in Germany. Russian cultural pundits dismissed film as highly simplistic ("food only for the
eyes"), whereas theater, according to its legion of devotees, appealed to
the most profound human emotions.[4] Theater lovers further argued, with
markedly elitist overtones, that cinema pandered to the primitive tastes of
the "crowd," theater to the better elements of society.[5]

The movies, moreover, had a distinctly international flavor that displeased nativists at a time when Russian nationalism was on the rise. The
chief problem for these nationalist critics was the lack of spoken language
in films (which of course pleased internationalists). For most Russian intellectuals, who were strongly influenced by Romanticism, the Russian
language was the very essence of Russian culture.

There were other issues as well for those suspicious of film. As long as
foreign films dominated the screen, and foreign firms monopolized the
market, Russian cinema could not possibly be accepted as "Russian" art.
These (predominantly French) films might pretend to focus on Russian
subjects, but they were never authentic enough. No foreigner, it was argued, could ever hope to understand the "Russian soul."[6] French technology might conceivably be welcome under certain carefully controlled

circumstances, but those supposedly puerile French fabrications of Russian life would never be.[7]

Even worse, some writers asserted, the ubiquitous foreign travelogues, a standard part of film programs that would seem to be quite harmless and even useful, introduced Russian children to Notre Dame Cathedral, the Louvre, and the palace at Versailles before they had had a chance to learn about the equally splendid wonders of Russian cultural monuments. To be fair, some cultural critics were more cosmopolitan and derided such "primitive nationalism." Nonetheless, the fact that such sentiments were widespread and bound to spread wider yet threatened to inhibit the development of the cinema and perhaps lead to governmental restrictions.[8]

In this time of rising nationalism across Europe, only a few leftist circles in Russia found the supranationalism of silent cinema a virtue.[9] Most Russian critics, even the most reasonable ones, believed that Russian movies were innately profound and truthful, unlike the superficial and deceptive European product.[10] These sentiments not surprisingly intensified during World War I.

Another problem the cinema industry faced in its quest for respect from the powerful Russian cultural establishment was the very novelty factor that attracted audiences in the first place. By classifying the movies in the same category as other "sensational" novelties of the time, the guardians of high culture cheapened the reputation of film. These vaudeville and cabarets acts to which the elite objected sound quite amusing: Miss Volta, the "living electric accumulator," whose 500,000 volts of power enabled her to light lamps and cigars with her fingertips; "Kiki, the world-famous cinema poodle"; the Lilliputians (a midget couple who sang duets); or Les Armands, a troupe of fox terriers who performed "unbelievable stunts."[11] We can certainly understand, however, why artistically oriented directors and producers would want to distance themselves from Miss Volta.

The fact that cinema, unlike the other arts, was so clearly a "commercial affair" also made it suspect to the intelligentsia, who deeply distrusted business in general and capitalism in particular.[12] But by 1910, a few prominent writers like Lev Tolstoi and Leonid Andreev (and a bit later, Andrei Belyi) evinced a positive interest in film. Tolstoi, for most the oracle of Russian culture, had allowed himself to be photographed for films and had deemed cinema "a good thing," to the delight of filmmakers.[13] Others, like Mikhail Artsybashev, Leonid Andreev, Zoia Barantsevich, Vladimir Maiakovskii, and Anastasiia Verbitskaia (author of The Keys to Happiness), wrote screenplays. It would be a mistake, however, to overestimate the support of writers for the cinema in its infancy. Most fervently hoped that cinema was merely a passing phenomenon.[14] In fact, the general (non-film) press tended to oppose cinema so vigorously that every time a favorable article about a particular film or the industry appeared, the cinema community rejoiced.[15] This was especially so if a journal "respected by the intelligentsia," like *Contemporary World* (*Sovremennyi mir*), published an article on film, even if it limited its praise to the connection between film and scientific advancement (not a topic of much intrinsic interest to Russian movie moguls).[16]

THE COUNTEROFFENSIVE

Like some American exhibitors at the same time, the Russian film community realized the importance of crafting and projecting a positive image. Studios and critics (and it must be kept in mind that with the exception of *Cine-phono* the trade journals were studio publications) set out to present the film community as a group of solid, cultured, educated, civic-minded citizens. Some of the ways filmmakers chose to do this now seem quaint. One of the first targets was "illiteracy" in advertising; a campaign was launched to purge misspellings and grammatical errors from movie advertisements and intertitles.[17] A few argued, with darkly nationalistic aspersions, that these language mistakes could be traced directly to the "foreign" influences at work in Russian cinema.[18]

As the movie industry sought to enhance its image as a purveyor of high-class entertainment, the physical condition of the screens also required attention. Konstantin Paustovskii remembered the one in the Kiev theater he attended as a boy as a "wet gray cloth" on which an "ominous green light flickered" and across which "black spots darted."[19] If the screen were the symbolic "mirror of the cinematographic soul," obviously it should not be dirty and torn.[20] Linen was the material most frequently used at this time, and it needed to be cleaned regularly and replaced as often as necessary. False economy was a serious mistake.

At the same time that industry boosters sought to upgrade advertising and exhibition, film critics did not make the mistake of downplaying the marvels of cinema. Valentin Novus began a poem to the movies this way: "In our age of wonders / it is the most wondrous of all."[21] In carving out a niche for cinema within Russia's rich cultural heritage, many believed it important to establish that cinema symbolized and celebrated all that was good about modernity.

Far from being "unintelligent" and "awful," as snobs had early maintained, cinema vividly and accurately reflected the complicated textures and rapid tempos of modern life.[22] In a world that moved all too quickly, cinema was the sole invention that captured, conquered, and exploited both space and time. With so much happening so fast, cinema was an "undying witness," perfectly preserving memory.[23] And cinema, through the wide variety of people found in its audiences, was the art that best represented the democratic spirit of the twentieth century. This last point was particularly stressed in 1911, in connection with the commemoration of the fiftieth anniversary of the abolition of serfdom.[24]

In the 1910s, emboldened by the public's unabashed and unabating attraction to the movies, film critics moved from their defensive positions to the offensive. Why continue to apologize and justify? One critic in Khanzhonkov's elegant journal *Pegasus* (*Pegas*, after his trademark symbol), which the producer launched in order to position cinema squarely among the "legitimate" arts, paraphrased Flaubert on the subject of mass taste:

> The public isn't at all stupid. In questions of art, the only stupid ones are:
> 1. Ministers of culture
> 2. Directors of theaters
> 3. Publishers
> 4. Editors-in-chief of newspapers
> 5. Authoritative critics.[25]

Indeed, wasn't it ironic that the trashy "boulevard" or kopek (penny) press dared to criticize the cinema industry for films like *Sashka the Seminary Student* (*Sashka seminarist*) or *Sonka the "Golden Hand"* (*Sonka zolotaia ruchka*) when they published material no less sensational?[26] Whom was one to believe: the critic N. Ezhov, who labeled the cinema repertory "pornographic" and "tasteless"? Or the brilliant and popular Silver Age writer Leonid Andreev, who wrote: "I really love cinema and believe in its future (not only greatly, but colossally)"?[27]

Directors also joined the frontlines of the culture wars, standing staunchly against those elitists who claimed ownership of Russian culture. *New Times* (*Novoe vremia*) might attack film for its allegedly "crude" abuse of the classics, but director Petr Chardynin (who had adapted a classic or two for the screen) countered by praising the movies for introducing the great works of Russian literature to the masses who would not otherwise have the opportunity to become acquainted with them.[28] In fact, according to one commentator, cinema had a symbiotic relationship with literature. Films based on original screenplays did not, in her view, have the resonance of those based on classics or popular novels because the characters were unknown to the spectators, seen for the first time.[29] Literature was, therefore, the bride to cinema's bridegroom, never to be separated.[30] (*Literatura* is feminine in Russian; *kinematograf*, now an archaic term, masculine.)

The highest hurdle to overcome was, without question, the antagonism between cinema and theater, in part because of the persistent early belief that cinema was at its best no more than filmed theater. The arguments pro and con were quite inconsistent. A few prescient film critics argued that the theatrical and literary establishments' adversarial relationship with cinema was artificial and unnecessary. To each his own: "Theater is theater. Cinema is cinema."[31] Why create hierarchies and artificial competition when there was an audience for both? In fact, cinema might just become the legitimate theater's "best friend," because it has the power to record and preserve the performances of the best actors, who will forever rise like "sleeping beauties" to delight audiences.[32] Theater aficionados, therefore, wrongly slighted cinema. They should deign to recognize that film can do certain things (e.g., represent the fantastic) much better than theater. The reverse was also true, of course: Hamlet's soliloquy, it was argued, could never be adequately represented in (silent) film.[33]

It was obvious that cinema challenged theater for some of the same audiences. The novelty factor aside, films, being mechanically reproduced, were a much more consistent and widely distributed form of entertainment than theater.[34] Moscow Art Theater's great director Konstantin Stanislavskii, in his own words "not a special admirer" of cinema, attempted to find the silver lining in this cloud. He argued that the movies provided much-needed competition to theater, so that the latter would not be tempted to rest on its laurels and thereby stagnate.[35] A cartoon that appeared in 1913 in the journal *New Satyricon* (*Novyi satirikon*) presented a less sanguine view of these fears. It shows Melpomene being strangled by strands of film from a movie camera. She cries: "Dramatists, artists, poets, help! Cinematographic films are strangling me!"[36]

Cinema had its special champions, of course, who found film superior to both literature *and* theater. Leonid Andreev and Vladimir Maiakovskii were prominent voices for this point of view.[37] This small but highly vocal and visible minority believed that the sooner film emancipated itself from its reliance on theatrical and literary talent, the better.[38] Here the debate foreshadows the culture wars of our own times. Why, these film enthusiasts argued, had the book been privileged over other storytelling vehicles? After all, "it's only part of life, not all of life . . . it's only part of culture and progress."[39] And as for film, it "isn't silent — it speaks loudly, universally; it shouts to all classes."[40] Cinema was not ersatz art, not a carnival sideshow (*balagan*), but the "seventh" muse.[41]

This idea of cinema as "seventh" muse was not a widely held view; after all, how many of the films of Russian production even pretended to be art? The *potential* of cinema as art was, however, recognized by a few outside the film community. Russian futurists loudly (and logically) proclaimed their support of cinema as the art of the future, as did other modernists. Interestingly, some snide movie critics snubbed this support. They felt cinema was too good for the futurists and argued that the futurists *needed* cinema to reinvigorate a fading movement, since their ideas were "already uninteresting to many."[42]

Another way to bolster cinema's respectability was by emphasizing its potential to fulfill an important educational function, especially in an illiterate (or, at best, marginally literate) society. (The titles could be read aloud by a barker.) As already mentioned, the movies could acquaint the nonreading public with Russian literature by bringing literary adaptations to the screen. Cinema, mainly in its documentary aspects, might also serve as a "living newspaper," especially important in a society as far-flung and multi-ethnic as the Russian empire.[43] The war spurred recognition that film could become a historical document, providing a record of the conflict, and the idea that the cameraman was "not only a spectator but also a witness" gained significance.[44]

The emphasis on the didactic potential of film became pronounced in the Soviet period, but before the Revolution this kind of rhetoric was halfhearted. If the cinema community really had believed in the primacy of film's didactic function, then studios and distributors should have been concerned with taking cinema to the countryside, which they were not. Nor did studios evince interest in making films for children. They didn't even tone down the sensationalism of their often salacious adult fare. Sometimes on holidays, theaters devoted an early evening program to children's fare, but managers were hard put to obtain suitable films.[45]

A few observers found the pleasures of the movies childlike, like "fairy tales" (*skazki*), especially when compared with theater, but most realized the menu was markedly adult in its orientation.[46] Certainly films like the Thiemann studio's *Camp of Terror* (*Lager uzhasa*), advertised as "The Apotheosis of Horror!" wouldn't serve the juvenile audience as educational fare.[47]

Russian children, however, loved the movies despite (or because!) of these defects, and concerns over the potentially pernicious influence of cinema did not abate. It is true that Konstantin Paustovskii's father escorted the family to the cinema to introduce them to "one of the most magnificent novelties of the twentieth century," comparing it in importance to the invention of the steam engine.[48] He was, however, apparently a parent of rare vision (Paustovskii's mother, on the other hand, strongly disagreed with the value of the novelty).

In 1914, a Russian version of the U.S. Payne Fund study appeared. The left-liberal, highly respected "thick" journal *European Herald* (*Vestnik Evropy*) published the results of a survey conducted among 1,482 students from sixteen schools (locations, ages, class, and other important sociological data were not included in the report). Thirty-eight percent of the children admitted their preference for movies over books, finding film more concrete, more realistic, more experiential than the written word. Most of these young movie fans cited the frequent violence depicted on screen as a particularly thrilling and enticing aspect that drew them to the movies. According to the report's author, A. I. Zak, a few especially bright children rejected cinema as "stupid and tasteless," but he feared that the cinema would soon assume the "character of an epidemic," consuming susceptible youth in Russia as it had in the West.[49] In an another study Zak conducted ("Cinema and Juvenile Criminality," cited by Joan Neuberger in her book on Russian hooliganism), he tells of the daredevil deeds of young Tatiana. The thirteen-year-old had become a thief to finance her movie habit and dared to escape from her locked room by climbing down a drainpipe because "people did such things all the time in the movies and survived."[50]

Aleksandr Pasternak, whose recollections were first cited in chapter 2, had a remarkable gift for rendering the immediacy of long-ago experiences. He described the excitement children felt this way:

> What if everything twitched and jerked? It was still the movement of the immovable, and we accepted it as such; not as a travesty of the smooth,

uninterrupted flow that is nature itself, but as its documentary proof and evident confirmation. Grateful and reverent, we left the little hall with a wonderful feeling of having participated in a world of visible miracles, a sensation so strong that this is what I remember now, while the pictures which summoned it to life have been utterly forgotten.[51]

THE WAR YEARS

The debate over the value of cinema intensified after 1914, with renewed nationalist vigor. The Skobelev Committee, constituted during the war to produce progovernment propaganda films and named after the popular nineteenth-century Russian general and nationalist, stressed the "democratizing" role of cinema as a purveyor of mass (patriotic) culture in its organ the *Screen of Russia* (*Ekran Rossii*). The campaign to promote cinema as an intrinsic part of the government's war effort was carried out most energetically, however, in the pages of Ermolev's *Projector* (*Proektor*).[52]

Producer Iosif Ermolev believed that the imperial government had levied unduly harsh taxes on film and was restricting the growth of the film industry at a time when cinema could best serve the state.[53] He hoped to convince the government that cinema was a key component in building national solidarity, especially in time of war, and should therefore be granted concessions. *Projector's* articles reworked familiar themes but with patriotic twists.

Projector writer Fedor Mashkov argued, for example, that in wartime, Russian cinema was as important to the nation as Russian science.[54] Another article in the journal stressed that cinema served as a culturally unifying force, by disseminating the Russian classics to the illiterate.[55] Furthermore, the case was once again made that film could serve as a "living diary," or official record, of the events of the day.[56] Finally, Ermolev claimed (through his surrogates on *Projector's* staff) that the war had not only given the industry an overall economic boost but inspired a new realism that had helped cinema further develop into a respected art form.[57]

The problem was, as we shall see, that during the war Russian movies became ever more sensational. Movie advertisements, dripping with blood, promoted films about Satan and satanism, including the Ermolev studio's own *Satan Triumphant* (*Satana likuiushchii*). Even *Projector* critics admitted that cinema could better support the war effort if film scenarists moved beyond their favored themes of unrequited love, rampant misery, and the ubiquitous "suffering woman."[58]

The urgency of Ermolev's message intensifed after the February Revolution (March by the Gregorian calendar) and even more after the Bolshevik Revolution in October (November). Ermolev urged filmmakers to unite to serve the new Russia, and he proceeded to help found ONO, the first producers' association. But how could ONO, or any other group, succeed in making new films, given the nearly complete absence of raw film stock? Inadequate and unpredictable supplies of electricity kept movie theaters dark most of the week, further damaging the industry.[59] Why, *Projector* asked, was the new regime so hostile to the cinema?[60] After all, filmmakers had proven that they could cooperate with any government, and the studios were busy churning out revolutionary "sensations" like Petr Chardynin's 1917 film *The Bourgeois, Enemy of the People* (*Burzhui — vrag naroda*).[61] Given the undeniably bourgeois origins and orientation of Russian cinema, this was ironic indeed.

Whatever one thinks of the Bolshevik nationalization of the film industry in 1918, there can be no doubt that they well understood the ideological threat Russian commercial cinema posed to their utopian visions. This will become even clearer as we discuss the dominant themes, images, and genres of early Russian films in the following chapters.

PART II

Fragments from
a Film Program

5

Sex and Suicide

A DEEPLY VIOLENT EROTICISM CHARACTERIZED THE SENSATIONAL melodramas that were the staple product of native Russian cinema. Even after the passage of more than eighty years, these films still have the power to shock, so dark and intense are the emotions portrayed—and so gifted are the portrayals. In this chapter, we will begin to explore some of the most significant of these films, in order to understand what they reveal to us about the travails of "modern life" in Russia on the eve of revolution. But first, an important caveat is in order.

WHY "FRAGMENTS FROM A FILM PROGRAM"?

About 20 percent of early Russian cinema survives, a respectable proportion compared with other national cinemas, although only about one-third of the extant films have been reconstructed and restored so that scholars may view them. Of those that have been restored, many are still in fragments, making narratives sometimes very hard to follow, even for those familiar with the different narrative conventions of early cinema. There are also serious gaps, most notably in the Ermolev company's titles. Iosif Ermolev took as much of his archive with him as he could carry when his company left Russia in late 1918 or early 1919, and these pictures are presumed lost. To a lesser extent, this is also a problem with the Thiemann studio's titles, so that, for example, the box office hit *The Keys to Happiness* survives only in a few stills held in the Russian State Archive of Literature and Art and in the published screenplay. And yet, based on my reading of hundreds of synopses and reviews in the film press, the surviving body of work is remarkably representative of the themes, genres, and directorial styles of the time.

As we have already noted, the first fifteen years of film production every-where focused mainly on short subjects: travelogues, novelties, screwball comedies, literary and historical sketches in the tableau style. Not until around 1910 do we see the first attempts to develop coherent narrative structures that would enable film to tell longer and more complex stories, with cinematographically specific aesthetic flourishes. Melodramatic tales of deeply erotic violence emerged immediately in Russia. By drawing on a wide variety of original sources—folktales, classics, popular literature—as well as aesthetic styles, Russian cinema quickly asserted itself as an art of synthesis that provides remarkable images of a society in distress from the pressures of modernization and class change. It also provides, not co-incidentally, remarkable contributions to the history of early film art.

NARRATIVE EXPERIMENTATION

An attractive early example is *Rusalka* (1910), adapted by Vasilii Gon-charov and Vladimir Siversen from Pushkin's retelling of the folktale about the seductive river sprites of Russian lore. *Rusalka* stars Aleksandra Gon-charova and Andrei Gromov, who often worked together and were main-stays of the period drama (discussed in detail in chapter 7). In this picture, Gromov plays the prince who is the lover of a miller's daughter (Goncha-rova). She learns he is leaving her to marry a woman of his own class, and despite his attempts to pay her off with a gift of jewels, the young woman refuses to take comfort and mysteriously vanishes. She rematerializes at the prince's wedding feast and again at his marriage bed. She has become a *rusalka*, the Russian folkloric vamp.[1]

Eight years pass. We see that the prince has scorned his wife and with-drawn from real life. Obsessed with his visions of his past love, he is even-tually drawn by forces beyond his control to the mill, where he finds that the miller has gone mad. At the mill, the *rusalki* surround the prince and lead him to the river where he drowns himself. He is not, however, really dead. He has become a captive of the nymphs who live at the bottom of the river. Goncharov moves the well-known story along quickly, with rela-tively restrained use of the fantastical elements. Tales of the supernatural were especially popular at this time, regardless of the medium, so we can safely assume that *Rusalka* was a film that likely enjoyed widespread appeal.

But at this time of genre formulation, replication of the sex-and-violence motif was not easy, even within the same studio, as *The Sorrows of Sara* (*Gore Sarry*, 1913) indicates. One of the Khanzhonkov studio's "Jewish" films, *The Sorrows of Sara* stars Tatiana Shornikova as Sara and Ivan Mozzhukhin as her husband, Isaak. Because Sara is unable to have children, she is forced to divorce him, against both their wishes. Isaak, after unsuccessfully attempting to thwart these plans to part him from his beloved wife, decides to hang himself. Naturally, he easily finds a fine hanging rope conveniently located in Sara's bedroom. The film ends with Sara wandering through the cemetery, looking for Isaak's grave. She collapses weeping beside the headstone. The "Jewish" films of this time, produced by Khanzhonkov and other studios, were largely intended for the ethnic audience, and like *The Sorrows of Sara* tended to present the Jewish community in a highly negative fashion.

The Sorrows of Sara survives only in a fragment (now running 20 minutes),[2] but even the skills of Ivan Mozzhukhin cannot save it from its obvious schematism. The "Jewish public" who previewed the film at a special studio screening held at the Continental theater apparently enjoyed it nonetheless and overlooked the fact that Jewish actors are not playing the main roles.[3] Given the pervasive anti-Semitism in Russia, however, it must have seemed to them to be a reasonably sympathetic portrayal.

A more typical example from the same year, that foreshadows themes and preoccupations common to this genre, is *Behind the Drawing Room Doors* (*Za gostinoi dveriami*, Ivan Lazarev and Petr Chardynin, 1913). This film is preserved in a fragment (now approximately 36 minutes) that lacks the beginning, the end, and titles. While it is hard for the present-day viewer to reconstruct the story with precision, the emotions the directors intended to convey are nonetheless quite clear.

A couple (young woman, older man) arrive at an artist's studio, decorated with a modernist painting in the deranged style of the Russian artist Mikhail Vrubel. The woman, who initially affects an exaggerated hauteur, is to have her portrait painted. She and the handsome young artist are drawn to each other; their flirtatious smiles and gestures quickly intensify, and they ignore the artist's mistress glowering in the background.

In the next scene we see the older man, the artist, and the young woman strolling in a park (shot on location); when the older man decides to rest on a park bench, the two continue alone. As soon as they are out of his sight, they begin kissing passionately. Up to this point, in the absence of titles that undoubtedly would have explained relationships, one has assumed through body language that the older man is the woman's husband.

It seems at this point, however, that he is her father, as he discovers the lovers and happily joins their hands. The two men embrace.

The artist now must deal with his mistress, who while attempting to slash her rival's portrait, cuts her lover's hand instead. He nurses his troubles at a cafe in the company of several seedy characters. One is a "new woman," who is smoking and allowing herself to be crudely caressed by one of the men. The artist soon learns from his déclassé companions that his new fiancée is a prostitute. This news, of course, puts the identity of the "father" once again in doubt; is he our "heroine's" pimp? The artist angrily confronts his fiancée and threatens her with his pistol. Then we see him in his studio slashing his portrait of her, after which he shoots himself.

By the standards of the day, this is a typical but artistically unremarkable film, although its narrativization reveals the sensationalism that drew audiences to the movies. Compared with better Russian films made around the same time, the mise-en-scène is sparse, as though for the set of a play (the outdoor scenes excepted). The camerawork is static, with most shots set at long or medium range, and the editing is abrupt. As Kristin Thompson has pointed out, it is important to remember when assessing movies of this period that some stylistic conventions of early cinema like the static camera and the long shot were not necessarily "primitive."[4] But certainly today's spectator would find the acting and screenplay much less convincing than other contemporaneous examples.

What makes *Behind the Drawing Room Doors* worth discussing at all is the development of particular motifs that were ubiquitous in early Russian cinema. In terms of class, the film focuses on the demimondaine, and even the seemingly respectable couple turns out to be not so respectable after all. Morals, both public and private, are not what they should be: illicit sexual relations are portrayed openly, as is the hypocrisy of the double standard. The "guilty," if we can even identify them, are not punished; bad women always triumph. Violence (actual or implied) is rampant: knives and guns abound, and the weak, duped man takes (or tries to take) his own life.

If Russian film melodrama had not moved beyond this kind of schematic narrativization to more complex melodramatic forms, it would hold interest only for the most fanatical fans of early cinema or for devotees of Russian fin de siècle culture. Another early example, however, better shows the potential of filmed narration. This was Aleksandr Ivanov-Gai's *The Daughter-in-Law's Lover* (*Snokhach*, 1912), an approximately half-hour film made for the Khanzhonkov studio, starring the versatile Ivan Mozzhukhin. What a difference a talented actor, capable director, and decent script could make!

Snokhach is an untranslatable term that refers to a cruel and distasteful sexual practice in Russia's patriarchal rural communities: fathers forcing themselves sexually on their sons' wives. How common this was in modern Russia is a matter of debate, but it was common enough to inspire "campaigns" against the practice, especially in the Soviet period, to educate young women about their rights to resist these sexual predators.[5] Mozzhukhin plays Ivan, a drunken ne'er-do-well with a pretty, gentle wife, Lusha (Tatiana Shornikova). His father, skillfully portrayed by the character actor Arsenii Bibikov, is presented as a stereotypical peasant patriarch; furious with his worthless son, he threatens him with a pitchfork. Lusha is not much better, at least in terms of peasant values—although she begs her husband to stop drinking, she too is sweet and lazy. She spends most of her time daydreaming while others work in the field.

The father slowly realizes that he is attracted to Lusha, even as he berates her for her laziness. While dancing with her, he kisses her, impulsively, surprising them both. When he finds her alone in the garden (beautifully filmed outdoors, in natural light), he embraces her. She breaks away, runs to find Ivan in the fields, and uncharacteristically insists on taking his place behind the plow.

Next we see the besotted father drunk, staggering between the rows of grain in the fields. Ivan and father begin drinking together; Ivan, not the man his father is, passes out. The father then goes in search of his prey; he envelops the terrified Lusha—and there is a well-timed and dramatic break. Lusha is now disheveled, weeping piteously, her apron stained; the *snokhach* is sleeping in a drunken stupor. Lusha attempts to escape her fate in a boat (another well-shot outdoor scene), but returns after a mysterious encounter with a hermit and what appears to be the ritual sacrifice of a chicken.

The worst has come to pass: Lusha is pregnant and has become the focus of village gossip. Determined to control her fate and end her misery, she hangs herself. In the final scene, Ivan weeps over her body as curious villagers gather. His father, who appears quite deranged with grief, begs his forgiveness.

In certain respects, *The Daughter-in-Law's Lover* is as atypical of pre–Great War melodrama as *Behind the Drawing Room Doors* is typical. The most important difference is the setting and social orientation. Most Russian movie melodramas were urban, concerning the middle and upper classes and the problems of modern life, whereas *The Daughter-in-Law's Lover* is deeply rooted in the countryside and in peasant tradition. But the movie is among the first signs we have of the "paradigm shift"[6] in Russian cinema — from a filmed *tableau* or "attraction" to a movie that is a *movie*, consistently articulated in a cinematic idiom.

The Daughter-in-Law's Lover is not a rudimentary filmed play, but a story that can be told much more effectively on the screen than on the stage. Its themes of violent sex, incest, death are integrated not just through what is *shown* on the screen, but also by how these scenes are cut and edited. The interestingly composed outdoor shots, a marked contrast from the artificial backdrops of the theater and films like *Rusalka*, became a defining characteristic of early Russian cinema, which Russian critics liked to explain by pointing to the Russian's "special" relationship to nature. Finally, Ivan Mozzhukhin may have begun his career on the stage, but his acting was instinctively cinematic. Other important Russian stage actors were able to make this transition, too.

EVGENII BAUER

As capable as Ivanov-Gai proved himself to be in *The Daughter-in-Law's Lover*, the master director of the contemporary melodrama was, without a doubt, Evgenii Bauer. Bauer entered the film world relatively late (given the fast pace of change), at a time when audiences were beginning to tire of filmed *tableaux*. He proved himself to be the man for this pivotal moment in the evolution of Russian cinema: a film artist of great originality and pictorial skill who was able to synthesize and transform the elements of the new art. Although Bauer's work was little known in the West in his time, his talents were world-class, and his best movies rival those of his European or American peers.

An important early work, one of the finest in his oeuvre, was *Twilight of a Woman's Soul* (*Sumerki zhenskoi dushi*, 1913), a full-length feature (about an hour) co-produced by Khanzhonkov and Pathé. Bauer used the extra length not for mere "sensation," though the picture is certainly sensational, but to craft a well-developed narrative of multiple betrayals. A beautiful young noblewoman, Vera (Nina Chernova), meets Maksim (V. Demont), a working-class ruffian, while on a charity mission with her mother, Countess Dubrovskaia. Pretending illness, Maksim later lures

Vera back to his hovel and rapes her. After he has passed out, she kills him — and goes on with her life. She eventually falls in love with the handsome Prince Dolskii (A. Ugriumov) but is racked with guilt over her crime, which is shown in a series of flashbacks. When Dolskii proposes marriage to her, Vera sees him *as Maksim* and faints.

Vera is determined to tell her lover her dark secret. He vows that nothing will ever change his love for her, but she, fearful, keeps putting off the moment of truth. A letter she writes on the eve of the wedding goes astray, in typical melodramatic fashion, so she does not break the news to him until after they are married. The shock and disgust on Dolskii's face need no words, and without any hesitation, Vera leaves him.

Years pass. The Prince has become a dissolute and unhappy playboy; Vera has become the famous actress "Ellen Kay." Recognizing her at the opera *La Traviata*, he realizes that he still loves her. In an interesting counterpoint to the plot of *La Traviata*, Vera coolly rejects Dolskii, whereupon he returns home and shoots himself in the heart.

This quintessential "Bauer film" prefigures many issues important in Russian cinema and transcends the clichés of melodrama. In stylistic terms it is a remarkable combination of Bauer's aestheticism (with elaborate detailing of set and costume) and realism — in its vivid picture of urban poverty and decay. The beautifully decorated interiors not only reflected elite style of the day, but formed it as well. Rooms are underfurnished and elegantly draped, with masses of lavish flowers and potted palms. Costumes are similarly detailed: when Vera leaves the Prince, slowly walking away from the house dressed in a gorgeous washed silk coat trimmed with fur, she looks so exquisite that one wonders how he could ever let her go. Her hair is also radically chic, worn short and marcelled (though a short time later, it has mysteriously grown — a continuity glitch).

Camera and lighting techniques are quite modern, that is, definitely cinematic rather than theatrical. Light and shadow are employed for psychological effect: for example, when we first see the unlucky Vera in her house, she is shrouded in darkness. Bauer eschewed the long-range shots and static camera of many of his peers, favoring the medium close-up to achieve intimacy and, remarkably given the date, a tracking camera following the heroine as she walks away from everything she has known. There is even a scene shot in deep focus, when Maksim sneaks into Vera's bedroom to spy on the forbidden fruit and leave the fateful note luring her to him. Finally, Bauer skillfully utilizes long takes and painterly compositions to characterize Vera in repose.

Urban poverty, however, is not aestheticized. Garbage and decaying rubble surround the workers' tenements, with their broken windows signifying the broken lives within. The men in the slum are gambling and drinking when Vera and the Countess arrive; their bowing and scraping seem patently insincere, even sinister. The smell in Maksim's room is so bad that the Countess covers her nose.

Bauer also provides a complex portrait of elite lifestyle that moves beyond the obligatory cafe and restaurant scenes of his contemporaries, although there are plenty of those. In addition to high society eating, drinking, and dancing, we see other leisure and cultural activities like opera going, fencing, and target shooting. We even witness the Prince employing a private detective to find Vera a year after she has decamped abroad to create her new identity.

Finally, Bauer's vaunted "psychologism" is much in evidence here, through the kind of nuanced acting that only the movies can capture. Even the minor characters exhibit the telling touch: Dolskii flicks an invisible speck from his white glove while consulting with the detective; the rigid and correct Countess recoils slightly and brushes off her dress after Vera impulsively embraces her. But of course Vera is almost always at the center of our attention, so we must examine her characterization most closely.

Vera is a complicated woman, who appears deeply depressed at the emptiness of her life. Her efforts to find meaning by helping the poor end in degradation and tragedy. From this point on, she is not only alienated from her own milieu, but afraid of the world outside as well, yet she reveals herself to be resourceful and strong. She is not a passive victim and takes the life of the man who has wronged her (whatever we may think of this act of personal vengeance). Vera is also devoted to truth and cannot see the meaning of a love where she would have to continue to conceal what has happened to her. Vera replies to the Prince's wordless horror at her revelation with a look of withering scorn at his conventionality. And at the end, although she is emotionally shaken by his renewed declarations of love, she is proud of her control over her emotions, and her discipline in refusing to jettison her career for this unworthy lover.

Bauer continued to develop the motif of strong woman/weak man, but with a different twist, in his 1914 film *Child of the Big City* (*Ditia bolshogo goroda*), another superlative effort. Here he deals with the corrupting factors of urban life more directly and critically than he did in *Twilight of a Woman's Soul*. A naive and poor orphan girl, Mania (Elena Smirnova) must support herself as a seamstress after her mother dies from consumption. She becomes the mistress of a rich young man, Viktor (Mikhail Salarov), who initially is attracted by her unaffected innocence. Viktor becomes her Pygmalion and transforms sweet Mania into the cold, elegant, and spendthrift "Mary." After Mary has spent all Viktor's money, she abandons him and moves on to his friends. In desperation, he attempts to see her one last time. She refuses, and he shoots himself.

Child of the Big City is more obviously a message film than is *Twilight of a Woman's Soul*. There is no true protagonist; the characters are all unsympathetic, shallow pleasure seekers. Viktor is an even more unlikeable fellow than Dolskii in *Twilight of a Woman's Soul*. He and a friend "pick up" Mania as she looks longingly in the display window at a jewelry store. The two cads decide to amuse themselves by taking her to a fancy restaurant, where her table manners leave something to be desired. Viktor relishes his superiority over her, even her fear as he takes her in his arms. When their roles are reversed in the second half of the film, Viktor is truly pitiful, cowering in his obsession and degradation. He luxuriates in revenge fantasies, but unlike a "real man," he is unable to carry them out.

Mania, of course, is a victim, too, like many other poor girls "done wrong" in early melodrama. Her triumph over victimization and her rise to modern womanhood, however, differ from Vera's in *Twilight of a Woman's Soul*. Mania has become a vamp, moving from one worthless man to the next as soon as she has sucked him dry. She is, therefore, no longer the Russian "Mania," but the Western "Mary." As Mary, she is glamorous and calculating; with a cruel smile and cigarette in hand, she informs Viktor — in *writing* — that since his means are exhausted, he needs to find a less expensive mistress.

Bauer's aestheticism is pronounced in this film, and he was criticized for it. The beautifully decorated sets, the painterly compositions, the stately pacing (which even his contemporaries sometimes found too slow) seemed here not a means to an end, but the end in itself. As a *Cine Journal* critic put it: "in places one very much gets the feeling that a director–scene painter and not a director-artist produced this picture."[7] To be fair to Bauer, however, he wanted to show the seductive glamour of this way of life, and he succeeded with great flair.

In contrast to the leisurely pace of much of the picture, its final scene is mesmerizing and definitely cinematic. It is worth examining its innovative construction, which relies on a great deal of crosscutting, in some detail. The crosscutting between glum Viktor in his stark room and gay

Mary, surrounded by her many admirers, sharply emphasizes their different lifestyles. As Viktor writes her begging for one last meeting, we see Mary dancing. This scene is shot tantalizingly through drapery so that the viewer becomes a true voyeur, catching Mary only in glimpses as she sweeps by.

Now that Viktor's money and his manhood are gone, a voyeur is all he can ever hope to be to Mary. He slowly walks to the club, his hopelessness and doom evident in every heavy step — as Mary dances the tango, the first time this dance appears in a Russian-made film.[8] Mary scornfully dismisses the note and tells her maid (oh, cruel insult!) to give him *three* rubles. Outside, Viktor staggers in shock; inside, seen by means of a daring, high overhead shot, Mary dances ever more frenetically. Viktor shoots himself. Mary and her friends are startled to see the body on the steps. She reacts first with disgust, then, laughing mirthlessly, walks *right over* his corpse, and steps into her waiting automobile. "On to Maxim's!" reads the closing intertitle.

In many ways, *Child of the Big City* is the emblematic Russian cinema melodrama. Woman is vampire: a ruthless sexual predator, powerful and indestructible. Man, on the other hand, is a weak, feminized victim of his erotic impulses, master of nothing. It is a remarkably unmediated portrait of (male) society's angst, symbolized in the stereotypically gendered ways that are so well described in Bram Dijkstra's recent book on the portrayal of male psychic trauma in fin de siècle cultures, *Evil Sisters.*[9]

Bauer's next major film was *Children of the Age* (*Deti veka*, 1915), a nuanced and sophisticated depiction of his favorite themes of glamour and corruption. The film stars Vera Kholodnaia as Maria and Arsenii Bibikov, who was so effective as the father in *The Daughter-in-Law's Lover,* as Lebedev. Here we see one of Russian cinema's most vivid portrayals of class conflict and the tensions engendered by capitalism.

The beauteous Maria lives a modest, middle-class life with her husband, a young banker (I. Gorskii), and their new baby. One day, while shopping at what appears to be the Petrovskii Passage shopping arcade in Moscow, Maria meets an old school friend, Lidia (V. Glinskaia), now a wealthy society matron. The two women begin socializing with each other, but Maria's husband does not fit in well with Lidia's glamorous circle of friends. A rich industrialist, Lebedev, is attracted to Maria at a party and arranges with Lidia to meet Maria alone. Surprised and repelled, Maria resists Lebedev's advances, so he retaliates by using his influence at the bank to have her husband fired (although Maria does not know this).

Lebedev then lures Maria into his web through a combination of guile, alcohol, and force, while her hapless husband is out job hunting. Ruined and guilt-ridden, the sorrowful Maria leaves her husband and child to become Lebedev's mistress. Next the unscrupulous Lebedev sends word to Maria's husband that he has a job for him, when in reality he has authorized an attorney to pay the husband a significant sum to grant Maria a divorce and give her custody of the baby. The horrified and heartbroken young man refuses, starts a fight, is thrown out of the office, and goes home to shoot himself.[10]

Transcending the narrative clichés of the genre, *Children of the Age* is an intensely moving film, superbly acted by all the principals, especially the matchless Vera Kholodnaia as Maria. It is a chilling portrait of sexual guile, exploitation, and violence. Maria has apparently married "beneath herself," and when she resumes her friendship with Lidia, her pleasure in taking up her old way of life again seems innocent and charming. Maria loves her husband and her baby, but she enjoys flirting with the men who are showering her with attention at Lidia's party. Lidia's role as procuress for Lebedev is ambiguous. Lidia claims that she wants Maria to live the sort of life to which she is accustomed, and which she deserves because of her great beauty, and yet it may be that Lebedev has somehow entrapped Lidia as well.

Lebedev is a man who feels entitled to take whatever he wants (and Bibikov plays this elegant "gentleman" as convincingly as he did the peasant patriarch in *The Daughter-in-Law's Lover*). He is not, in fact, any kind of gentleman. When he surprises Maria on her outing with Lidia at the park, he grabs her and attempts to kiss her without any of the niceties of seduction. Later, after Lebedev has arranged for Maria's husband to lose his job, Lebedev and Maria meet again at a picnic Lidia has arranged. Lebedev literally drags the very drunk Maria off into the woods, in a scene that leaves no doubt as to what happened next. Then, in a truly horrifying and exceptionally well-staged scene, we see Lebedev and Maria in his chauffeur-driven car; he is kissing her as she struggles to break free. Maria is so desperate that she actually manages to jump out of the car and run down the street. Lebedev chases her, catches her, and roughly forces her back into the vehicle. "She's having hysterics," he coolly advises the male passersby who have stopped to look and wonder, uneasily, if she is a damsel in distress. They shrug and move on. Lebedev resumes his groping and kissing; Maria, thoroughly brutalized, no longer resists him. She has given up — on herself and on her past life. No one will help her.

That this disturbing tale unfolds against a backdrop of luxury makes it all the more powerful. Bauer makes provocative use of both his lushly decorated interiors and equally gorgeous outside scenes of parks, forests, gardens. His shot composition, lighting, and camera angles and movement are also very effective. These make the popular outdoor summer activities like boating and picnicking look very enticing indeed, as do the sexy gypsy dancers Lidia has hired to entertain her guests (which reflects the gypsy "craze" of the time).

The subtleties of class differentiation are quite apparent, as when Maria's honest and straightforward husband reveals himself to be ever so slightly out of place at Lidia's party. His discomfiture with the "beautiful people," and theirs with him, is obvious. And the fact that the malevolent predator Lebedev is identified as an industrialist rather than as a prince is no accident. As we shall see, despite the fact that the movie moguls were themselves capitalists, they often played to the audience's fears of capitalism (which was, of course, no more than "good business").

AFTER BAUER

Bauer's accidental death in the summer of 1917 left a gaping void in the world of Russian cinema. No one could make this kind of film as well as he did. Two late examples of the genre by other accomplished directors are, however, worth noting: Petr Chardynin's *Be Still, Sadness, Be Still* (*Molchi, grust, molchi*, 1918) and Iakov Protazanov's *Little Ellie* (*Maliutka Elli*, 1918).

Be Still, Sadness, Be Still pairs two of the most important stars of the Russian screen—Vera Kholodnaia and Vladimir Maksimov—in a story that, according to the Soviet insert to the print, epitomizes "the values of the bourgeoisie": the belief that one can buy and sell anything and the emphasis on appearance and material possession. These are certainly the values of Russian melodrama, but whether or not they actually exemplified the values of the Russian bourgeoisie is another matter. Regardless of the truth of the portrayal, the fear of the effects of encroaching commercialism on Russian life is obvious in many of these pictures.

Be Still, Sadness, Be Still records a staple of Russian popular culture: the circus. Kholodnaia plays a circus performer named Paola (or "Pola"), whose extraordinary beauty naturally attracts the constant harassing attentions of numerous men. She is defended by her partner, Loria (played by the director, Petr Chardynin), a clown-acrobat who drinks heavily. Eventually Loria is critically injured when he performs drunk, and the crippled Loria and Paola are forced to become street musicians. Their theme song is the mournful "Be Still, Sadness, Be Still." A group of young gentlemen (Ivan Khudoleev, Vladimir Maksimov, Vitold Polonskii, and Osip Runich) who saw and admired Paola at the circus decide to invite the two to perform at their private "bachelor" party, at which Paola is the main attraction. The young men vie for her attention, give her an expensive necklace, and offer Loria (who is very drunk) money to turn her over to them. Outraged, Paola leaves and refuses to return to the streets to perform. But when they are truly destitute, Paola returns to offer herself to one of the young men, the artist Volyntsev (Maksimov).

As Loria sinks deeper into poverty, Paola enjoys her life as a rich man's mistress—for a while. Eventually her lover becomes too possessive for her taste and temperament: he doesn't like going out to see the gypsy performers she adores, he doesn't want her to sing at a restaurant. When he attempts to sell her to a younger rival, Telepnev (Polonskii), she pridefully departs to another man in this "incestuous" circle. Her new lover, an inveterate gambler, has lost a huge sum of money, 64,000 rubles. Desperate, he devises a plot to rob a friend, the very Telepnev whom Paola refused. While Paola unwittingly serves as decoy, distracting the party by singing for them, her lover sets off the alarm as he attempts to break the safe. Unwilling to face the shame of exposure, he shoots himself with the gun he has stolen from Paola's dresser.

Be Still, Sadness, Be Still is not up to the level of most Bauer films, but Neia Zorkaia says it was a major box office hit in 1918.[11] The plot is absurdly complicated, with many loose ends (like the narrative function of the clown Loria). The sets are schematic, the camerawork pedestrian. Kholodnaia and Maksimov struggle to invigorate the thin material. And yet we see the persistence, even after the Revolution, of the theme of a woman who, forced by circumstances to sell herself, nonetheless triumphs over the weak men who surround her. Throughout, Paola manages to retain a certain dignity and even a measure of integrity.

Protazanov's film *Little Ellie* (from the Ermolev studio) is markedly different from *Be Still, Sadness, Be Still* and a very distinctive piece of work. It is, perhaps, the most shocking film in Russian cinema, and yet it does not vulgarly exploit its story of child rape and murder for its sensational aspects. (The title was, nonethless, usually excluded from Soviet filmographies of Protazanov's work.)

Little Ellie takes place in an unnamed, apparently Scandinavian country and is a psychological melodrama, constructed in a complicated series of flashbacks, that represents Protazanov's most stylistically sophisticated work up to that time. The ubiquitous Ivan Mozzhukhin plays Norton, the mayor of the town, who in the opening scene is examining his bruised arm and torn shirtsleeve. Next we see him at the home of Clara (Nataliia Lisenko), where detectives are questioning her about the disappearance of her young sister Ellie, who has been found murdered in the woods.

Norton comforts Clara, even taking her to the scene of the crime, and a year later they plan to marry. The murder remains unsolved. Despite his evident love for Clara, Norton behaves increasingly strangely. He has frequent panic attacks when reminded of Ellie's death, as when someone finds an empty cigarette packet at the murder site or when the police visit Clara to give her a portrait of her sister. Norton goes alone to Ellie's grave, clutching his left arm as though it were once again wounded. Drawing a gun and pointing it at his heart, he intends to kill himself but decides instead to return home to write a confession.

Clara surprises him writing the letter, and they have a violent argument as he safeguards the incriminating document. From this point, his psychological condition severely deteriorates. He wakes from fitful sleep screaming. He goes to mail the letter, then doesn't. He asks Clara to give it to the detective herself. He confesses to the murder and begs her forgiveness. In shock, she goes to the police station with the letter but changes her mind and burns it instead. Norton meanwhile has killed himself.

Mozzhukhin excelled at this kind of psychological drama (as he had shown in Protazanov's *Queen of Spades*, to be discussed in chapter 6), and his breakdown, guilt, and sexual ambivalence are finely tuned. The most remarkable aspect of *Little Ellie*, however, is the nonlinear way the story is told, through the use of flashbacks and crosscutting. There are two kinds of flashbacks in the picture: brief intrusions of memory and narrative flashbacks.

The first flashback is narrative and occurs when Norton first sits down to confess. He recalls how he met Clara, at a school function where Ellie was receiving an award as an outstanding student. Norton then befriended the two sisters, visiting their home often, though Ellie feared him. The second, when he has awakened from a nightmare and rushes screaming from his door, is a vision of the child lying dead on the path. The third and final flashback, which is stunning in its intensity, details the murder and what led up to it.

This flashback is completely subjective and self-exculpatory, chillingly accurate in its portrayal of the mindset of a child molester. Norton has convinced himself that he turned to Ellie for "love" only after realizing that Clara was oblivious to his affection for her. Ellie, after all, resembled Clara so much and indeed acted like a little lady when Norton escorted her into a party on his arm. She was flattered by his attentions, at least in Norton's mind. On the day of the murder, Norton has been drinking heavily. He meets Ellie "accidentally" on her way home from school; he persuades her to take an alternate route through the woods. He begins kissing and caressing her — she bites his arm and breaks away. As he chases her, he is caught in a blurred closeup, the cameraman apparently running along beside him. There is a quick cut to the present, with a shot of Clara trembling in horror, then back to the past. The killing was an "accident"; as Norton grabbed her and flung her down to the ground, she hit her head on a log. Later, we see him hurrying back through the woods to retrieve her cap, which he presents to Clara two days after the murder as just "found."

Little Ellie takes the preoccupation of Russian cinema with sexual degradation and exploitation to a new extreme, but the focus here is on the perpetrator, rather than on the redemption of the victim. A particularly disturbing factor is Clara's tacit complicity in Ellie's "seduction" and her role as accomplice after the fact when she destroys the confession. But like Bauer's best work, Protazanov's film is much more than a sensational exploitation of the most terrible of all crimes: it is also a psychological exploration into the world of a rapist-murderer. No wonder that the puritanical Soviet film critics thought it best to "forget" this early work from a director who had become one of their favorites.[12] Oddly, a *Cinema Gazette* critic labeled it "one of the most conventional melodramas in the cinema repertoire," which "does not contain any of the interesting and vivid moments so essential for the screen." This reviewer claimed that the final flashback produces an "unpleasant impression" of "excessive tension and intensity."[13] Nowhere in the review, however, is the source of this "unpleasantness" explicitly described.

All these films bear strong resemblances to one another and typify the stock plots of the sex melodrama, especially at the turn of the century, when the sensuous woman became the embodiment of male angst.[14] The erotic leads to degradation and death; class conflict and gender conflict are closely related. What does this mean? (Does it have any meaning?)

Certainly the new social patterns that resulted from Russia's rapid, partial, and late "modernization" engendered anxiety, especially urbanization and industrialization, the breakdown of the old caste system, and increasing freedom for women. Cities were seen as nests of corruption, poverty, and exploitation; the materialism engendered by capitalism led to betrayal; the independent woman robbed man of his strength and character; when classes mixed, especially "new" middling classes, trouble followed. These themes will be further reinforced by the films that are the subject of the next chapter.

6

Murder and Mayhem

THE EROTIC OBSESSIONS AND PROFOUND MISOGYNY THAT CHARACTER-
ize the films previously discussed clearly preoccupied Russian filmmakers
as these issues preoccupied their society. Sexual conflict is also a major
theme of this chapter. The difference in content between these films and
those in the previous section is admittedly extremely subtle, useful primarily for organizational purposes. In this variation of the melodrama, however, violence is directed outward, toward the offenders, rather than in-
ward, toward the self. This means, therefore, that conflict tends to lead to
murder rather than to suicide (although sometimes the murderer subse-
quently commits suicide to avoid punishment) — and that there is slightly
less "psychologism" in this rubric. But more important than any arbitrary
distinctions is the remarkable consistency we can see in styles and themes
over time.

FIRST EFFORTS

Two of the earliest examples of the murder-and-mayhem films come from
the Khanzhonkov studio, *Drama in a Gypsy Camp near Moscow* (*Drama v
tabore podmoskovnykh tsigan,* 1908) and *The Peddlers* (*Korobeiniki,* 1910).
Drama in a Gypsy Camp near Moscow, directed by Vladimir Siversen, is a
kind of early docudrama featuring "real gypsies" from a gypsy encamp-
ment in the environs of Moscow. A gypsy girl goes off with her lover; he
kills her for no apparent reason; there is great consternation among the
gypsies when they discover her body; the murderer kills himself. The schematic development and lack of obvious motivation for the actions are not
unique to this picture but are, as we have already seen, generally characteristic of early experiments with film narrative.

The plot of *The Peddlers*, based on a folksong by N. A. Nekrasov, although simple, is considerably more developed. Two peddlers, one young (Andrei Gromov), the other old (Vasilii Stepanov), head off on their route. A sinister-looking man (garbed in black) watches them counting their money; later this man emerges from the forest to confront them on their path. He murders them, boasts about his deed in a tavern, and is arrested.

Initially, the picture looks like another clichéd "peasant" film: picturesque vistas, painted backdrops for the "interiors," lots of bowing and kissing. But a few of cameraman Vladimir Siversen's stylistic touches elevate it. When the young peddler meets his girlfriend (Aleksandra Goncharova), the camera pans away from them as they sink down in a field, embracing. The murder scene is very nicely staged and photographed to build suspense. The robber walks right into the camera with his gun and *pretends* to shoot them — before taking the hapless men completely by surprise by *actually* shooting them.

Vasilii Goncharov's 1912 film *The Brigand Brothers* (*Bratia razboiniki*, based on a poem by Pushkin) has an even better developed plot and characters and employs the then-novel narrative device of a framing story surrounding a long flashback. (In Pushkin's 1821 original, the "flashback" is anticipated by the dying robber recounting his exploits.) A man (the versatile Arsenii Bibikov) joins a group of ruffians lounging and drinking by a river. "Let me tell you of my grief," says he — and proceeds to recount his life in crime. Orphaned at an early age, the man must care for his younger brother (Ivan Mozzhukhin) when their stepmother throws them out. The two little boys trudge away to an unknown future. Years pass. We next see them as young men working as farm laborers for a rich peasant (Vasilii Stepanov), but when the younger brother's carelessness leads to the death of a calf, the peasant fires them. The peasant's daughter (played by an actress recorded only as "Dolinina") is loved by both brothers. She, however, prefers the younger and leaves home to join him. Her outraged father follows and attacks his daughter's lover with an ax. In a scuffle, trying to protect his brother, the elder accidentally kills the old man. The two brothers and the victim's unrepentant daughter all flee.

First they live as beggars before eventually turning to highway robbery. The older brother ruthlessly kills their prey, despite the younger's protestations. (The girl has disappeared from the story.) In the course of a dramatic prison break and pursuit, the younger brother, always the weaker, dies from his injuries. The older buries him with great sorrow, and this is the end of the flashback. Returning to the present, the man announces to his audience that in honor of his brother's proclivity to mercy, he sometimes spares the lives of old men he robs.

In addition to Goncharov's skillful employment of various cinematic techniques, we can also admire the way he has developed the character of the older brother. The film's sociological explanation for crime is interesting and believable — as well as gendered. (Victimized men kill other men in these pictures; victimized women, on the other hand, "ruin" men.) Goncharov does not, however, glorify criminal exploits in the way such popular (and criticized) serials as *Sonka the "Golden Hand"* did; he seeks, rather, to understand.

Most sensational of the rural melodramas, however, was the first film from Grigorii Libken's Iaroslavl studio, *Merchant Bashkirov's Daughter* (*Doch kuptsa Bashkirova*, 1913). The picture was released as *Drama on the Volga* (*Drama na Volge*) and advertised, as noted earlier, as a "colossal success."[1] Directed by Nikolai Larin, this was a "docudrama" alleged to have been based on a recent tragedy that struck a little too close to home. (Remember Libken's reputation for dirty dealing, discussed in chapter 1.) "Merchant Bashkirov" allegedly sued to have the name of the film changed; hence the altered title *Drama on the Volga*. According to the *Cine-phono* announcement: "The title has been changed because the heroine's surname is identical to that of some well-known merchants in a certain town on the Volga — by sheer coincidence, of course."[2]

Bashkirov's daughter Nataliia loves Egorov, her father's clerk, but papa has other ideas, arranging a marriage for her with an elderly merchant business associate. Nataliia's mother, a drab middleaged woman whom we see standing quietly in the background of several early scenes, informs her of the betrothal plans. The mother, despite her meek appearance, turns out to be a central character who actively aids the young woman in her rebellion against the patriarch. When Nataliia summons Egorov to tell him about this awful turn of events (her "engagement"), the mother allows the young couple to be alone together, first on a walk by the Volga and then in the girl's bedroom. Seeing the tyrant Bashkirov returning home unexpectedly, his wife alerts the two lovers, and Nataliia hides Egorov under the enormous feather mattress on her bed.

After old Bashkirov departs once more, the two women discover to their horror that Egorov is dead, smothered under the feather mattress. Mother once again takes the initiative and pays their handyman to dispose of the body. He, however, begins to blackmail them, first for more money, then for sexual favors from Nataliia. The distraught young woman eventually submits to the handyman in his hut, but when he peremptorily summons her to the tavern, where he has been bragging to his buddies about his "conquest," she decides to take action. After the drunken men have passed out, she first raises an ax to the handyman's head, then decides instead to block the exit and torch the tavern, killing all the witnesses to her shame. We see her running from the conflagration, clearly deranged.

Merchant Bashkirov's Daughter is often used as an exemplar of the extremism of Russian cinema melodrama. The picture is certainly "over the top," but no more so than any of the daytime dramas on American television today, and well within the parameters of the melodramatic tradition. And although audiences at the end of the century may be reluctant to label the choices Nataliia and her mother make to resolve their problems as "feminist," unlike many of the heroines of early cinema, they are not waiting helplessly for men to save them, nor do they act like victims, at least not consistently.

Fine cinematographic technique, as well as the solid acting of the unknown cast, also elevates *Merchant Bashkirov's Daughter* from the merely sensational. Indeed, it is a largely successful marriage between Russia's artistic and tabloid cultures. There are several very beautiful shots, as in the scene when the lovers embrace in silhouette, framed by the arch of a bridge, as we look past them to the Volga. They then walk down the path and out into the light. The scene where the handyman disposes of the body by stuffing it into a barrel and then taking it out and dumping it into the river is well staged and cut for suspense, as is the next scene when the fishermen "net" the body. The rape is understated, but still presented in a way that is sympathetic to the victim, as Nataliia trembles and struggles in the odious blackmailer's embrace.

Another early example of melodrama-with-murder, *The Secret of House No. 5* (*Taina dom no. 5*, 1912), is a Russian Pathé studio production, directed by Kai Hansen. Although it is not, therefore, a truly authentic "native" Russian picture, it is still useful to examine it in this context. Movie critics often claimed that no one could make a "Russian" movie better than a Russian director—and a comparison of *The Secret of House No. 5* with *Merchant Bashkirov's Daughter* helps illustrate that point very well.

The plot is positively straightforward compared with most of the others considered here. The "courtesan" Elsa, her lover Darskii, and her best friend Veksel are an inseparable trio, but Darskii is falling in love with a younger, much prettier woman. Veksel lures Darskii to House No. 5 by wagering him that he will be scared of spending the night there, a murder scheme he has borrowed from a newspaper article (the penny press of the times, avidly read by the lower middle classes in the cities, was filled with such lurid stories). Veksel and Elsa kill Darskii and stage it to look like a suicide.

There is essentially no character development in this sketchy melodrama, nor are there any cinematographic elements of interest. It is formula filmmaking at its dullest, with none of the bizarre twists Russian directors loved. The ingredients are right enough, focusing on the entertainments popular among the urban elites (and therefore aspired to by others): gambling at a casino, dining at a restaurant featuring the ubiquitous gypsy dancers, riding in a carriage in the park. The orientalist fad is also evident here: Elsa wears a kimono, and her flat's decorations are vaguely "oriental." But she is too crudely manipulative to be the kind of heroine any young woman would want to emulate. In Evgenii Bauer's films, by contrast, Russian audiences were given what they wanted to see and experience: beautiful and glamorous people who rode in automobiles, not old-fashioned carriages; who lived in lavishly but tastefully decorated mansions, not tacky apartments.

EVGENII BAUER

One of Bauer's most provocative films was his 1915 *Daydreams* (*Grezy*). A well-to-do gentleman named Viktor Nedelin (Aleksandr Vriubov) has suffered terribly since the death of his adored young wife, Elena (N. Chernobaeva). Nedelin has, however, a beloved memento: Elena's luxurious tresses, which he keeps in a glass box. He frequently takes the hair from the box to kiss it. This macabre fetish will lead him to murder.

Out on a walk one day, Nedelin spies a woman walking alone down the street. She strongly resembles Elena (and indeed, is again played by Chernobaeva). Nedelin eagerly follows her into a theater, where Giacomo Meyerbeer's opera *Robert the Devil* (*Robert le diable*) is playing.[3] It turns out that this woman is an actress, playing one of the corpses who rise from the coffins to become dancing sprites. Nedelin is convinced that the actress, called "Tina" in Western fashion, is his wife reincarnated and arranges to meet her. Tina, a calculating soubrette, is determined to take whatever advantage she can of Nedelin. For the time being, his obsession flatters and amuses her, but this does not last long.

Tina wants Nedelin to give her some of Elena's clothing and jewelry.

This he will not do, although he allows his good friend the artist Solskii to paint Tina dressed as Elena. The troubled Nedelin cannot separate completely from either his dead wife or the grasping Tina, not even after his concerned housekeeper quits in frustration. Solskii (Viktor Arens) tells him what should be obvious, that Tina is unworthy of his affections. Nedelin's love affair with Tina is tumultuous, with constant arguing and recriminations. When Tina derisively says, "Go lie down with your dead wife," Nedelin retaliates by beating her, but she taunts him one last time. Here Tina crosses the line: she grabs the sacred tresses from their box and mockingly dances around Nedelin's sitting room with the hair wrapped around her neck like a boa. Enraged, Nedelin strangles her with it.

During World War I, hints of necrophilia in the movies became common enough to concern critics. These critics, who presented themselves as friends of cinema, feared societal backlash as directors and producers continued to push the limits of the acceptable in films like *Daydreams*. The mysticism and interest in the supernatural that characterized Russian society during the war years also figure prominently in this film.[4] Elena's ghost appears in *Daydreams* on two occasions, after Nedelin's first attack on Tina, and just before her murder. The ghost seems to sanction her widower's actions, offering her purity in sharp contrast to Tina's crassness.

This is one of the few occasions where we see Bauer employing a conventionally pure "Victorian" female image. Elena has a sweet, bland face; long, flowing tresses; a loving, retiring manner; and, of course, she is dead ("the only good woman is a . . . "). Tina, on the other hand, is bold and vivacious, with her hair done up in a modern style. We see her initially as the *flâneuse* who so disturbed European men in the modern era: striding along, alone, in a public space, looking at a strange man directly, openly, without shame or fear.[5] If the passive Elena, who has fulfilled middle-class society's expectations, has been taken from her adoring husband, then how can a dangerous, déclassé woman like Tina be allowed to live? And Tina most certainly presents a grave danger to the social order: she drives a decent man like Nedelin to the brink, to a crime of madness and passion.

Bauer returned to the female-centered films for which he was noted in *A Life for a Life* (*Zhizn za zhizn*) and *The Dying Swan* (*Umiraiushchii lebed*), both made in 1916. *A Life for a Life*, which was based on a novel by the French writer Georges Ohnet, featured an all-star cast: Vera Kholodnaia as Nata, the adopted daughter of a wealthy businesswoman/ industrialist; Vitold Polonskii as her lover, Prince Bartinskii; Ivan Perestiani as her husband, Zhurov, a rich merchant; Olga Rakhmanova as the mother and woman of affairs.[6] The plot is unusually complicated, even for a Bauer film, and offers sharp criticisms of the behaviors of both the new and old elites.

Two young women, Nata and Musia (Lidiia Koreneva), have grown up like sisters in the Khromov household, although only Musia is Mrs. Khromova's biological daughter; Nata is adopted. Now that the girls are of marriageable age, the distinction that never mattered before now matters very much. Nata has no money; Musia has a great deal.

But Nata has her own kind of capital. She, unlike the sweet-faced Musia, is strikingly beautiful, and when the handsome wastrel Prince Bartinskii enters their lives, it is Nata whom he invites to "come look at my collections." They quickly become lovers. The merchant Zhurov, who introduced Bartinskii to the Khromovs, has long hoped to marry Nata, so he calculatingly advises the Prince to woo Musia instead. In accordance with the conventions of the melodrama, Musia genuinely loves the roué Bartinskii and is innocently unaware that Nata is involved with him. Against her mother's advice, Musia gladly accepts his marriage proposal. Zhurov's plan has worked, for the unhappy, jilted Nata now agrees to *his* proposal of marriage.

The two women have a lavish double wedding ceremony. On the sisters' wedding day, Nata confesses to Mrs. Khromova that she and Bartinskii have been having an affair. Although deeply disturbed, Mrs. Khromova persuades Nata not to tell Musia, and the weddings go off as planned.

The Prince's behavior as a married man confirms Mrs. Khromova's worst fears. He resumes his "riotous life" (as the intertitle informs us), particularly at the harness races, where he gambles heavily. The besotted Musia turns control over her money to him (married women in Russia had long retained legal rights over their own financial resources). In the meantime, Nata is sulking prettily as Zhurov's pampered wife.

Finally, at Mrs. Khromova's birthday party, Nata and Bartinskii resume their passionate affair, not realizing that Musia, innocently looking for her husband, has seen them kissing as they sink onto a divan, an unusual example of woman as *voyeuse*. (The spectator, however, is left to imagine the rest.) Heartbroken though she is, Musia still maintains her heroic silence and composure. Musia is now more alone than ever before, as the Prince and Nata rendezvous even in public places.

The film comes to a climax when Zhurov discovers that Bartinskii has forged his name as co-signer of a note to cover one of his many debts, and he alerts Mrs. Khromova. Musia, confronted with this impending scandal, finally breaks down and tells her mother about Nata and Bartinskii; Mrs. Khromova informs Zhurov, who plans a phony business trip to trap the lovers. Caught together in Nata's bedroom, the lovers are at Zhurov's mercy. Zhurov has planned to kill them both for revenge, but then decides that it would be more humiliating for Bartinskii to have him arrested for fraud and jailed instead. As the police surround the Bartinskii house, Mrs. Khromova hands him his pistol and tells him to "be a man." Bartinskii, however, has no conception of a gentleman's honor, so Mrs. Khromova must act to save her daughter's reputation. She kills her son-in-law herself and puts the gun in his hand to make his death look like a suicide.

In the relatively unsympathetic role of Nata, Kholodnaia did not command the screen with her usual panache. Perhaps this explains why her film husband, Ivan Perestiani, complained in his memoirs that he could not understand why she was so beloved an actress (as discussed in chapter 3). The other principals—Polonskii, Perestiani, Rakhmanova, and especially Koreneva as Musia—strengthen the film immeasurably through their acting. The framing and staging of individual scenes represent some of Bauer's finest work; he carefully places characters within the frames, thereby indicating their changing relationships to each other and their world. Bauer's use of crosscutting and parallelisms is also effective, as when he cuts from Musia embracing her mother (pure love) to the Prince embracing Nata (illicit love).

As always in a Bauer film, set design and decoration were elaborate. As a *Cine Journal* critic noted, tongue-in-cheek: "Columns, columns, columns . . . columns in the parlor, in the office and on the fireplace, columns here, there, and everywhere."[7] The reviews of the film were so good that *Cinematographic Herald*, a Khanzhonkov studio publication, compiled a number of excerpts in an unusually long feature article on the picture.[8] Even Ermolev's rival *Projector* praised it but could not resist the temptation of suggesting that the film was "too Western," not an inconsequential charge, considering burgeoning Russian cultural nationalism. For some, *A Life for a Life* was seen as too dependent on "outward beauty," which "has weakened those elements which are typical of Russian film art—inner beauty, the beauty of psychological truth and spiritual feeling."[9]

Any such shortcomings notwithstanding, *A Life for a Life* is an extremely effective picture. *The Dying Swan*, based on Zoia Barantsevich's popular novella and starring a real ballerina, Vera Karalli, as the mute ballerina Gisella, is even better. Gisella is caught among three men: her loving and protective father (Aleksandr Kheruvimov), with whom she lives; Viktor (again, Vitold Polonskii), her handsome and tender lover; and the deranged artist Count Valerii Glinskii (Andrei Gromov). Madness and the eroticization of death are as important here as they are in *Daydreams*, but even better developed and therefore more believable.

Count Glinskii is determined to capture death on canvas but is suffering from a painter's block. A friend (Ivan Perestiani) tells him he might find inspiration by seeing the famous ballerina Gisella dance her signature role, the Dying Swan. The dance (of which we are treated to bits) mesmerizes Glinskii; Gisella agrees to sit for a portrait, in the costume and pose of the Dying Swan. Glinskii works like a man truly obsessed; his friend becomes fearful, as does Gisella's father. Viktor, who has recently reappeared in Gisella's life, proposes to her. Gisella, her face alight with joy, goes to Glinskii's for her final sitting. Outraged, and fearful that her *look* of happiness will ruin his painting, he calmly breaks her neck, returns her to the "correct" unnatural pose, and continues to paint. The closing shot could have served as a frontispiece for Bram Dijkstra's *Idols of Perversity*, a study of the distortion of the female image in Western art.[10]

Karalli was a phenomenally gifted silent screen actress and apparently a big box office draw. In the promotions for *The Dying Swan*, for example, her name appeared in letters more than double the size for those of the title.[11] As an actress, Karalli exemplified the grace and melancholy of fin de siècle culture. Her emotional range was considerable, and Barantsevich's scenario (which she had adapted from her novel herself) gave Karalli full scope.[12] Gisella, despite her handicap, is a young woman of some independence. Soon after meeting Viktor while on vacation with her father in the Crimea, she begins meeting him alone for walks and drives. When she inadvertently sees Viktor kissing another woman, she takes action: she and her father leave so that she can attend ballet school. She decides to accept Glinskii's invitation to paint her portrait; she likewise accepts Viktor's proposal without seeking anyone's approval; she continues to sit for Glinskii even though she is concerned about his unbalanced behavior and has had a terrible nightmare in which a nun tells her she will soon die. True, Gisella doesn't smoke cigarettes (the telltale sign of the modern woman), but she has a career and wears a wristwatch (two other potent signs of female emancipation).

Visually the film is a pure delight. Once again, Bauer had created and found interior and exterior settings suited to his painterly style. His use of natural light, artificial light (flashing lights signify the beginning of Gisella's dream), and a fast tracking camera makes this film look fresh and vital even after the passage of more than eighty years. Like *A Life for a Life*, *The Dying Swan* received excellent reviews, which the Khanzhonkov studio used to full advantage in promoting the film in the *Cinematographic Herald*.[13]

SATAN TRIUMPHANT

Bauer's stylistic and thematic unity marks him as a true *auteur*, and his oeuvre is unmatched. Nevertheless, of the "murder and mayhem" melodramas, Iakov Protazanov's *Satan Triumphant* (*Satana likuiushchii*, 1917) was in a class by itself. A full-scale, two-part "blockbuster," *Satan Triumphant* epitomized the "decadence" of Russian cinema (and of the empire on the eve of revolution), as far as Soviet film historians were concerned. It also reflected the late imperial society's fascination with satanism.[14] (Its surviving print runs just over one hundred minutes at current projection speed, but the end of the first part has been lost.)

Like Protazanov's *Little Ellie* (discussed in the preceeding chapter), this film takes place in a Scandinavian setting and stars Ivan Mozzhukhin. Here Mozzhukhin is at his most flamboyant, playing the dual roles of Pastor Talnoks and his son, Sandro Van-Gogen. In the first part of the film, Talnoks, a fire-and-brimstone preacher, busies himself making life as bleak as possible for his flock. He encourages his late wife's sister, Esfir (Nataliia Lisenko), to live platonically with her husband, the hunchbacked artist Pavel (P. Pavlov). He also demands that Esfir stop playing the piano and criticizes Pavel's paintings. This unhappy situation is too tempting for Satan (A. Chabrov) to pass up.

One dark and stormy night, Satan arrives at the pastor's house, disguised as a lost traveler. He quickly insinuates himself into the minds and souls of everyone in the household, suggesting to Esfir that life at the pastor's is too dull for a pretty young woman; to Pavel, that he needs to assert his spousal rights; to the pastor, that he is sexually attracted to his sister-in-law, Esfir. Satan's piano playing, especially of the "Hymn Triumphant," mesmerizes all of them, and the seeds of Satan's suggestions begin to take root. Pavel tries to force his wife to have sex (she fights him off), and the pastor also makes sexual advances to Esfir.

Talnoks begins to suspect that their disruptive guest is Satan; this is confirmed when the pastor sees a two-hundred-year-old drawing of Satan in an antique shop and recognizes in it a portrait of the traveler. But Talnoks is helpless before the greater power of untrammeled evil. He steals the drawing and tacks it up in his room *covering* a portrait of the Madonna and Child. This drawing serves as a symbolic figleaf in a later scene as it is superimposed over Esfir and Talnoks, who are lying in his bed in adulterous embrace. The ending of part 1 is no longer extant, but Talnoks dies making love to Esfir in his church under the portrait of Satan! The church collapses in protest at this sacrilege, and Talnoks is crushed by a log.

The second half of the film begins with a brief recapitulation in flashbacks of the first part, so that it would have been understandable to those spectators who had not seen the beginning. Many years have passed; Esfir lives with her son by the pastor, Sandro, now grown and a famous pianist. One day Sandro discovers the music for the "Hymn Triumphant" and becomes literally possessed as he plays it. His personality is transformed: he is rude to old women, gambles, goes to whorehouses, loses the love of his fiancée, Inga (Vera Orlova), and attempts to strike his mother, who has realized what is happening. Satan begins socializing with his new recruit, encouraging him to develop his powers. When Sandro plays the piano for the prostitutes at the brothel, they dance in a frenzy until one collapses, dead. The film ends with Sandro and Satan toasting their partnership.

With this film, Protazanov and Ermolev were obviously taking advantage of the complete collapse of the censorship in 1917. Protazanov had run into censorship trouble with the Russian Orthodox Church on several occasions, particularly over his desire to adapt Tolstoi's *Father Sergius* (*Otets Sergii*, discussed in chapter 7), so he must have enjoyed twitting the church elders with this enjoyably outrageous film. And *Satan Triumphant* is outrageous, playing its sensationalism to the hilt. It is also not too farfetched to suggest that the conservative businessman Ermolev might have seen "Satan Triumphant" as an apt metaphor for the revolution which was threatening his movie empire.

The acting in *Satan Triumphant* is quite uneven, making it a one-man show for Ivan Mozzhukin, whom one critic described, with specific reference to this film, as "virtually the most exciting screen actor in the Moscow *pléiade*."[15] Although *Satan Triumphant* is broadly drawn, there is effective use of crosscutting, superimposition, and especially dissolves. (The dissolve was a rare transition in Russian cinema at this time.) We must also consider it a sign of Ermolev's resolve and determination that the studio would mount such an ambitious film at such a late date.

CODA

Of course not every major melodrama of early Russian cinema fit neatly into the "murder and mayhem" or "sex and suicide" rubrics, but a glance at some of those that did not helps us to understand the popularity of the sensational among urban audiences even better. Films based on Jewish life, for example, tended to work over the theme of the arranged marriage. The sad, relatively restrained *To Life* (*L'Khaim*, 1910), directed by André Maître and Kai Hansen, was a Russian Pathé production, apparently widely distributed to Jewish communities outside Russia.[16] Beautiful Rakhel, daughter of Rabbi Moise, dutifully gives up her lover Sholom for an arranged marriage. A year (and a baby) later, Sholom returns and effortlessly persuades her to leave her husband for him. She takes her young child with her. Five years pass before she and Sholom surreptitiously return to visit her now inexplicably impoverished husband. He apparently doesn't recognize them, but after she has gone, he collapses weeping. *Cine Journal* published a letter from a viewer, one "M. S. S." from the town of Kerch, praising the film for its positive portrayal of Jews.[17] A review reported that the entire town of Mogilev had rushed out to see this "cinematographic pearl."[18]

Another relatively sympathetic portrayal of Jewish life can be seen in the Mintus (Riga) studio's film *The Wedding Day* (1912). *The Wedding Day* also concerns an arranged Jewish marriage, but its surviving print is too fragmentary to construct a coherent plot. Its chief historical interest lies in the fact that Mintus rounded up a group of itinerant Jewish actors to play the parts, so it provides a rare documentary example for theater students of what this style of acting looked like.

Many of the Russian melodramas that eschewed the usual highly sensational elements of the most successful films focused on "upstairs/downstairs" themes of class divisions. Vasilii Goncharov's *The Peasants' Lot* (*Krestianskaia dolia*, 1912) is one of these. Masha (Aleksandra Goncharova) enjoys a happy life as the daughter of a well-off peasant. She loves Petr (Ivan Mozzhukhin), he loves her, and their parents have agreed to their marriage. Then her world comes crashing down when her parents' property and home are destroyed in a major fire. Petr's parents no longer find the match suitable, and anyway, Masha has to go to the city to work as a maid to help support her family. Seduced by the master of the house (but paid off handsomely), the wretched Masha returns to her village. Now her parents can rebuild their house, but she has to see Petr and his unpleasant, jealous new wife daily.

There is not much to remark on stylistically in this film, which is nicely, if conventionally, made. The gifted Mozzhukhin is wasted as Petr, who doesn't have much to do in the story, but Goncharova is convincing, especially as she gains confidence in her new city life. She likes the stream-lined style of her maid's skirt and blouse, and streetcars no longer amaze her. Yet she is not sophisticated enough to resist the master's blandishments. Near the end of the film, however, there is a remarkable and beautifully composed scene, showing peasant girls dressed in their finery walking down a hill to church on converging paths. Masha, in the left foreground, is palpably and achingly alone.

The Wet Nurse (*Kormlitsa,* 1914) is one of Petr Chardynin's most interesting pictures for Khanzhonkov. Duniasha (T. Lashchina) is a maid who is seduced by the rich son of the household, Georgii (N. Pomerantsev), and betrayed by a cunning butler (Vitalii Brianskii). After being alerted by the envious butler, Georgii's parents discover the couple embracing in Duniasha's tiny room. She is fired (the cad making no protest). She creeps home to her elderly parents; her father attempts to beat her when he learns she is pregnant. She fends him off, but he throws her out.

Duniasha has become an outcast. She is jeered by her neighbors, and destitute, she has to fight off various lewd bounders before a woman shelters her and her child. Some time has passed. Now Duniasha is a wet nurse — oh, coincidence! — for Georgii's child; he has married the noble-woman (Sofia Goslavskaia) to whom he was engaged when he was sleeping with Duniasha. The two women become friends, and Duniasha confides her story. When the wife realizes that her husband is also the father of Duniasha's child, she decides to leave him and take their baby with her. The two women go together to redeem Duniasha's baby from the tene-ment, presumably to a new life of female solidarity. Georgii is left alone, pondering his miserable existence before the fireplace, a theme reprised in a different way in Abram Room's 1926 film *Third Meshchanskaia Street* (*Tretia Meshchanskaia,* known in the West as *Bed and Sofa*). But at least the pitiful Georgii doesn't kill himself, which makes the ending unusual for this genre, as we have seen.

Evgenii Bauer's 1914 picture *Silent Witnesses* (*Nemye svideteli*) presents a sharp portrait of class conflict, in contrast to the gender conflict of *The Wet Nurse.* Nastia (Dora Chitorina), the childlike teenaged granddaughter of the doorman (Aleksandr Kheruvimov) at a very grand house, enters service as a favor to the peasant maid Variusha. Variusha wants to return to her husband and children in her village, but the mistress won't release her without a replacement. The grand dame is going to the Crimea and can't possibly leave her poor son Pavel (Aleksandr Chargonin, another among the legion of languid Russian gentlemen) to fend for himself without a maid.

Nastia initially enjoys her role as "witness" of the high life in the household: motorcars, telephones, gorgeous clothes, fine food, graceful conversation. Pavel adores the elegant but standoffish Ellen (Elsa Kriuger), whose slim silhouette seems to have stepped from a fashion magazine of the period. The fact that she calls herself "Ellen" rather than the Russian "Elena" is an important early sign of her negative (Westernized) character. A cold-blooded schemer, she seeks to make him jealous with a double deception. Determined to marry Pavel for his money, she "pretends" that she is attracted to Pavel's friend, the slick Baron (Viktor Petipa), who is in truth her secret lover. When the Baron breaks off their nonexistent engagement, Ellen goes running to Pavel for the comfort that he is only too happy to give her. After Pavel and Ellen marry, Ellen and the Baron take up where they left off.

The problem for Nastia is that in the midst of all this high-class doubledealing, *she* has fallen in love with Pavel and has become his lover in the course of consoling him about his disappointment over Ellen. When Ellen decides to marry him, Pavel predictably dumps Nastia. Ever observant and loyal to the end, Nastia realizes what is happening between Ellen and the Baron and confronts them, but the innocent girl is powerless before such perfidy. The vengeful Ellen takes Pavel away, and Nastia is left behind, bereft.

Silent Witnesses is as skillfully directed as all Bauer films. The set of the mansion, with its grand staircase and art deco rooms, exudes good taste. The role the telephone plays in forwarding action (arranging clandestine meetings between Ellen and the Baron, for example) is an especially modern device, as is Bauer's use of the split screen during these conversations. Given the brilliantly overwrought inventions of Russian melodrama, however, I suspect that the window into high society the film offered did not fully compensate for its relative lack of energy and passion compared with other Bauer films.

But the most unusual of the melodramas on the upstairs/downstairs theme came from the prolific Iakov Protazanov: a film with a happy ending! This rare, feel-good movie was *The Maidservant Jenny* (*Gornichnaia Dzhenni*, 1917 or 1918). As Yuri Tsivian has noted, it had to be set abroad because "in Russia, such a turn of events [the happy ending] would have seemed forced."[19]

Jenny (Olga Gzovskaia), the daughter of a destitute but genteel widow, decides that she must swallow her pride and find work. She fails a typing test for a secretarial position, her first choice of work. She refuses to try out for a job as a chorus dancer in a variety theater, feeling that it is too degrading. She therefore decides to become a maid for a wealthy household (and is not above forging a letter of recommendation for herself). At this point all resemblance between Jenny and Duniasha of *The Wet Nurse* ends.

The young gentleman (Vladimir Gaidarov) of the household where Jenny works is not the cad we have become used to in Russian cinema. A war hero, he was wounded at the front when his airplane crashed. The aviator quickly realizes that Jenny is not "really" a maid. Not only is she beautiful, she also plays the piano and reads English. Almost all the other members of the household, high and low, are displeased with the attention the young man pays her. His mother (Olga Kondorova) is, naturally, concerned about what she sees as a mésalliance. One of the household's manservants (Dmitrii Bukhovetskii), whose unseemly advances Jenny has rebuffed, tries (unsuccessfully) to get her fired by planting some silver in her room. The climax comes when a guest attempts to embrace Jenny; the aviator challenges him to a duel and is wounded. After Jenny has nursed him back to health, but refused his offer of marriage, she discovers that she is the Countess Champierre![20] All is well.

This pleasant, well-acted film would be thoroughly unremarkable in any context except the Russian. An honorable hero. A respectable heroine. A straightforward story. What a surprise! The style of the film, with its closeups and fades, is modern enough, but the only "radical" plot element occurs at the end, when Jenny cuts across authentic class barriers by asking the butler François (Iona Talanov, who trusted her in the incident of the "stolen" silver) to drink to her happiness, and they shake hands. This democratic ending may well have been a salute to revolutionary times.

It is fitting to end this discussion of Russian film melodrama with an examination of the last film by the master of the genre, Evgenii Bauer's *To Happiness* (*K schastiu*, 1917). Bauer suffered a fatal accident while making this picture on location in the Crimea in the summer of 1917, and it was released posthumously, in September. *To Happiness* features a most unusual love triangle: a middle-aged lawyer, Dmitrii (Nikolai Radin); a wealthy widow, Zoia (Lidiia Koreneva, who was so good in Bauer's *A Life for a Life*); and Li (or "Lee," Taisiia Borman), her teenaged daughter, who is going blind.

Dmitrii desperately wants to marry Zoia, who has been his lover for more than ten years. Zoia, however, insists that they must wait until Li is "settled." Dmitrii and Zoia, for their parts, are completely unaware that Li is in love with Dmitrii; Zoia has concealed her relationship with Dmitrii so skillfully that Li thinks they are just friends.

As Dmitrii is getting ready to give Zoia an ultimatum, she decides to take Li to the Crimea for her health. While on this vacation, Li is befriended by a young artist, Enrico (Lev Kuleshov, the future Soviet director, who was also art director on the film).[21] Her mother mistakenly believes Li has fallen in love with Enrico and joyfully sends this news to Dmitrii, who then happily joins them for a holiday. Enrico continues to court Li, but now that Dmitrii is around, she plays the part of the melancholy, lovestruck maiden. No one suspects that Dmitrii is the true object of her affections until Enrico proposes to Li in a leafy bower. Dmitrii and Zoia approach the young couple but are hidden from sight, so that they can hear this conversation unseen. To their horror, Li tells Enrico that she loves Dmitrii and that "without this love I shall die."

Dmitrii leaves for home immediately. Li, grief-stricken, confesses her love for him to her mother ("Mama, why did he leave? I'll die without him"); Zoia, ever the selfless mother, promises to help her win him! Dmitrii, however, reveals himself to be the most sane, mature, and honorable male character in Russian cinema. He is revolted by this thought (near the beginning of the film, he tells the family doctor that he thinks of Li as his own daughter) and continues to refuse Zoia's truly pathetic pleading. As Zoia begs him, on her knees, he stands like a statue. Li appears on the scene, and her mother tells her Dmitrii won't marry her. He, however, unleashes the real blow, informing her that he won't because he loves someone else, namely, her mother. Li immediately loses what remains of her sight.

Li's hysterical blindness is a fitting symbol for all the blindness in this film. Dmitrii believes in the possibility of happiness with Zoia, a most unrealistic hope given her obsessive love for her daughter. Zoia fails to realize that her overprotective coddling of her daughter has retarded her emotional development; Li looks, dresses, and acts like a very young and immature adolescent (and strongly resembles Lillian Gish). Enrico believes that Li's mooning and sighing are for him. And Li is truly blind to everything in her world. The beautiful outdoor scenes in the Crimea show nature in its glory: the craggy beach, lush greenery, sunlit paths — in sharp contrast to the unnatural and unhealthy relationships between and among these characters.

Class conflict, dysfunctional families, sexual manipulation and deception, violent solutions to insoluble problems . . . this was the stuff of Russian melodrama, and material that speaks to us at the end of the twentieth century much more directly than do the one-dimensional heroines and villains of early American cinema. There was, however, a little light in the darkness of the standard repertory, the topic of our "intermission."

INTERMISSION

Fun and Foolery

RUSSIAN AUDIENCES DID NOT HAVE TO FACE A DIET RESTRICTED TO THE racy "gloom and doom" films described in the previous two chapters — as superb as many of these were. It would be absurd to think that class and gender conflicts were always front and center even in such politically and economically troubled times. Theater managers always included a comedy or an animated picture on the program for variety. As already noted, French comedies dominated throughout the prewar period, but this did not mean that Russian filmmakers failed to mount any challenge to the French hegemony. Some Russian efforts are worth examining — and are even quite funny.

THE SHORTS

Many of the earliest examples of native Russian filmmaking were in fact comic or satiric and provide additional insights into style and experimentation. Not surprisingly, many of these first efforts were quite derivative of French comedy, with the novelty factor of cinema clearly paramount. A good example is a very short (now four-minute) movie from the Drankov studio, *The Diligent Batman* (*Userdnyi denshchik*, 1908), directed by N. Filippov, who also stars as the unlucky and clumsy valet. The picture is shot in a single take. The batman sits on a pin, breaks a pile of dishes, eats the contents of a pot, gets shoved out the door, and comes back to do it again. This is comedy at its most basic but no different from what we see in other national cinemas at a similar stage of development.

There was also experimentation with animation. In the now two-minute film *Play on Words* (*Igra slov*, 1909), we are presented with rather charming, still cartoon illustrations of sayings like "She lost her head" and "He has one foot in the grave." The simplicity of these line drawings

The movies enter the streets, as depicted in this 1913 cartoon by I. Stepanov entitled "Old Russia Is Risen!" (Courtesy of Milestone Film & Video, New York, N.Y.)

Drankov Studio's "sensational" poster of the 1908 film *Stenka Razin*
(Courtesy of Milestone Film and Video, New York, N.Y.)

Postcard of Vera Kholodnaia, the "Queen of the Screen"
(Courtesy of the Yuri Tsivian Collection, Chicago, Ill.)

Publicity photo of Vera Karalli (Courtesy of
Milestone Film and Video, New York, N.Y.)

Publicity photo of Nataliia Lisenko (Courtesy of
Milestone Film and Video, New York, N.Y.)

Postcard of Ivan Mozzhukhin, the "King of the Screen"
(Courtesy of the Yuri Tsivian Collection, Chicago, Ill.)

Postcard of Vladimir Maksimov (Courtesy of
the Yuri Tsivian Collection, Chicago, Ill.)

Postcard of Vitold Polonskii (Courtesy of
the Yuri Tsivian Collection, Chicago, Ill.)

Publicity photo of Evgenii Bauer, early Russian cinema's auteur
(Courtesy of Milestone Film and Video, New York, N.Y.)

Still from Ivan Lazarev and Petr Chardynin's *Behind the Drawing Room Doors*, 1913 (Courtesy of the Yuri Tsivian Collection, Chicago, Ill.)

Still from Aleksandr Arkatov's *The Chrysanthemums in the Garden Bloomed Long Ago*, 1916 (Courtesy of the Yuri Tsivian Collection, Chicago, Ill.)

Still from Ivan Lazarev's *Merchant Bashkirov's Daughter*, 1913
(Courtesy of Milestone Film and Video, New York, N.Y.)

Frame enlargement from Petr Chardynin's *The Peddlers*, 1910
(Courtesy of the Paolo Cherchi Usai Collection, Rochester, N.Y.)

Frame enlargement from André Maître and Kai Hansen's *Lieutenant Ergunov*, 1910
(Courtesy of the Paolo Cherchi Usai Collection, Rochester, N.Y.)

Frame enlargement from Petr Chardynin's *The Boyar's Daughter*, 1911
(Courtesy of the Paolo Cherchi Usai Collection, Rochester, N.Y.)

Frame enlargement from André Maître and Kai Hansen's *Princess Tarakanova*, 1910
(Courtesy of the Paolo Cherchi Usai Collection, Rochester, N.Y.)

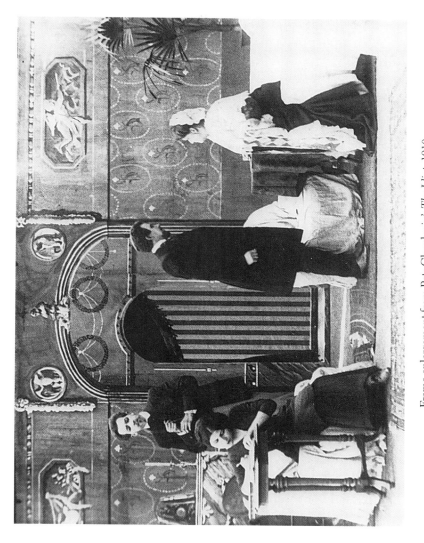

Frame enlargement from Petr Chardynin's *The Idiot*, 1910
(Courtesy of the Paolo Cherchi Usai Collection, Rochester, N.Y.)

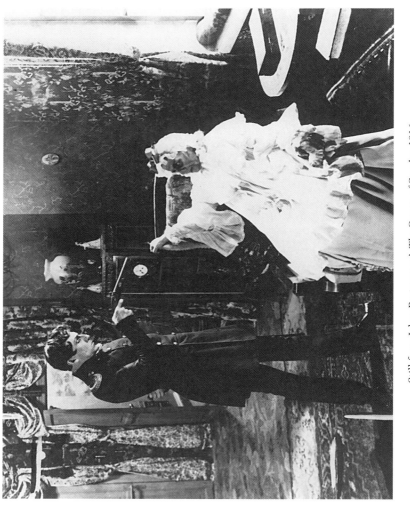

Still from Iakov Protazanov's *The Queen of Spades*, 1916
(Courtesy of Milestone Film and Video, New York, N.Y.)

is strikingly modernist and unlike the ornate, Beardsleyesque illustrations common to the magazines and advertisements of the day.

One of the best early examples of Russian narrative film comedy came from Russian literature, with an admixture of French style. Kai Hansen adapted Chekhov's *Romance with Double Bass* (*Roman s kontrabasom*) for the Russian Pathé studio in 1911. Although the Russian credentials of this film are rather thin, Czeslaw Sabinski ("Cheslav Sabinskii" in Russian), who became a leading director in the Soviet period, served as scenarist and art director for the picture.

The premise of *Romance with Double Bass* is classical farce: a woman falls asleep while fishing by a river; the man with the "double bass" decides to go swimming in the same area. Two strolling jokesters steal his clothes. The man with the double bass runs off in a panic when he discovers he has no clothes (carrying his bass case, of course). In the meantime, the woman, upon waking from her nap, undresses so that she can enter the river to retrieve her line, which has snagged. While she is in the water, the tricksters return to steal *her* clothes. As she frantically scurries down the road in her underwear, she meets the bassist who offers to hide her in his case. But when he spies the thieves with their clothes, he chases them, leaving her quite unaware of events, locked in the bass case lying by the road. Two men passing by naturally decide to carry the case to the cafe where the film began, and when they open it, to everyone's surprise and amusement, the half-clad woman emerges. The plot is well suited to the technical possibilities of filmmaking at this time, and Hansen's picture is a charming example of early silent comedy. Moreover, as the *Cine-phono* reviewer solemnly noted, the subject matter was "treated . . . with all the respect owed to the name of Anton Pavlovich [Chekhov]."[1]

COMEDY FEATURES

A more ambitious but equally charming farce was Petr Chardynin's 1913 adaptation of Pushkin's *The Little House in Kolomna* (*Domik v Kolomne*). Here Ivan Mozzhukhin, famed for his "psychological" portrayals in movie melodramas, had a rare opportunity to show off his comedic gifts (and battled with director Chardynin over how far they could take the humor without running the risk of being too risqué).[2] Mozzhukhin played a double role as a fun-loving young guards officer who pretends to be a (female) cook in order to spend more time with his lover, the flirtatious

Parasha (Sofia Goslavskaia). Parasha's starchy widowed mother (Praskovia Maksimova) is completely taken in by the impersonation, even though "Mavriusha" is highly incompetent — as well as comically unfeminine. Cross-dressing and sexual role-playing were a common theme in early film comedy and in cabaret (Aleksandr Galinskii was a popular Russian *transformator*, or female impersonator, of the times).[3] Certainly Mozzhukhin appears to be enjoying himself immensely as a clumsy and not-so-attractive woman.

One very funny scene shows Parasha (who is in on the joke) teaching "Mavriusha" how to gesture like a woman; another shows him "helping" Parasha dress; yet another involves "Mavriusha" doing calisthenics with her skirt hitched up. The joke comes to a predictable end when mama returns home from church unexpectedly to find "Mavriusha" shaving his beard in her boudoir. She screams and faints. The cinematography and mise-en-scène of this film are humdrum, but the pacing and acting are not, and it still elicits chuckles at exactly the right moments.

By 1914, the gifted Evgenii Bauer was applying his talents to full-length comedy. The best example was *Cold Showers* (*Kholodnye dushi*, a double entendre in Russian which also means "frigid souls"), a satire of sex and sexual identity (what else?!), starring Bauer's wife, Lina Bauer, a talented comedienne. *Cold Showers* is quite a complicated farce, carefully constructed in discrete episodes to set up the main action. We first see the cheerfully provocative heroine Lina (the character borrows the actress's name) flirting with two men on a train, one her "Captain" (P. Lopukhin), another the smitten Pierre (Sergei Kvasnitskii), whom she obviously has only just met. Next, she is drinking champagne in a private room in a fancy hotel restaurant, where Pierre has followed her. Cut to her bedroom, where we see her in a nightgown coyly pulling the draperies while Pierre anxiously waits in his hotel room for her signal. In the morning, we are not quite sure with whom she has spent the night, because the Captain suddenly appears on the scene once again. He catches her sneaking a few kisses with Pierre and angrily chases him away. Lina is certainly not ashamed of being found out; in fact, she is delighted at the discovery, and she falls on her knees before the Captain in mock repentance.

The poor Captain, it seems, is but one of a host of men supporting her in the manner to which she has become accustomed. Lina has numerous lavish desires and numerous debts to match. In her quest for luxury, she is soon shuttling many men, each believing he is her "one and only," in and out of her apartment. She manipulates them not only with her charms, but with alcohol, sleeping potions, swooning, and not a little guile.

The pace of her amorous manipulations becomes delightfully frantic. Pierre returns, to be shoved into the "cold shower" of the title to hide from the Captain, who has come to rescue Lina from her debts. Another lover dresses like a woman and is introduced to the Captain as her *matiushka* (a quaint term for "mother"); when Pierre emerges from the shower soaked, he is boldly presented as the "cook Fatima" (another orientalist allusion). The Captain to his credit sees straight through "Fatima," a brawl ensues, a posse of police arrive, *they* are shoved into the shower. Everyone ends up at the police station. It's a very funny screwball comedy, skillfully staged and directed.[4]

Not as scintillating as *Cold Showers*, and therefore more representative of the typical comedy, was another Bauer film, *The One Thousand and Second Ruse (Tysiacha vtoraia khitrost*, 1915). An inept and unloved husband (S. Rassatov) cannot understand women, his unfaithful wife (as usual, Lina Bauer) in particular. He studies a self-help book, a "handbook of Eastern Wisdom" that tells the secrets of "1,001 womanly ruses," to no avail. Her husband's spying and attempts to apply his newfound knowledge only make the woman bolder: she pulls up her skirt in public and sneaks cigarettes in her bedroom. By telephone, she arranges a rendezvous with her lover (again, Sergei Kvasnitskii) in her own home, while her husband is sleeping next door. When she is about to be discovered, as she expected and indeed hoped for, she shoves her lover into the closet. Her husband, however, refuses to play the outraged cuckold and slyly demands to know the "1,002d ruse."

The One Thousand and Second Ruse is an ambiguous film that on the one hand gently mocks some of the more obvious conventions of the melodrama, including those in Bauer's own films. Directors almost always characterized the modern (or "new") city woman as uncommonly bold, especially in public. Moreover, her smoking was a dead giveaway; new women smoking cigarettes were as ubiquitous in early Russian cinema as they were elsewhere. Russian readers would likely have recalled that Tolstoi had used smoking as a sign of Anna Karenina's moral decline some forty years earlier.[5] (But on the other hand, *The One Thousand and Second Ruse* plays into what would nowadays be regarded as some rather offensive female stereotyping.)

These examples are plot-driven, rather than star-driven, comedies. As we have already seen in chapter 3, the immense popularity of the French comic Max Linder made it difficult for the personality comedy to develop in Russia at this time (just as the popularity of Charlie Chaplin in the Soviet Union in the 1920s inhibited Soviet comedy actors from developing an original style). One successful exception to this rule was the Czech-born comic Anton Fertner, whose persona in Russian cinema was known as "Antosha," a hapless Everyman. Among the funniest of the Antosha films was Eduard Puchalskii's *Antosha Ruined by a Corset* (*Antosha korset pogubil*, 1916, Lucifer studio). The premise is simple: Antosha, who has had a lively party in his flat in his wife's absence, has to clear everybody out and clean up when his wife decides to return home unexpectedly early. But he has failed to notice, until the last minute, the corset that one of his guests has left behind. This corset has nine lives; Antosha simply can't dispose of it. He throws it out a window, in the fireplace, on the street, "loses" it in a crowd . . . , no matter what he does, the corset always finds its way back into his hands.

Fertner, who looked like a respectable middle-aged businessman, had a low-key manner that made the hoariest clichés of the sex farce seem fresh, as in the scene in which he takes the party from the cafe back to his apartment wearing a woman's plumed turban, while one of his lady friends has his top hat on. Another very funny bit shows the drunken guests elaborately tiptoeing into the parlor to avoid waking the servants, then boisterously dancing around the table before collapsing in happy exhaustion. Poor Antosha in the end is caught out by his fame. In a remarkable, self-reflexive nod to Fertner's true movie stardom, one of Antosha's fans has recognized him and insists on returning the corset.

FANTASY ANIMATION

Comedies were not the only light films available to Russian audiences. Cinema fantasies, or "trick films," like those of the French filmmaker Georges Méliès, were as popular in Russia as elsewhere. They inspired the "insect animation" or "animal puppetry" of Wladyslaw Starewicz ("Vladislav Starevich" in Russian). Starewicz (1882–1965), an entomologist by training, was born in Moscow to Polish parents. He was reared, however, in Kovno (now Kaunas, in Lithuania), where he moved in 1886 after his mother's death so that he could live with his aunts. After making a few nature documentaries, Starewicz returned to Moscow in 1911 to join the Khanzhonkov studio.[6] A fascinating description of his techniques for making the "puppets" appears in the filmography *Silent Witnesses*.[7]

Most of Starewicz's films for Khanzhonkov were quite inventive and very short. *Merry Scenes from the Lives of Animals* (*Veselye stsenki iz zhizni zhivotnykh*, 1912) provides us a charming, approximately six-minute look at a grasshopper band, a parade of butterflies, and some beetle friends dancing a popular dance, the shimmy. A good example of the fables Starewicz loved to render was an adaptation of Krylov's *The Dragonfly and the Ant* (*Strekoza i muravei*, 1913), which contrasts the fates of the industrious ant and the lazy, carousing, violin-playing dragonfly. A Russian winter brings "need and want" to the dragonfly, while the self-satisfied and vindictive ant, warm in his snug log cabin, refuses help and shelter.

Starewicz even used the insect puppetry in a combination live action–animation war fable *The Lily of Belgium* (*Liliia Belgii*, 1915, made for the government-sponsored Skobelev Committee for war propaganda). Perhaps this isn't "entertainment" per se, but it certainly is a very gentle example of wartime politicking that was quite suitable for children to view. A beautiful little girl (played by Starewicz's own daughter) asks her grandfather to tell her the story of the lily. He does, using the world of nature as the setting for his allegory of bestial Germans and brave Belgians. "Servants of violence," played by beetles, use the courageous lily as a bridge to ford the rivulet in their expansionist march, but, thankfully, the "root lives" (as the intertitle proclaims) and the lily will survive.

Starewicz also experimented with animated narratives. *The Cameraman's Revenge* (*Mest kinematograficheskogo operatora*, 1912) develops a funny little story, directed to adults, in only about twelve minutes. Business takes our beetle protagonist, Zhukov by name as well as by nature (*zhuk* is beetle in Russian), to the city, where he, quite naturally, goes to a club to "relax." There he finds a lovely dragonfly to keep him company. Zhukov and the dragonfly go to the "Hotel d'Amour," but unbeknownst to them, they are being filmed by a *paparazzo avant la lettre*, the grasshopper "cameraman." Zhukov, tired of the hubbub and bustle in the city, arrives home to find his wife with her lover, an artist. After a brief scuffle the lover flees, and Zhukov, who decides he needs to spend more time with his wife, takes her to the cinema. There they see the film *The Unfaithful Husband*, which stars none other than Zhukov himself. In shock, he escapes through the screen. How did this happen? The grasshopper cameraman, as we see, moonlights at this theater as the projectionist. It's a clever and fresh film, "with splendid acting by the beetles, whose gestures and movements were completely like those of human beings," according to one critic.[8]

A Gogol story inspired one of Starewicz's most ambitious films, *Christmas Eve* (*Noch pered Rozhdestvom*, 1913), a "satanic" film with a comic folkloric twist. The Devil (played by Ivan Mozzhukhin, who is virtually unrecognizable in full devil makeup and regalia, complete with tail) and the plump, saucy, and lascivious village witch Solokha (Lidiia Tridenskaia) conspire to wreak havoc in a Ukrainian village on Christmas eve. Riding together on Solukha's broomstick, the Devil and the witch steal the moon, making it difficult for the local men to find their way to the tavern.

The Devil then creates a phony snowstorm, forcing the old man Chub (Pavel Knorr) back to his house, where his pretty daughter Oksana (Olga Obolenskaia) has a visitor, Solukha's lovesick son, the blacksmith Vakula (P. Lopukhin). But the Devil's plan to have Chub catch them together goes awry; Chub thinks it can't be his hut, or, according to the intertitle, "the blacksmith wouldn't be in it." Indeed the only house the village men appear to be able to find in the dark is Solukha's; as each appears, she stuffs the visitor she already has, including the Devil, into a sack.

For the latter-day viewer, this story is much more appealing on the page than on the screen, and the movie seems to go on and on in a rather incoherent way. Vakula, who has been looking for the Devil to take him to St. Petersburg, finds him in the sack he was carrying. Eventually, Vakula returns with Catherine II's slippers (the "tsaritsa's shoes") that Oksana has demanded in order to marry him. All ends happily and in a flash-forward we see the young couple with their son hammering away in the smithy. The Devil is being tormented and taunted by other devils for doing good instead of evil.

Audiences of the time certainly must have found some of the special effects appealing, especially the miniaturization of the Devil so that he could hide in Vakula's pocket while at Catherine's court. But the overall darkness of the film and its rural setting (not very well realized) do not easily lend themselves to the demands of film comedy. Starewicz, inventive though he was with beetles and grasshoppers, did not work particularly well with actors, and even Ivan Mozzhukhin's considerable talents could not save this picture.

Lighthearted fun rarely drew more than halfhearted efforts from Russian filmmakers. It seemed to them not really "Russian," unlike the melodramas they turned out with such zest and skill and artfulness. So it makes sense that even when fulfilling their civic duty to enlighten the "dark" masses in their largely illiterate society by making historical films or adaptations of Russia's great literary classics, filmmakers turned to melodrama with relish, as we shall see in the next chapter.

7

History and Literature

As already discussed in chapter 4, cinema entrepreneurs wanted film to be more than "mere" entertainment. Largely responding to the criticisms of the cultural pundits in the intelligentsia, filmmakers fervently promoted the movies as an entertaining and therefore effective form of education. Adapting important historical events and the classics of Russian literature to the screen would fulfill cinema's educational function, they hoped, at the same time bringing them the respect they yearned for as middle-class producers of culture. This idea of cinema as a tool in the service of public education was as important in the earliest years of Russian cinema production as it was elsewhere. As we shall see, however, it proved to be a dead end, although the idea was revived with vigor in the Soviet Union in the 1920s.[1]

THE COSTUME DRAMAS

Historians have long debated whether any film can ever be "real" history. Silent film is, after all, primarily visual and emotional and not a particularly good medium for the transmission of ideas. Most of the first Russian "historical" films were, not surprisingly, costume *tableaux* from early modern Russian history or from folktales. These reflected contemporary interests in the Russian past, of course, but also historical themes that could be adapted to the public's well-known fondness for lurid details. Certainly none of these could be considered a serious effort at interpreting Russia's history, a challenge that would be taken up in earnest in the first decade after the Revolution.

A good example of the early historical *tableau* is Vasilii Goncharov's 1908 *A Sixteenth-Century Russian Wedding* (*Russkaia svadba XVI stoletiia*), in which Aleksandra Goncharova and Andrei Gromov replicate the marriage rituals of that time in a suitably stylized fashion. The studios had to be very careful not to get into censorship trouble by too harsh a depiction of any Romanov ancestor, which meant that historical subjects were mainly selected for their pictorial or legendary value. This stricture was not too onerous, since it probably suited directors' and audiences' tastes in any event.

The film that usually bears the honor of being the first native Russian film is a narrative example of this genre: Aleksandr Drankov's politically conservative rendition (based on a popular song) of Stenka Razin, the seventeenth-century peasant rebel. In Drankov's *Stenka Razin* (1908), the rebel (played by Evgenii Petrov-Raevskii) is no socialist people's hero, but rather a violent, drunken brigand. The film opens showing the wild revels of his gang, both on their boat on the Volga River, and then in a forest clearing. Razin's slave mistress, identified in an intertitle as a "Muslim Princess," shimmies provocatively for the men, but they are jealous of Razin's possession of her and plot to make him believe she is unfaithful. It's not too hard to convince Razin of her perfidy, and with little ceremony, the suspicious rebel leader flings the Princess to her death in "Mother Volga." There is not much "history" here, but a good enough story with an overlay of "orientalist" color.

Compared with the simple retelling and unimaginatively static camera of Drankov's *Stenka Razin*, a Franco-Russian costume drama directed by Kai Hansen and André Maître for the Russian Pathé studio, *Princess Tarakanova* (*Kniazhna Tarakanova*, 1910) comes off reasonably well. This is an adaptation of a play by Ippolit Shpazhinskii about an incident from the time of Catherine II (the Great) and stars a number of noted theater actors. Empress Catherine (N. Aleksandrova) learns from her lover Count Orlov (Nikolai Vekov) that Princess Tarakanova (V. Mikulina) is claiming to be, as an intertitle informs us, the "sole and lawful ruler." Orlov conspires to trick the Princess onto a frigate, where she is arrested and transferred to the Peter-Paul Fortress. When the Princess complains to Catherine about the conditions of her imprisonment (separated as she is from her maid and her possessions), she is transferred to a dungeon (a much worse place). "Exhausted by her sufferings," according to the intertitle, the Princess dies — or in another version of her doom, shown as an alternate ending, she is drowned in a flood that pours through the windows of her cell.

The camera here is as motionless as it is in *Stenka Razin*, but what makes *Princess Tarakanova* a more interesting film is that Hansen and

Maître take some care to develop Catherine's character over and above the demands of the plot. Catherine, ever the intellectual in this depiction, is usually seen at her desk, writing. She is also seen holding forth with her ladies-in-waiting at a salon, her little dog on her lap. Nonetheless, a contemporary critic felt that "one simply feels like laughing" at the inaccuracies of the historical milieu (a judgment this historian feels is unduly harsh).[2]

Petr Chardynin directed many costume vignettes for the Khanzhonkov studio, and a look at two of his earliest efforts indicates that the love-and-violence motif of the contemporary melodrama was likely to be an important aspect of historical films, too. In *The Lady Orsha* (*Boiarina Orsha*, 1910), a young lady (Aleksandra Goncharova) waits for a tryst with her lover, Arsenii (Andrei Gromov), while her father's guards are drinking and carousing outside. A jester spots the lovers and alerts the father (played by Chardynin himself, who frequently acted in his own films). Arsenii is dragged away to a cell, but he is rescued by his men. Some time later, he returns to the manse with a large force of men, kills the father in a particularly brutal fashion by stabbing him in the back, but he is too late. Arsenii discovers the skeleton of his lady love. Her father locked her in her room, to starve to death. Again we see the interplay of love and violence, with violence triumphant as it was in most of the Russian movie melodramas.

Chardynin reworked these themes in *Vadim* (1910), another film set in vaguely "olden times" (but loosely based on Lermontov's story about the Pugachev rebellion). The hunchback Vadim is picked up for vagrancy and becomes a slave (*kholop*) of the lord. The lord is attempting to seduce his stepdaughter, Olga, who runs to Vadim for protection and revenge. Vadim then recruits a renegade Cossack gang to launch an attack on the lord's estate. Heads fly. Vadim finds Olga with her lover but overcomes his jealousy. Here Chardynin combined the typical with the unusual (for Russian cinema): love and violence with the rare touch of "happily ever after."

Films set in the nineteenth century were less common than those taking place earlier owing to the censorship. Vasilii Goncharov came much closer to the present in his 1910 Gaumont picture *The Life and Death of Pushkin* (*Zhizn i smert Pushkina*). The story of Pushkin, his beautiful and putatively unfaithful wife, and Pushkin's ill-fated duel with D'Anthès, is, of course, the very stuff of melodrama and never failed to interest Russian audiences. In this picture Goncharov is exceedingly restrained, indeed, reverential, as he arranges for us a series of *tableaux vivants*: Pushkin throwing snowballs, Pushkin reading, Pushkin taking exams, Pushkin reading . . . Critics were unforgiving; one wrote (making the film sound much more interesting than it really is):

> Servility and tasteless licentiousness — these, in the director's eyes, form the basis of Pushkin's character. No, let's just forget these Russian-made films. . . . Best to continue watching those hackneyed foreign films: there, at least, one doesn't come across offensive and ignorant attitudes toward that which is most dear — our inner culture.[3]

As we have already seen, studios became convinced around 1912–13 that Russian audiences were sophisticated and attentive enough to enjoy much more complex cinematic narratives, and the historical genre likewise evolved in this direction. In 1914, for example, the Khanzhonkov studio came out with the full-length historical melodrama *Prince Sere-brianyi* (*Kniaz Serebrianyi*), co-starring the ubiquitous Aleksandra Goncharova and Andrei Gromov, who specialized in historical portrayals. The cinematographer was Louis Forestier, the French-born cameraman who was enormously influential in Russian cinema.

Prince Serebrianyi, unlike many other Russian costume dramas, is historically specific, set in the sixteenth century during the reign of Ivan IV (the Terrible). The film opens with happy, dancing peasants, whose enjoyment is destroyed by a gang of marauding *oprichniki* (soldiers who terrorized the countryside at the behest of the tsar). A handsome young prince drives these blackguards off. He then visits a downcast young noblewoman, whom he apparently loves, to the displeasure of her father, who has promised her to another. After a series of arrests, imprisonments, betrayals, and mayhem (all of which were indeed characteristic of sixteenth-century Russia), the Prince is saved by the local peasants he once helped. It is, however, too late: his beloved has taken holy vows and joined a convent. Despite the complexities of the plot's twists and turns, *Prince Serebrianyi* is reasonably easy to follow — and daringly liberal in its portrayal of the antagonistic relationship between the elite and the people.

The historical genre never evolved much beyond *Prince Serebrianyi* in terms of narrative complexity. Audiences apparently became bored with the sameness and remoteness of these vehicles, and during the Great War the spicy contemporary melodramas, which were much more interesting as art and entertainment, dominated the market. But after revolution overthrew the Romanovs early in 1917, we can see some of the ways in which the historical genre might have evolved had it not been for the Bolshevik coup eight months later. (The Bolsheviks, of course, had their own agenda for cinema.)[4]

Now it was possible to depict revolutionary history on the screen, and Aleksandr Drankov rushed into production a film about the socialist revolutionary leader Ekaterina Breshko-Breshkovskaia, *Granny of the Russian Revolution* (*Babushka russkoi revoliutsii*, 1917). "Granny" was Breshko-Breshkovskaia's revolutionary sobriquet, belying her pivotal role in organizing terrorist action for her party. Drankov was apparently already convinced that the radical socialists would win out over the democrats, because his director, Boris Svetlov, who was to go on to work in the Soviet period, constructed the film like a hagiography, in tone reminiscent of the Goncharov film on Pushkin discussed above.

Breshko-Breshkovskaia is overjoyed that her parents will let her pursue her education; she announces to her circle that they must be prepared to fight to the death for the people; she runs a peasant school; she is arrested, again and again and again. ("And prison again" is an oft-used intertitle, but hardly necessary.) The final scene of the film is missing; what remains, however, draws the movie to a close at a suitable point: Breshko-Breshkovskaia's triumphant return from exile.

One of Evgenii Bauer's last films, made the year of his death, was what we might call fictionalized contemporary history. This was *The Revolutionary* (*Revoliutsioner*, 1917), starring Ivan Perestiani as a fictitious revolutionary known as "Grandad." In 1907, as the police begin their final sweep of arrests to bring the Revolution of 1905–7 to a close, the revolutionary is hiding in his brother's flat. His brother betrays him to the police, apparently motivated by a desire for self-preservation. After languishing for a while in a prison cell that has seen many other political prisoners (as evidenced by the wall graffiti they have left behind), Grandad lives the hard life of exile in Siberia. During his ten years in Siberia, Grandad loses his closest friend, Levitskii, a distinctly Christlike figure whom he takes outside for one last look at Mother Russia.

Before leaving Siberia to return home after the February Revolution, Grandad prays at Levitskii's grave, swearing in an intertitle, "Comrade, your sacrifice was not in vain!" "Freedom's martyr" returns home to admiring friends and family, including his faithful daughter (played by the popular writer Zoia Barantsevich) and now-grown son (Vladimir Strizhevskii). But there's a problem: the son is a defeatist and a Marxist, whereas Grandad believes that "The salvation of the revolution lies in a victorious end to the war." Grandad persuades his son and his son's friends to abandon their defeatist ways; the old man and the young one go off together to win the war!

Although far from Bauer's best work, this is a most interesting film in historical terms, because it is so strongly anti-Bolshevik (the Bolsheviks were the central force behind popular demands to end the war in 1917). *The Revolutionary,* whose main character, Grandad, is not in any obvious way revolutionary, also shows the essential conservatism of Bauer and the Khanzhonkov studio at this time. One did not have to be a Bolshevik to be offended by this warmongering Christian! Ivan Perestiani took some care in his Soviet memoirs to distance himself from this picture ("once again it was a case of me [*sic*] totally disliking myself as the author of the scenario and the actor in the main role"), but he admitted that *The Revolutionary* elicited an enthusiastic reaction from the appreciative audience.[5]

In short, historical films never became a coherent genre in artistic terms, or a particularly successful one. The most talented directors, Bauer and Protazanov, usually avoided them, finding much more scope for their creativity in the contemporary melodrama. The directors who did make these films had to be very wary of running afoul of the censorship, especially as the regime became more historically conscious and protective of its historical legacy at the time of the tercentenary of the Romanov dynasty in 1913. Intellectuals, not surprisingly, were little impressed with the "historical" content of these pictures, so they never served their intended purpose of gaining recognition from the cultural establishment. By 1914–15, studios had definitely become disenchanted with the genre, which probably reflected their analysis of box office potential as well.

THE LITERARY CLASSICS

Literary adaptations for the screen fared better. They came in two types: the "classics" (Lev Tolstoi and earlier) and popular contemporary novels, a few of which have since become classics in their own right. The reverence for the classics that characterized educated Russia, especially the nascent middle classes, meant that directors and scenarists had virtually no artistic license in adapting the stories to the screen. The cultural elite invariably criticized all attempts harshly, and from watching some of these efforts, we can easily understand why. Of course critics' expectations were unrealistic, given the technical parameters available to directors at this time.

Petr Chardynin was an extremely versatile director, this very versatility perhaps a reason why he is lightly regarded today. (Unlike Evgenii Bauer, he failed to develop an identifiable style as *auteur.*) In 1909, Chardynin produced a synopsis of Nikolai Gogol's *Dead Souls* (*Mertvye dushi*), with Chardynin himself taking the role of Nozdrev. Because the surviving print is so fragmented, it's difficult to know what Chardynin intended, but the film, even when intact, probably was designed to appeal to viewers who already knew the story. (Indeed, more than one critic believed that advance familiarity with any film's story was essential for a profound viewing experience.)[6]

This is confirmed by Chardynin's 1910 rendition of Fedor Dostoevskii's *The Idiot* for the Khanzhonkov studio. Again, no viewer who had not already read the book could possibly follow the plot — and that was the point. It was a cinematic *illustration* of the novel, another example of the role intertextuality plays in interpreting these sources. It would be a serious error to label these films "primitive" without understanding the conventions behind them. Yet even given the 1910 spectator's different expectations, artistically speaking *The Idiot* falls short of the best contemporaneous efforts at literary adaptation. The sets and costumes are inaccurate, and the static shot placement and unvarying length of the takes (by Louis Forestier) make viewing dull. (We should note, however, Forestier's explanation in his memoirs that at this early stage of his Russian career he and Chardynin communicated mainly by sign language, with one of the director's "precisely five words of French" being *couper* [cut]!)[7]

In 1911, the Khanzhonkov studio presented a look at peasant life in an oddly lighthearted adaptation of Nikolai Ostrovskii's *In a Busy Place* (*Na boikom meste*). Directed by Petr Chardynin and shot, once again, by Forestier, *In a Busy Place* gives us what now amounts to nine minutes of various comings and goings, with lots of people flirting and kissing. A 1916 version of *In a Busy Place*, which also survives only in fragments, appears to have been much truer to the original text in its dark look at the deception, jealousy, and generally bad behavior of its characters.

Lev Tolstoi was much more problematic for the censorship than Gogol, Goncharov, or Dostoevskii, and it was difficult to obtain approval to adapt many of his works because of the Russian Orthodox Church's strong opposition. The most important adaptation of Tolstoi at this time was certainly

Iakov Protazanov's *Father Sergius* (*Otets Sergii*, 1917), to be discussed below. But Protazanov's most notorious "Tolstoian" film was his early "docu-drama" *The Passing of the Great Old Man* (*Ukhod velikogo startsa*, 1912).

Protazanov co-directed this film two years after Tolstoi's death, with Elizaveta Thiemann, who also played the role of Tolstoi's daughter and protector Aleksandra. Tolstoi's widow, Sofia Andreevna, whom O. Petrova portrays very unfavorably, successfully sued to have the picture banned in Russia, but that publicity served to enhance its box office abroad.[8] As is well known, an intense domestic battle raged within the Tolstoi household during the "great old man's" final years, as the Count continued to reject the material world that his wife so valued.

Protazanov's Tolstoi is the man of legend: eager to help peasants and the downtrodden. (According to Protazanov, the actor Vladimir Shaternikov, who played Tolstoi, "was totally unlike him in appearance" but was completely transformed through a remarkable makeup job.)[9] The greedy and haughty Sofia Andreevna, on the other hand, will only sell land to peasants for the highest possible price, has thugs roaming the estate to attack a poor woman gathering scrap wood, and so on. Tolstoi signs his book rights over to his longtime associate (and his wife's bitter enemy) Chertkov (Mikhail Tamarov) and changes his will. He thinks of killing himself until he is stopped by a vision of his sister, a nun.

Tolstoi then decides to visit her in the convent, where he is joined by his daughter Aleksandra. On October 31, 1910, in flight from his much-feared wife, the "great old man" finds deathbed refuge at the station at Astapova. The film ends with a newsreel shot of the Count on his bier followed by a slow pan of the sky as Jesus welcomes him to heaven.

Five years later, between the February and October Revolutions, Protazanov was at last able to make the film adaptation of his most heartfelt desire: *Father Sergius*. This version of Tolstoi's story of the naive officer who becomes a monk and faith healer after a failed love affair is deservedly famous, primarily for Ivan Mozzhukhin's nuanced portrayal of the title role. Prior to the fall of the Romanov dynasty, the story had been considered too incendiary to be filmed on two counts: the highly negative portrayal of Nicholas I, the tsar's great-grandfather, and Father Sergius's inability to conquer his sexual desires.

Protazanov did not compromise on either issue. Vladimir Gaidarov depicts Nicholas I, whose public persona was that of an upright family man, as a duplicitous adulterer, who seduces young noblewomen. Nicholas's current mistress is Countess Marie Korotkova (Vera Orlova). The Countess has attracted the attentions of Prince Stefan Kasatskii (Mozzhukhin), the "model officer" who has heretofore obeyed his father's dying wish to follow a military career. Kasatskii is, however, drawn to the high life at court and persists in pursuing Marie despite her rebuffs, unaware of her relationship with the tsar. Nicholas urges Marie to marry in order to provide a respectable front to their relationship (nineteenth-century rulers generally preferred married mistresses with complacent husbands, in the event of potentially embarrassing pregnancies). Marie easily entices the besotted Kasatskii, but on the advice of her mother, she decides to confess the truth to him on the eve of their wedding. Horrified, he breaks their engagement and becomes a monk, not because of any religious conversion, but to purge himself of sexual feelings.

The rest of the film concerns the incomplete transformation of Kasatskii into the holy man Father Sergius. Although he is "far from Petersburg," absorbed in a life of obedience and prayer, he cannot escape his sexual impulses. Erotic daydreams, of Marie waiting for him in her nightgown, kissing him passionately, frequently intrude. When Sergius is transferred to a monastery near a city, one of his former army comrades comes to visit him. This visit rekindles so many unresolved doubts that Sergius enters a hermitage, in an effort to distance himself further from the real world, but he is still plagued by images of his former fiancée.

In the film's most famous episode, Sergius receives a visit from the beautiful, unstable, and manipulative gentlewoman Mme. Makovkina (Nataliia Lisenko, Mozzhukhin's real-life wife), who intends to seduce the hermit prince as a diversion. Sergius yields to her pleas that she is lost and cold, allowing her to enter his abode. Instantly attracted to her, he flees to an adjacent room. She begins undressing, calling out to him for help, pretending to be ill. To quell his emotions, he takes an ax and chops off his index finger. Blood dripping, he comes to her saying, "I cannot help you." The foolish woman is struck with remorse, and a title informs us that she entered a convent the following year.

Nearly twenty years have passed since Sergius forsook the world. Since his encounter with Mme. Makovkina, he has gained a considerable reputation as a healer. This proves to be his ultimate undoing. One day a merchant approaches him, begging him to heal his daughter, who is mentally disturbed. The deranged girl, whom her father describes as "afflicted by the devil" and "afraid of sunlight," is also a lascivious minx. As soon as she is left alone with Sergius, she puts his hand on her breast and embraces him. Fadeout to a shot of the girl, in her shift, sleeping on Sergius's pallet.

Distraught, he creeps out to find his ax, but is stopped by a priest who offers to "chop wood" for him. Sergius then flees the monastery to become a wandering pilgrim, who begs for food and occasionally teaches the peasants to read. Still, he cannot purge his memories of his former life. Eventually he is arrested and deported to Siberia for not having any identity papers.

This psychological drama required an actor of Mozzhukhin's caliber to effect Sergius's long and complex transformation successfully, and this was the kind of role in which the versatile actor excelled. A less subtle actor might well have resorted to broad gestures and expressions; here we see the fabled "twitch" in his jaw that Vladimir Nabokov remembered from his youth. Vera Orlova and Nataliia Lisenko are irresistible, showing once again director Protazanov's great gifts in working with actors.

Tolstoi was arguably the most revered figure in contemporary Russian literature of the time, but the most adapted author was the beloved and relatively safe Aleksandr Pushkin. Pushkin's works provided an almost endless supply of good story lines. Given his early proclivities for literary adaptions from the classics, director Petr Chardynin could not fail to "do" Pushkin as well. He filmed Pushkin's psychological melodrama *The Queen of Spades* (*Pikovaia dama*) in 1910, again with Forestier on the camera. Although Chardynin had pulled together a good cast, with Aleksandra Goncharova as Liza and Petr Biriukov as German, the state of cinema narrative at the time could not do justice to the complexities of Pushkin's tale of mysticism, greed, and madness. But Chardynin did portray the Countess's ghost in a clear and believable way and also German's "vision" of the secret of the three cards.

Six years later, in 1916, Iakov Protazanov undertook another filming of the story, for the Ermolev studio, with Ivan Mozzhukhin as German. *The Queen of Spades* was a major success for both the director and the actor, who worked extremely well together. Protazanov's effective use of flashbacks and crosscutting and Mozzhukhin's nuanced facial expressions and body language expressed German's growing obsession beautifully, in a way that Chardynin's earlier film never could. (The jealous Vladimir Gardin noted in his memoirs, however, that the movie had to be good, given that Protazanov spent six months filming it at a cost of twenty-five rubles a meter.) [10]

The picture opens with a group of officers playing cards. The dour German, however, never plays but watches his friends for hours. To amuse the party, one of the officers tells a tale about his grandmother's youthful adventure with gambling and how the Countess had saved her honor by learning a particular sequence of three cards guaranteed to win at chemin de fer. Although the other young men laugh at the story and shrug it off, German cannot stop thinking about it.

He begins lurking outside the old Countess's house and intrigues to seduce her young ward, Liza (Vera Orlova). Eventually he succeeds in winning Liza's trust and finds his way into the house. German confronts the Countess (Elizaveta Shebueva) late one night when she returns from a ball, and brandishing his pistol he demands to know the secret of the three cards. She dies from fright. One night, after he has been drinking heavily, she "appears" to him and tells him that a three, a seven, and an ace need to be played in order on consecutive nights.

German is introduced to a private high-stakes gambling club. The first night he bets forty thousand rubles, plays the three, and wins. The second night, he bets his entire winnings from the night before, plays the seven—and wins again. The third night, he again stakes everything he has and plays what he thinks is an ace. The ace, however, has turned into the queen of spades. The queen's face is the Countess's, and German goes mad.

Protazanov used all the tricks that were available to filmmakers at this time to tell this compelling story. There are two major flashbacks: first when the young officer is "telling" his grandmother's story, we see it as a story-within-a-story. Second, we see a flashback as a dream; when the Countess is dozing after the ball, she remembers herself as a young woman (here played by T. Duvan). One of her many lovers comes to her through a long passageway and a secret door—and then with a start she returns to the present and finds German in her room. Protazanov also employs the split screen effectively, to show German in the present, along with German's fevered imagination of his winnings. The use of crosscutting is equally sophisticated for the time, especially in the sequence where German is waiting for his opportunity to enter the house while the Countess and Liza are at the ball. The mystical aspects are well presented: the ghost of the Countess lacks corporeal distinctiveness and fades as she slowly walks away from him. Superimposition, naturally, was another important device: the Countess's face superimposed over the queen of spades, cards floating all over German's room in the asylum.

As good as Protazanov's *Queen of Spades* was, it received some reviews that were so devastatingly negative that Ermolev studio rivals were almost certainly conducting a "campaign" to counteract the film's popularity. For example, the Khanzhonkov journal *Pegasus* devoted *six* pages to excoriating *The Queen of Spades* in one issue. "Veronin," Valentin Turkin's pen name, declared that "G. [*sic*] Protazanov showed in his production of *The Queen of Spades* that he doesn't feel the brilliant simplicity of Pushkin's beauty."[11] Damning words from one Russian to another. (Of course, Ermolev was not above the same sort of thing, and his organ *Projector* regularly attacked Bauer films.)[12] The independent publication *Cine Journal*, however, believed the film a great success (although its critic "G." thought Mozzhukhin's acting, florid to the modern eye, "too reserved").[13]

The other important Pushkin film from the Ermolev studio before the postrevolutionary emigration was Aleksandr Ivanovskii's *The Stationmaster* (*Stantsionnyi smotritel*, 1918).[14] Ivanovskii, like many others, stayed behind and became a premiere director of Soviet costume dramas in the 1920s, but this loose version of *The Stationmaster* is perhaps his best-realized film. Everyone from a crochety old lady on the stagecoach to an angry government official softens at the spell cast by the stationmaster's beautiful daughter Dunia (again, wonderfully played by Vera Orlova). Ivanovskii's techniques are up-to-the-minute with good pacing and short takes (although he does rely heavily on iris transitions, which were already outmoded in Russian cinema).

The station is a place where we see a great mingling of the classes. A flirtatious young officer who arrives at the station decides that he will stay and seduce Dunia. This the lieutenant does by feigning illness: "Your smile is the best medicine" reads the intertitle. The doctor, of course, realizes it is all a pretense but is bribed to join in the conspiracy. When the lieutenant is "well" enough to return home to St. Petersburg, he tries to persuade Dunia to go with him. Finally, she agrees to go on a short ride with him; she never returns.

The stationmaster (well acted by P. Pavlov) collapses in grief when he realizes that his daughter Dunia is gone. While he is in the hospital, the doctor reveals the hoax, and the grieving old man travels to the capital to find his beloved daughter. When he does, she screams and faints, and a hussar rudely forces him out. Three years pass. The old man is dying of a broken heart; he "sees" Dunia and believes that she has returned to him, but she is only a hallucination. He has a flashback to the hussar's pushing him out the door and collapses and dies. Another year goes by. Dunia returns to find her father dead. She has a flashback to their happy days together and kneels at his grave weeping.

Pushkin's story "The Stationmaster" is among his most subtle and delicate, and the danger in any retelling is to concentrate on its melodramatic narrative elements in a banal way. Ivanovskii avoids doing this through excellent casting and construction. Vera Orlova is particularly strong in this role, and she makes the transition from naive young girl to rich man's mistress heartbreakingly believable — as is her epiphany when she kneels at her father's grave. Ivanovskii does, however, manipulate the narrative to fit new social sensibilities. It is no longer social satire, but straightforward social criticism, stripped of Pushkin's irony.

As we have seen, adaptations of literary classics were as uneven as the historical films, but at least they had the advantage of first-rate stories, ready-made. Therefore, a few, like Protazanov's *Queen of Spades*, made a genuine contribution to the evolution of Russian film art. The best among these may also have served an educational function of introducing less cultured audiences to the importance of these artistic monuments. But directors and producers always faced the unwelcome possibility that an "indelicate" treatment could unleash a storm of abuse from the hypersensitive literati. Problems of this sort were unlikely in filmic adaptations of the already "scorned" works of a Mikhail Artsybashev or an Anastasiia Verbitskaia, the two most commercially successful novelists of the day. And the classics, fascinating though they might be, were too far removed from the demands of "real" life, that is, the modern, urban lifestyle that the typical filmgoer either enjoyed or aspired to enjoy. Even if there were lessons to be learned from the great works of Russian literature, how valuable were they in the fast-paced modern world? At a time when everything was changing, it seemed more logical to turn to the newest muse for a guide to life.

8

The Guide to Life

THE HISTORICAL MOVIES AND FILMED ADAPTATIONS OF LITERARY CLAS-
sics did not, in the end, bring cinema the respectability its producers
craved. They were simply too literal and — ironically — too literary. As we
have seen, cinema's "paradigm shift" from novelty to "seventh muse"
had already occurred — in the contemporary film melodramas, which
achieved considerable artistic substance by the middle of the Great War.
Unconstrained by slavish loyalty to the icons of Russian culture, yet remaining distinctively Russian nonetheless, even the most ordinary among
them created new models and codes by which to guide Russians through
the perils of modern life. A reexamination of the social codes of the melodramas discussed in chapters 5 and 6 will make this plain.

PUBLIC SPACES / PRIVATE LIVES

One might be tempted to conclude, after reading the film "programs"
described in the previous chapters, that the lessons to be found in the
movies were complex and morally ambiguous ones about infidelity, sexual
exploitation, vengeance, and death. As we know, some critics feared that
the dominance of these themes in cinema would corrupt the morals of
young and old alike. The rash of suicides in movie theaters described in
chapter 2 might be construed as evidence to support this view. Yet as any
survey of the penny press and the popular literature of the period shows,
the movies in fact mirrored not only the motifs of Silver Age high culture,
but also well-entrenched tabloid interests in suicide, murder, and the general mayhem of city life, all of which were part of the "hyperstimulus" of
modernity. This fictitious world, as depicted in movies and pulp novels, as
well as in the "high class" entertainments of artists like Leonid Andreev
and Andrei Belyi, provided its consumers respite from, as well as answers
to, the real problems of modern Russian life.

Although the pace of change in Russia at times seemed glacial compared to the dynamism of Western Europe, it is nonetheless clear that
Russia was no longer "eternal" and traditional, especially in the urbanizing areas west of the Urals. The proliferation of advertisements in the
newspapers for all kinds of self-help manuals indicates the yearnings of the
middle and working classes for a guide to the rules and manners of "civi-
lized" life. The movies provided living, visual examples that neither literary texts nor photographs could match.

First, there was the question of how to behave on the street, an especially pressing concern for women. Even respectable women might
now proceed unaccompanied on the streets for the new leisure activities
of shopping and window-shopping (which should not be confused with
the tedious domestic chore of provisioning the household). Browsing in
the shopping arcades of Petersburg and Moscow provided new opportunities for social contact: in *Children of the Age* (a telling title), Maria becomes reacquainted with her old school friend Lidia while shopping. But
on the other hand, window-shopping women should not allow themselves
to be picked up by strange men as the naive orphan Mania is in *Child of
the Big City*, or the result would likely be sexual exploitation and moral
corruption.

The street in early Russian cinema presented both pleasure and danger
to both men and women. People in the movies are mainly seen on the
street "strolling," long a favored public activity in Russia. In *Daydreams*,
Viktor Nedelin's aimless wandering is interrupted when he observes Tina,
sashaying seductively, with her provocative sidelong gaze. He is almost
compelled to follow her to the theater. Despite the continued popularity
of walking for pleasure, the car has replaced the carriage as the vehicle of
choice for the wealthy, whether aristocrats, nouveaux riches or demimon-
daines. In *Children of the Age*, for example, Maria tries to escape Lebedev
by leaping from his car, but the male passersby on the boulevard nervously
look the other way.

Likewise, parks presented opportunities for both amusement and danger. Sophisticated picnics are featured in *Children of the Age*, as sites of
uncomplicated pleasures—as well as seduction. (Those wooded glades
provided excellent opportunity for concealment.) In *Silent Witnesses*, the
duplicitous Ellen and her lover, the Baron, rendezvous at a public park
quite openly, seemingly oblivious to the possibility of discovery.

Cafes and restaurants present other acceptable, if not always entirely
respectable, public spaces for the intermingling of the sexes and the
classes. The private rooms that could be hired in restaurants often served

as the site of trysts. Restaurants like those in *Child of the Big City* and *Be Still, Sadness, Be Still* offer more than meals and public "privacy"; they also purvey ready-made entertainments. The well-known popularity of gypsy-style music and dance is amply documented in the movies, as are the latest Western dance crazes, which will be discussed below.

Even "high class" entertainments like the theater, opera, and ballet are sometimes featured in early Russian cinema, although mainly in Bauer films like *Daydreams*, *Twilight of a Woman's Soul*, and *The Dying Swan*, which are almost always in a class of their own. Interestingly enough, the movies themselves rarely appear as sources of entertainment (as they do later in the 1920s in self-referential Soviet films like *The Cigarette Girl from Mosselprom* or *Mary Pickford's Kiss*);[1] Starewicz's *The Cameraman's Revenge* provides one rare exception. We know, however, from the complaints of the culture police that movie theaters, especially the back balconies, immediately became popular as a warm, safe, and sometimes luxurious haven for young lovers.

So "the street" or public space in the Russian movies of the 1910s, in partial contrast to the unrelentingly gloomy German street films of the 1920s, is an ambiguous zone where many possibilities exist, both positive and negative. The same paradoxes appear in the purely private space of home, which is not always depicted as a refuge from the trials of the world. Regardless, filmmakers showed cinematic models for "home" as an aesthetic space and demonstrated new tastes in interior design very effectively.

The contrast between the modern and the traditional can be well illustrated by taking the interiors of *Merchant Bashkirov's Daughter* and comparing them with those in any Bauer film. The indoor sets of *Merchant Bashkirov's Daughter* represent small-scale merchant notions of prosperity perfectly: tiny, overfilled rooms, with overstuffed upholstery (including the conveniently gargantuan feather bedding that smothers the lover) and large, heavy furniture. Wallpaper is fussy, nondescript paintings are hung near the rafters, voluminous draperies block light. In short, the set design presents the typical, overdressed interior of the nineteenth-century European or American bourgeoisie.

The private spaces in Bauer films (like *Twilight of a Woman's Soul* or *To Happiness*) present a sharp contrast to this kind of overdressed claustrophobia and represent the "space of private fantasies."[2] Of course, as critics joked, there were "columns, columns, columns." Rooms are spacious and airy, with very high ceilings (convenient for the overhead shots Bauer liked to use). The typical moviegoer, who came from the lower professional groups or the petty bourgeoisie, naturally would not be able to afford this kind of enviable spaciousness, but there were other design aspects that could be appropriated, or at least imitated.

The atmosphere in Bauer homes is one of lightness. Draperies are translucent, to take advantage of available illumination. Plants, especially large ferns, are strategically placed for a "greenhouse" effect that partially erases the line between indoors and outdoors. The large rooms are made even more spacious by a relative lack of furniture (compared with *Merchant Bashkirov's Daughter*), and what furniture there is has clean, neoclassical or *style moderne* lines. Paintings and other decorations are sparse. The enterprising middle-class urban homemaker could in fact emulate this look much more cheaply than she could the expensive hand-carved furniture and tapestries that had signified the height of good taste at the end of the last century. And she would have the satisfaction of knowing that she was "à la mode" and, therefore, very Western.

One of the most fascinating aspects of the depiction of private space at this time was the spectator's view into the most private space of all: the bedroom. The bedroom shown in the movies, especially in Bauer films, is more than a place to sleep; ideally, it is also a place for contemplation, a place to express one's individuality. Literary heroines, of course, have long retreated to their bedrooms as the sole place in the house they can call their own, and we see such gracefully decorated rooms visually depicted in *Twilight of a Woman's Soul* and *To Happiness*. But men can now enjoy this luxury too; the rare example of the masculine sanctuary can be seen in *Silent Witnesses*, where Pavel's room is a combination bedroom and study, complete with telephone. Of course, the bedroom is also the site where the unconscious manifests itself in dreams or nightmares: witness the vivid nightmare scene in *The Dying Swan*, where Gisella sees disembodied hands emerging from all sides to take hold of her slim neck.

"THE DREAM WORLD OF MASS CONSUMPTION"

There were other dreams evident in the movies. The "dream world of mass consumption"[3] that spectators saw in the movies was, unlike Gisella's nightmare, enticing and desirable. The connection between cinema and the development of consumerism is well-known.[4] Considering the relative underdevelopment of the mass press in Russia, compared with Western societies, cinema logically served an especially important role in reinforcing the new materialism of a nascent capitalist society.

The role of shopping as a new form of entertainment has already been mentioned. While it was certainly a gendered, predominantly female activity, men must have delighted in certain aspects, especially car shopping. We see plenty of automobiles in the movies, like the one that carries Mary and friends to Maxim's restaurant after Viktor's suicide in *Child of the Big City*. These cars, in the movies owned by glamorous and immoral young men, were heavily advertised in the press and bore jazzy monikers like the "Metz" and the "Hupmobile."[5]

Women, however, were not merely consumers. Consumption was not seen as an end in itself; it was not vulgar accumulation of goods. Consumption needed to be followed by transformation, the transformation of woman into a work of art.[6] Now it was not only gentry women who could achieve this. Women viewers could appreciate and imitate the spare elegance of Ellen in *Silent Witnesses*, even if they sympathized with the tender Nastia in terms of the movie's plot. They would certainly hem their dresses above the ankle, as Ellen and other screen beauties did. Vera in *Twilight of a Woman's Soul* and Nata in *A Life for a Life* dress with exceptional taste and grace, and their coiffures have a simplicity to match. The rotund and overdressed style of matrons and merchant wives (as well as the plain and natural look of peasant girls) is the stuff of comic relief, not admiration, in the contemporary melodramas.

Of course, *A Life for a Life*'s Nata and *Twilight of a Woman's Soul*'s Vera are played by two exceptionally beautiful women, Vera Kholodnaia and Nina Chernova, respectively, a fact that cannot be overlooked. Dress did not the woman make, but the female spectator could observe how even a less naturally stunning actress could transform herself through makeup and dress, as Lidiia Koreneva as Musia in *A Life for a Life* transforms herself from child to woman. With the addition of a wristwatch, even a simple shirtwaist dress would have a modern look. Modern beauty aids like tweezers and breast "enhancers" could help complete the ensemble.[7]

Since there was less creative leeway in male attire, the lessons in costuming that we see in the movies for men are more subtle. But Edwardian dandyism is noticeably absent from male dress, both for heroes (such as there are) and villains. Cool simplicity and a seemingly unaffected sense of style reigned, epitomized by Vladimir Maksimov's bland, beardless, and classically handsome face and slicked-back hair. It's the "matinée idol" look that persisted through the 1920s—and reinforced the many advertisements in the penny press for hair tonics and shaving creams.

MANNERS AND MORES

Apart from the vexing issue of dress, especially daunting etiquette issues faced the upwardly mobile in the new social landscape of urbanizing Russia. Two of the most critical of these, given the growing popularity of restaurants, were table manners and dancing. It is not surprising that the movies featured many such scenes, which the careful observer could use as a "living" etiquette book. The most instructive transformation occurs in *Child of the Big City*, especially in the early scene where Mania anxiously watches Viktor and his friends for cues on how to handle the array of silverware.

This is, however, Russia, not Britain. Even in Pygmalion-like films such as *Child of the Big City*, the atmosphere at meals is convivial, not stiff. The goal is to appear relaxed and self-confident; to enjoy oneself, but not in a boisterous, exaggerated, or vulgar manner. In the movies, anyway, it seemed that anyone might achieve the appropriate cool demeanor, with enough practice. The casual draw from a cigarette (for women as well as men) and the graceful tipping of a flute of champagne helped to create at least the illusion that one was well-bred.

Dancing the new dances was another area that required considerable sang-froid as well as skill. New dances rapidly became crazes and just as quickly fell out of favor. It was no longer enough to know the waltz and the mazurka. The tabloid press in particular was filled with advertisements for dancing lessons, gramophone records with dance music, and dancing instruction manuals.[8] One issue of the magazine *Contemporary Woman* (*Sovremennaia zhenshchina*), for example, provided detailed instructions on how to dance the exotically named Ta-Tao.[9]

The movies demonstrated "how-to" with verve. In addition to depicting gypsy dances, directors were especially fond of the tango, as was the rest of Russia.[10] There were numerous "tango" films, among them one Iakov Protazanov made for the Thiemann studio, which *Cine Journal* enthusiastically noted "couldn't be better."[11] Mary's tango in *Child of the Big City*, believed to be the first depiction of the tango in Russian cinema, is certainly among the most brilliantly filmed dance scenes in silent film. It beautifully illustrates the chilly, impersonal eroticism of the dance.[12]

Changing relations between the sexes and the enhanced opportunities for casual mingling in the cities' newly created public places also required new guides for acceptable behavior. Here we see a supercilious attitude toward old-fashioned modesty. The bowed head, shy glance, and downturned eyes characterize peasant girls (who are usually about to be sexually exploited), not the independent city woman, with her direct gaze and clearly expressed desires.

"NEW" WOMEN / "OLD" MEN

Early Russian film melodramas provide extended commentary on the sexual anxieties of the age, and a number of models and counter-examples for behavior in the modern world. On the surface, my accounts in previous chapters of sexually voracious women preying on weak-willed men may have appeared to resemble the prototypical American "vamp" Theda Bara presented in her 1915 film *A Fool There Was*. In *Evil Sisters*, Bram Dijkstra describes *A Fool There Was* as the distillation of Western discourse on male-female relations.[13] This would, however, be only a partial explanation of what we see in early Russian cinema. The Russian film world before the Revolution is certainly a universe in which the sexes are battling, but men are sexual predators as often as are women, and the clichéd virgin of early American films is rarely to be seen in Russian movies of the same time.

Sexual predation on the part of men typically results either from patriarchy or distinctions in class. It is clearly an aggressive action, without pretenses or protestations of love. Patriarchal rights manifest themselves most clearly in rural society. By raping his son's wife, the father in *The Daughter-in-Law's Lover* is "only" taking what is his according to village custom. Peasant women as a group are seen as particularly susceptible to sexual abuse and manipulation. The miller's daughter in *Rusalka* is beguiled by the attentions and gifts of the handsome young nobleman, who marries a woman of his own class. In *The Peasants' Lot*, Masha, who has gone to the city to work as a maid so that she can support her parents, falls victim to the calculating wiles of the master of the house.

Young urban working women also fall victim to their "betters." Mania in *Child of the Big City* is a notorious example. After all, Viktor and his friends corrupt *her* before she turns the tables on *him*. Young Nastia makes the mistake of falling in love with the mistress's son Pavel, innocently believing that sexual desire translates into love in *Silent Witnesses*. And in *The Wet Nurse*, Duniasha actually (and realistically) becomes pregnant as a result of her affair with the young master of the household. Finally, in a slightly different twist *Daydreams'* gentleman Viktor Nedelin uses the demimondaine actress Tina like a mannequin, dressing her up in his dead wife's clothing. When Tina attempts to express her own (admittedly mocking and manipulative) personality, Nedelin murders her, strangling her with his wife's hair.

Class differences can work the other way as well, but more rarely. In *Twilight of a Woman's Soul*, Vera falls victim to the poor worker Maksim while delivering him medicine. This, of course, is a brutal rape, rather than a misguided attempt at seduction. And the capitalist Lebedev's conquest of the poor gentlewoman Maria in *Children of the Age* must at least be considered a psychological rape; she first succumbs to his sexual advances while in an alcoholic haze, and he physically compels her to return home with him.

Male brute force is also at the center of the most horrifying tale of sexual predation in all Russian cinema. Recall how Norton chases down his prey in *Little Ellie*, raping and murdering a completely innocent child. And Satan, in an ironic sense the emblematic male, wreaks predictable sexual havoc in *Satan Triumphant*. "Esfir's baby" might serve as a latter-day subtitle of the film.

So when Russian film heroines turn around to suck men dry in classic vampire fashion, it can be construed as understandable anger or revenge (prefiguring *Thelma and Louise*), if not as fair play. In *Child of the Big City*, Mary becomes stronger and richer, as Viktor is destroyed, financially and psychologically, but who introduced her to this corrupt and parasitic way of life? It was Viktor, after all. In *Twilight of a Woman's Soul*, the pathetic Prince Dolskii commits suicide after the independent Vera refuses him, but he had in effect "abandoned" her to an uncertain future after she confessed her terrible tale of rape and murder. Dolskii saw Vera's victimization and revenge as moral degradation rather than as moral triumph. In *Be Still, Sadness, Be Still*, to name one more example, it is Paola who decides which men will receive her sexual favors, free of charge, after they attempt to buy her by paying off her friend, the drunken clown Loria.

Another important factor that moderates the sexual stereotyping of early film melodrama is that in Russian movies, a surprising number of women work. Lower-class women have typical jobs: maid, seamstress, wet nurse, actress, singer. They work out of necessity and often at considerable sacrifice, but they nonetheless appear to take pride in what they do. Upper class women turn to "high culture" pursuits: Vera becomes an opera singer after she walks out on her marriage (in *Twilight of a Woman's Soul*); Gisella is a famous ballerina (in *The Dying Swan*). But if necessary to support her mother, a noblewoman will become a housemaid, as in *The Maidservant Jenny*.

The lessons on gender relations to be derived from these films are, therefore, markedly ambiguous. Men may have seen in them confirmation of their fears that new social roles for females would empower women to the detriment of men. But in the screen battle between the sexes, women are no more often the victors than they were in real life. A feminist interpretation of this same body of work might see women being victimized in familiar ways, but fighting back. The image of a woman using her sexuality as a weapon, both offensive and defensive, is a cultural cliché of long standing, of course. We see in these films, however, the beginnings of some new paradigms.

Vera in *Twilight of a Woman's Soul* and the unsuspecting wife in *The Wet Nurse* are the most admirable examples of "new women." Both women leave their husbands to make new lives for themselves. Vera recognizes that she cannot live with a man who is disgusted by her tragedy (the rape); the young wife in *The Wet Nurse* chooses not to live with a man who has seduced and abandoned not only a defenseless woman, but his own child.

CLASS CONFLICT

It is typically difficult to separate class conflicts from gender conflicts, and that problem exists here as well. The social landscape of early Russian movies is, as we have seen, fragmented with class divisions. When classes mingle, trouble always arises. Given the "middling" social origins of the vast majority of producers, directors, and writers, not to mention that of the audiences, it is not surprising that the attitudes about the gentry that are presented in films are decidedly mixed. Although the gentry are usually seen as glamorous, they are also ineffectual, unproductive, and corrupt. The gentry lifestyle in the movies is self-indulgent, consisting of little more than conversation, intrigue, and entertainment.

Prince Bartinskii in *A Life for a Life* epitomizes the casual decadence that many believed characterized the Russian nobility in the twilight years of the empire. Bartinskii is a wastrel and a gambler, who marries one woman for her money, yet carries on an affair with her beauteous adopted sister. Not satisfied with sapping his wife's fortune, Bartinskii attempts to swindle a friend. Even when caught and threatened with prison and ruination, Bartinskii still cannot do the right thing to save the family's honor (and so his mother-in-law kills him).

Bartinskii's female counterpart in gentry perfidiousness is Lidia in *Chil-*

dren of the Age. Lidia, under the guise of being a friend to Maria, reintroduces her to the seductive world of wealth, luxury, and conspicuous consumption that Maria had left behind when she married her poor but worthy and hardworking husband. Once she has Maria hooked, Lidia then acts as a procuress for the sinister businessman Lebedev.

And then there is Count Glinskii, the insane artist of *The Dying Swan*, who breaks Gisella's neck for the sake of his painting. Glinskii is impersonated by Andrei Gromov in a highly negative fashion, almost as though he were a syphilitic degenerate. Indeed, Glinskii's abstracted and obsessive emphasis on form over humanity reinforces the worst stereotypes of the Russian nobility.

But there are numerous other examples of class tension, many of them already discussed. The films on the "upstairs-downstairs" themes provide countless glosses on the sexual double standard. In many smaller ways as well, we continually see the arrogance and cruelty of the upper classes toward their servants. In *Silent Witnesses*, little Nastia would not have entered service so early had she not desired to help the housemaid Parasha, who was separated from her family and longed to return to the village. The haughty mistress of the household couldn't have had less sympathy for Parasha's feelings. Only Nastia sympathizes, and her tenderhearted sympathies lead to her ruin.

Even when we turn to tales of village life, we see class tensions reflected in film, between rich peasants, known as *kulaks*, and poor peasants whose lives had improved little since the Emancipation of 1861. These problems were much talked about in the press, as peasant unrest continued to trouble the countryside, despite the fact that the fiftieth anniversary of the Emancipation was celebrated with a flourish in 1911. The Stolypin land reforms, which sought to encourage separation from the village commune and thereby favored the entrepreneurial peasant, continued even after Peter Stolypin's 1911 assassination. Although there is great debate about what the ultimate outcome of the Stolypin program would have been had war and revolution not occurred, in the short term it seems to have exacerbated class tensions in the countryside.

So it seems rather topical when Vasilii Goncharov chooses to film *The Brigand Brothers*, where the orphan brothers are essentially forced to turn to beggary and brigandage after their unjust treatment at the hands of a *kulak*. In *The Peasants' Lot*, Masha loses her status in peasant society, her fiancé, and ultimately her virtue when her parents are burned out of their home. Her fiancé's *kulak* family no longer considers her a worthy spouse.

And the cruel father in *The Daughter-in-Law's Lover* is clearly another rich peasant, who can afford to support—as well as to abuse—a lazy son and daughter-in-law.

Moving up the social ladder from peasant to merchant, we see a different set of class assumptions at work in *Merchant Bashkirov's Daughter.* Bashkirov never actually refuses to allow his clerk to marry his daughter, but the girl and her mother behave on the *assumption* that this will be so. They do not, therefore, actively protest her engagement to Bashkirov's elderly merchant business associate. It is this assumption of class difference that leads directly, though inadvertently, to the young man's death as he is smothered under the feather mattress where he is hiding from the father's wrath.

The transition from merchant to capitalist was also under way at this time. Despite the fact that many film producers were born into the merchant caste, and indeed were now *part* of the business community regardless of birth, the collective portrait in the movies is far from flattering. The intrigues of Lebedev and his banker friends in *Children of the Age* to deprive Maria's husband of his job are the cruelest example, but we also see others in *A Life for a Life.* The merchant Zhurov conspires against the happiness of his friend's daughter Musia by arranging to have his wastrel friend Bartinskii marry her so that Zhurov can have sister Nata for himself. In the same film, Mrs. Khromova, who has been identified as a wealthy industrialist, murders her hapless son-in-law Bartinskii and coolly arranges the gun in his hand so that his death looks like a suicide.

Another interesting social issue that emerges in the melodramas is the intersection of the demimonde with the respectable world. Classes intermingle at the peril of both, depending on the circumstances. In *Be Still, Sadness, Be Still,* it is not clear whether the young gentlemen were corrupted *before* they were seduced by Paola's remarkable beauty, or as a result of that seduction. *The Secret of House No. 5* is an even more ambiguous example. Darskii is murdered by the courtesan Elsa and her friend (or pimp) Veksel when he seeks to break off his relationship with her. Presumably, such a fate would not have befallen him if he had chosen more upstanding people with whom to socialize. In *Behind the Drawing Room Doors,* the markers for class identification are so ambiguous that it takes some time to identify the "heroine" as a probable prostitute (or at least a woman of very dubious character) who has latched onto the young artist for social advancement.

As this discussion has indicated, the contemporary melodramas had many messages encoded within them that moved beyond their entertainment and aesthetic aspects. The messages were subliminal rather than overt, and we can never know for certain if audiences really appropriated them in the ways I have suggested here. But as Boris Gasparov and more recently Eric Naiman have noted, Russian society's "life in art and its life in the 'real world' was blurred."[14] Naiman is referring specifically to literary models in this quotation, but I think that his observation is just as true for the cinematic models of this period. The intertextualities in Russian culture — literary, musical, theatrical, cinematic — were profound, and the border between "high" and "low" culture was so frequently transgressed that it threatened to become meaningless. So much the better.

CONCLUSION

Movies, Mirrors, and Modernity

EVGENII BAUER HAS FIGURED PROMINENTLY IN THESE PAGES, AND HIS shadowy biography, brilliant meteoric career, and abrupt demise serve as a microcosm for Russia's fragmentary and fragmented early cinema history. At the time of Bauer's death in the summer of 1917, he was filming *The King of Paris* (*Korol Parizha*). The picture was finished by Olga Rakhmanova and released posthumously. It survives without titles; watching it is very much like "seeing a dream" (to translate directly from the Russian *videt son*, "to dream"). The images are Baueresque to excess, especially considering that the year is 1917, when Russia was in revolution: extravagant flowers, bountiful food, crowds of servants, luxurious costumes, beautiful, modish people. (There is even the highly orientalized image of an Asian potentate and his entourage.) The acting in *The King of Paris* is also highly stylized and highly melodramatic. One of the most startling visuals in the film is a large mirror used to reflect various aspects of a theater foyer. The problem is that the reflections are all wrong: they couldn't possibly be reflected that way in nature.

The epigraph to this book quotes the *Pegasus* critic "Alek," who said that "the screen is a magic mirror in which . . . life in all its variety is reflected." [1] A dramatic statement, but how valid is it? Cinema is, of course, always a highly mediated reflection of life. To add to the complications and challenges of interpretation, the "mirror" in this case has been broken, and many of its pieces lost. As we have seen, the oeuvre is no longer intact, the production histories are scattered, the filmmakers languishing in the dustbin of history, and so on.

"THROUGH A GLASS . . ."

The partial reflections are nonetheless tantalizing and revealing, even if distorted to some degree. First, in the evolution of the Russian film industry, we have seen the rapid expansion and maturation of commodified cultural production in a society and economy that were far from "mature." Who could have predicted that a Europeanized, citified novelty like the movies would have such great staying power in a country that was not only poor, but also largely rural and very traditional? The timing was exactly right, and the entrepreneurial and artistic talents were there, even though they were sometimes of a distinctly "renegade" variety, as the preceding pages have demonstrated. The cottage industry nature of early film-making also helped, as did the relative concentration of the urban population. The Great War has often been cited in these pages as a key factor in the industry's "boom"—but war could just as easily have killed the fledging industry as bolstered it had it not been for the genuine talents residing there.

Second, scholars of pulp fiction, the penny press, and Russian popular culture like Jeffrey Brooks, Louise McReynolds, and Richard Stites have persuasively suggested that historians' unswerving emphasis for most of the last fifty years on Russian politics, political ideology, and political culture has provided not the grand narrative that is the stuff of classical history but instead a partial and misleading portrait of Russian society on the eve of revolution.[2] *The Magic Mirror* provides more evidence of the vitality, popularity, and surprising artistic maturity of commercial culture in a Russia that was "on the eve" of cataclysmic change. The arts, both high and low, had a synergistic relationship with the movies, each building on, and reinforcing, the achievements of the other. The urban public's desire for this kind of synthesized, commercial cultural production was apparently insatiable—and reflects the significant cultural changes that had taken place in Russia since the Emancipation. Furthermore, in the case of cinema, the dividing line between "high" and "low" culture, once an insurmountable barrier, had now become a line often crossed. The results were definitely noteworthy, if sometimes disturbing to conservative cultural critics.

Third, the close involvement of the Russian middling classes with the film industry provides a unique opportunity to study the personalities and issues involved with the building of a new small business community connected with technological innovation and urbanization. The blurring of class boundaries that we see in this story is at least as interesting and important a subject as the blurring of artistic boundaries. Valentin Bill's "forgotten class" can in part be rediscovered through the evidence in the movies.[3]

Finally, cinematic Russia sheds interesting light on the realities of revolutionary Russia. After the Revolution, Russian emigré historians often implied that class conflict was a fiction constructed by the Soviet government to support its Marxist-Leninist ideology. Yet the picture that has emerged in the second part of *The Magic Mirror* has surely been one of a society in deep crisis, riven by class conflict and gender anxieties. Early Russian movies were not optimistic tales of Horatio Alger-like heroes overcoming obstacles to find prosperity, love, and true happiness. Native comedies found their humor more often in irony and satire rather than in naive good cheer. Rather, we see a world of shadows darkening even the sunniest days, a world in which nothing is permanent. Status, wealth, beauty, health — all are likely to vanish in the world of the movies, as they were about to in "real" life. The apocalyptism of fin de siècle Russian culture found expression not only in the Great War, but also in revolution.

"MODERNITY" AND THE MOVIES

These observations lead me to the connections I see between Russian movies and Russian ideas about modernity. One might easily argue that the movies and institutions discussed here are no more than modernist kitsch, but I would like to suggest that that is a facile conclusion. One needs, of course, to differentiate between modernity and the high culture of "modernism." Irving Howe's classic essay of thirty years ago, "The Culture of Modernism," has been much criticized, but it provides a useful framework for analysis if one considers that he is really talking not about *modernism*, but rather about *modernity*, at least as we use the terms today.[4]

Howe rightly contends that any definition of modernity is "elusive and protean" and "hopelessly complicated." Synthesis of the modernist ethos, he says, is impossible, so that "pieces and patches, a series of notes" are the best one can muster by way of explanation.[5] It nonetheless seems to Howe that modern culture challenges society in important new ways. These challenges center on society's division, fragmentation, and extreme subjectivity and emphasize "freedom, compulsion, and caprice."[6] Compulsion and caprice, Howe argues, are expressed through perversity, which he defines as "surprise, excitement, shock, terror, affront," reminiscent of Georg Simmel's "hyperstimulus."[7] Because of these challenges that modernity poses to traditional sensibilities, especially its emphasis on perverseness, the culture police invariably attack modern cultural production as "unwholesome" and "decadent."[8] Finally, modernity is nothing if not apocalyptic. As Howe forcefully put it:

The modernist sensibility posits a blockage, if not an end, to history: an apocalyptic *cul de sac* in which both teleological ends and secular progress are called into question, perhaps become obsolete. Man is mired — you can take your choice — in the mass, in the machine, in the city, in his loss of faith, in the hopelessness of a life without anterior intention or terminal value.[9]

It seems unnecessary to belabor the point that this is precisely what early Russian cinema, as described in this book, was all about, regardless of whether or not its producers were conscious of what they were doing. Most were probably not; they were, after all, businessmen and purveyors of mass entertainment. (An *auteur* like Evgenii Bauer, on the other hand, probably *was* self-conscious to a certain extent, though we shall probably never find evidence with which to support the contention.) At every turn in Russian cinema, we see fatalism and corruption, obsession and fear.

For the present-day researcher, close to a century removed from the experiences of those times, there is no more "protean" an experience than watching one of these films without titles, without music, without credits, without context. While this is certainly an unnatural and even artificial exercise, it nonethless lays bare the visual elements of the film — and the powerful emotionality of Russian cinema — in a vivid and unsettling way. The extant minutes of Evgenii Bauer's 1916 picture *Iurii Nagornyi* (presently about three-quarters of an hour) provides one such startling, retrospective revelation. We cannot even be sure that the start of the film is actually the "beginning"; to make it even more disorienting, the print held at the Library of Congress has been taped in reverse, so that the images are mirror images (apparent in the reversed letters of signs, etc.).

First scene: a club or restaurant, many women smoking. One of the women moves from the public arena to the performing stage; she is a dancer à la Isadora Duncan. The next scene appears to be a posttheater party. Leaving the party, the dancer and an enigmatic, bearded man seem upset. The telephone rings; she seems angry — or frightened. The singer she has apparently recognized at the club arrives in his car, bearing flowers. She arranges herself on a divan. He tries to kiss her. When he leaves, she returns to the bearded man. Third scene: yet another party. Now she appears to be flirting with her would-be lover. They are drunk. She goes to his flat. Cut to the bearded man, pacing, biting his nails. He calls her. After some hesitation, she heads upstairs where the lover has passed out on the floor by the bed. She tips the candles to set a fire.

Now there is a long flashback, the temporal situation of which is initially confusing. A lovely young woman has been wooed and seduced at a party by the singer, who has plied her with liquor. Her guilt and grief lead her to suicide. Cut back to the framing story. The dancer is telling the bearded man about this tragedy. Who is the young victim? Her sister? Her friend?

The bearded man learns from the newspaper that his rival has survived the fire. The dancer goes to see him at the hospital. As his face is unbandaged, we see that he is now gruesomely deformed. She calmly, ruthlessly shows him his reflection in a mirror. He collapses, as she slowly walks out the door . . . That hideous reflection in the mirror is what lingers in the viewer's memory. Image has become meaning.

POSTLUDE

When Russian movie theaters began to reopen in the cities at the end of the Civil War (1918–21), Soviet film production was in its beginning stages, a subject I have treated in detail in *Soviet Cinema in the Silent Era*.[10] So few movies were produced that surviving prerevolutionary films, both Russian and foreign, initially supplied most of the repertory. Not surprisingly the Bolsheviks and revolutionary critics who sympathized with them found this a highly objectionable state of affairs. The movies of the 1910s were, after all, a "hideous reflection" of a decaying society and represented everything the Civil War had been meant to destroy, but had not destroyed.

As I indicated in the preface, my research over the past decade, first for *Movies for the Masses* and then for *The Magic Mirror*, has forced me to evaluate the extent to which Soviet cinema was really "new." Of course, there was much that *was* authentically revolutionary about it, especially if one focuses on the work of the avant-garde. But even among the most famous of these young men, one can see the strong linkages with the cinema (and the culture) that preceded them, notably in the case of Lev Kuleshov, the Bauer protegé who was the "old man" of the youthful avant-garde.

These continuities between Russian and Soviet film become even stronger when one examines early Soviet popular cinema (as opposed to the political cinema of Eisenstein and the avant-garde); this was the subject of *Movies for the Masses*. The contemporary melodrama and the historical costume drama both made impressive comebacks. Although thinly "Sovietized," I have argued that they owed much more in style and content to their Russian predecessors than they did to the veneer of Bolshevism.

Another important element of continuity lay in personnel: Iakov Protazanov, Vladimir Gardin, Petr Chardynin, Ivan Perestiani, Amo Bek-Nazarov, and Aleksandr Khanzhonkov were chief among many from the old regime who played key roles in building Soviet cinema. In fact, of the seventeen leading directors of Soviet cinema during the NEP, in terms of the number of films completed, *eleven* had begun their film careers before 1918.[11] This was less true among actors, but of the major Soviet silent film stars, one-third had acting experience in either the prerevolutionary theater or the movies.[12] And although the impact of this continuity in personnel cannot be quantified, we must remember that these are the movies with which the younger generation of Soviet directors grew up. As "hard-line" a director as the Communist and former Chekist Fridrikh Ermler was unafraid to recount that his love of the movies was born when he was a child, "hanging out" at the theater in Rezekne, Latvia, then part of the Russian empire.

Finally, there is the issue of cultural politics. Although I did not realize it at the time, the "theater versus cinema" debates discussed in *Soviet Cinema in the Silent Era* and the "entertainment or enlightenment" debates featured in *Movies for the Masses* simply recast in "Soviet-speak" the arguments of Russian critics discussed here in chapter 4.[13] Perhaps such debates were not a reinvention of the proverbial wheel, but they do indicate the extent to which old issues about the didactic functions of the cinema had not been resolved in Russia/USSR, continuing to occupy center stage long after Western pedants had abandoned their hopes of reducing cinema to an educational tool.

Russian cinema faded away, metaphorically as well as physically, but it emphatically did not die. One of the most important implications of this book is that Soviet cinema cannot be fully understood without reference to the rich traditions of Russian filmmaking.[14] And this is, of course, part of the "paradigm shift" of Western Russo-Soviet studies today. Now that the Soviet Union is no more, the linkages to the past take precedence over the disjunctures. *Plus ça change, plus c'est la même chose . . .* The influence of the new Russian bourgeoisie on Russian politics, economy, and culture has met with largely negative responses from both the intelligentsia and the "masses" — and a century after its birth, the Russian film industry is once again struggling to chart its own path amidst the pressures of commercialization, Westernization, and foreign competition.

NOTES

SELECTED FILMOGRAPHY

SELECTED BIBLIOGRAPHY

INDEX

NOTES

PREFACE

1. For a discussion of Pathé's Russian studio, see Richard Abel, *The Ciné Goes to Town: French Cinema, 1896–1914* (Berkeley, Calif., 1994), pp. 42–43.

INTRODUCTION: HISTORY AND FILM HISTORY

1. Daniel Brower, *The Russian City between Tradition and Modernity, 1850–1900* (Berkeley, Calif., 1990), p. 76.

2. Michael F. Hamm, Introduction, *The City in Late Imperial Russia*, ed. Michael F. Hamm (Bloomington, Ind., 1986), p. 3.

3. James Bater, *St. Petersburg: Industrialization and Change* (Montreal, 1976), p. 308; Joseph Bradley, *Muzhik and Muscovite: Urbanization in Late Imperial Russia* (Berkeley, Calif., 1985), p. 23; in Hamm, ed. *City in Late Imperial Russia*, see Michael F. Hamm, "Continuity and Change in Late Imperial Kiev," p. 110; Stephen D. Corrsin, "Warsaw: Poles and Jews in a Conquered City," p. 127; Frederick W. Skinner, "Odessa and the Problem of Urban Modernization," p. 211.

4. Hamm, Introduction, p. 3.

5. Daniel Orlovsky, "The Lower Middle Strata in Revolutionary Russia," *Between Tsar and People: Educated Society and the Quest for Public Identity in Late Imperial Russia*, ed. Edith W. Clowes et al. (Princeton, N.J., 1991), p. 249.

6. V. I. Lenin, *The Development of Capitalism in Russia* (Moscow, 1974), p. 510.

7. For an elegant recent presentation of Silver Age culture, see W. Bruce Lincoln, *Between Heaven and Hell: The Story of a Thousand Years of Artistic Life in Russia* (New York, 1998), chaps. 12–13.

8. Valentin T. Bill, *The Forgotten Class: The Russian Bourgeoisie from the Earliest Beginnings to 1900* (New York, 1959). This was the first analysis in English of the Russian "bourgeoisie."

9. S. Ginzburg, *Kinematografiia dorevoliutsionnoi Rossii* (Moscow, 1963), p. 10.

10. Ibid.

11. N. A. Lebedev, *Ocherk istorii kino SSSR*, vol. 1, *Nemoe kino* (Moscow, 1947), p. 5. This was, however, the only volume to appear since after its publication Lebedev was denounced in the anticosmopolitan campaign of this period.

12. Ibid., *Ocherk*, 1:5.

13. Ginzburg, *Kinematografiia*, p. 46.

14. Lebedev, *Ocherk*, 1:15.

15. B. S. Likhachev, *Kino v Rossii (1896–1926): Materialy k istorii russkogo kino*, vol. 1, *1896–1913* (Leningrad, 1927), p. 96. Likhachev died in 1934, and nothing else was published from his research until 1960; see below, note 28.

16. Ginzburg, *Kinematografiia*, p. 116.

17. Lebedev, *Ocherk*, 1:19–20.

18. Ibid., 1:20–21.

19. Ginzburg, *Kinematografiia*, p. 92.

20. Lebedev, *Ocherk*, 1:21, 26–27.

21. Ibid., 1:22; Ginzburg, *Kinematografiia*, pp. 59, 126.

22. Lebedev, *Ocherk*, 1:33.

23. Ginzburg, *Kinematografiia*, p. 102.

24. Lebedev, *Ocherk*, 1:30; Ginzburg, *Kinematografiia*, p. 131.

25. Vega, "Trezvaia Rossiia i kinematograf," *KZh*, nos. 1–2 (January 17, 1915), p. 59.

26. Ginzburg, *Kinematografiia*, p. 156.

27. Lebedev, *Ocherk*, 1:35.

28. B. S. Likhachev "Materialy k istorii kino v Rossii (1914–1916)," *Iz istorii kino: Materialy i dokumenty*, vol. 3 (Moscow, 1960), pp. 39, 45.

29. Ginzburg, *Kinematografiia*, p. 161.

30. Ibid., p. 158.

31. Ibid., p. 11.

32. Ibid., pp. 170–71.

33. Lebedev, *Ocherk*, 1:46. First names are given when known.

34. Ibid., 1:44–45, 47, 51; in Bernice Glatzer Rosenthal, ed., *The Occult in Russian and Soviet Culture* (Ithaca, N.Y., 1997), see especially Kristi A. Groberg, "'The Shade of Lucifer's Dark Wing': Satanism in Silver Age Russia," pp. 99–

134, and Maria Carlson, "Fashionable Occultism: Spiritualism, Theosophy, Free-masonry, and Hermeticism in Fin-de-Siècle Russia," pp. 135–52.

35. R. Sobolev, *Liudi i filmy russkogo dorevoliutsionnogo kino* (Moscow, 1961), pp. 154, 159.

36. Ginzburg, *Kinematografiia*, 191–92; for a detailed discussion of this issue, see Hubertus F. Jahn, *Patriotic Culture in Russia during World War I* (Ithaca, N.Y., 1995), chapter 3. See also Peter Kenez, "Russian Patriotic Films," in *Film and the First World War*, ed. Karel Dibbets and Bert Hogenkamp (Amsterdam, 1995), pp. 36–42. Leslie Midkiff DeBauche provides a counterexample from the United States at the same time in *Reel Patriotism: The Movies and World War I* (Madison, Wisc., 1997), passim.

37. Ginzburg, *Kinematografiia*, p. 137.

38. Ibid., pp. 137–38.

39. Ibid., p. 140; Likhachev, "Materialy," p. 88.

40. For a detailed discussion of Cibrario's activities after the Revolution, see Jay Leyda, *Kino: A History of the Russian and Soviet Film* (New York, 1960), pp. 126–28.

41. Ginzburg, *Kinematografiia*, pp. 213n, 261.

42. Likhachev, "Materialy," pp. 65–67.

43. Ginzburg, *Kinematografiia*, pp. 321, 367.

44. Ibid., pp. 323–31. As a Soviet historian writing in the early '60s, Ginzburg not surprisingly is quite hostile to these groups.

45. Ibid., p. 320.

46. Ibid., p. 322.

47. Thomas S. Kuhn, *The Structure of Scientific Revolutions* (Chicago, 1962).

48. Ben Singer, "Modernity, Hyperstimulus, and the Rise of Popular Sensationalism," in Leo Charney and Vanessa R. Schwartz, *Cinema and the Invention of Modern Life* (Berkeley, Calif., 1995), pp. 74–76.

49. See the full-page obituary with photos in *Niva*, no. 18 (1911). The examples in this paragraph are mainly drawn from *Niva*, 1908–11, but also from *Gazeta kopeika*, 1909.

50. Examples drawn from *Gazeta kopeika*, 1909–11, and from *Niva* and the supplement to *Niva*, 1909–1917.

CHAPTER 1: IN THE MOVIES

1. "Odessa i kinematograf," *Teatr i kino*, no. 28 (July 9, 1916), p. 12.

2. S. Ginzburg, *Kinematografiia dorevoliutsionnoi Rossii* (Moscow, 1963), p. 46.

3. Jay Leyda has attempted to detail the torturous rivalry between Drankov

and Khanzhonkov, a confusing tale; see *Kino: A History of the Russian and Soviet Film* (New York, 1960), pp. 29–34.

4. B. S. Likhachev, *Kino v Rossii (1896–1926): Materialy k istorii russkogo kino*, vol. 1, *1896–1913* (Leningrad, 1927), p. 60.

5. For a discussion of women as entrepreneurs, see Muriel Joffe and Adele Lindenmeyr, "Daughters, Wives, and Partners: Women of the Moscow Merchant Elite," in *Merchant Moscow: Images of Russia's Vanished Bourgeoisie*, ed. James L. West and Iurii A. Petrov (Princeton, N.J., 1998), pp. 95–108.

6. "Za piat let," *SF* 6, no. 1 (October 1, 1912), pp. 14–15; Ginzburg, *Kinematografiia*, p. 135.

7. "Italianskaia fabrika Gloria," *KZh* 4, no. 6 (March 23, 1913), p. 20.

8. See the advertisement for the new firm in *KZh* 5, no. 3 (February 8, 1914).

9. See the advertisements in *SF* 7, no. 9 (February 1, 1914) and no. 10 (February 15, 1914), [unpaginated].

10. Sorskii, "Khronika," *SF* 4, no. 16 (May 15, 1911), p. 9; advertisement for the Khanzhonkov studio, *SF* 5, no. 24 (September 15, 1912), pp. 6–7.

11. I. Mavrich, "Ob universalnosti kino," *SF* 7, no. 8 (January 18, 1914), p. 17.

12. The caste system in Russia, though rapidly disintegrating by this time, was still extraordinarily complex. For an excellent recent analysis, see Elise Kimerling Wirtschafter, *Social Identity in Imperial Russia* (De Kalb, Ill., 1997).

13. This view of Drankov has been softened in V. S. Listov and E. S. Khokhlova, eds., *Istoriia otechestvennogo kino: Dokumenty, memuary, pisma*, vol. 1 (Moscow, 1996), chap. 2.

14. See Yangirov's minibiography of Drankov in Yuri Tsivian, *Silent Witnesses: Russian Films, 1908–1919* (London and Pordenone, 1989), pp. 554–60.

15. R. Sobolev, *Liudi i filmy russkogo dorevoliutsionnogo kino* (Moscow, 1961), pp. 17, 29.

16. Mikan, "A. O. Drankovu," *KZh* 6, no. 23/24 (December 19, 1915).

17. Drankov & Taldykin announcement, *SF* 6, no. 17 (May 11, 1913), pp. 32–33.

18. *RS* (May 28, 1915).

19. Nikandr Turkin, "Zapisnaia knizhka Pegasa," *Pegas*, no. 11 ([November 1916]?), p. 84. (This is the final issue of *Pegas* held by the Russian State Library and lacks a front cover with the date.)

20. Ginzburg, *Kinematografiia*, p. 49.

21. Tsivian, *Silent Witnesses*, p. 284. As we shall see, *Merchant Bashkirov's Daughter* was only *advertised* as a blackmail melodrama but was in fact based on an obscure play.

22. See the advertisement for the picture, *KZh*, no. 16 (August 23, 1913), p. 104.

23. A. Bek-Nazarov, *Zapiski aktera i kinorezhissera* (Moscow, 1965), p. 39.

24. "Khronika," *SF* 7, no. 25/26 (September 27, 1914), p. 23.

25. "G. I Libken" and "Dmitrii Ivanovich Kharitonov," *KZh*, no. 20 (October 19, 1913), p. 32.

26. "Russkii amerikanets," *Teatr i kino*, no. 41 (October 8, 1916).

27. Mars, "Na fabrikakh Akts. O-va A. Khanzhonkov i Ko.," *KZh* 6, no. 9/10 (May 16, 1915), pp. 76–77.

28. [Christmas greeting from Khanzhonkov & Co.], *VK*, no. 122 (December 1916), [unpaginated].

29. [Untitled], *VK* 4, no. 88 (April 20, 1914), p. 17.

30. Advertisement, *VK* 4, no. 92 (June 21, 1914), pp. 2–3.

31. [Untitled], *VK* 2, no. 55 (December 29, 1912), p. 5.

32. *VK*, no. 118 (June 1916).

33. [Untitled], *Kulisy*, no. 4 (January 22, 1917), p. 14.

34. Ginzburg, *Kinematografiia*, p. 161.

35. See Thiemann studio advertisements in *SF*, no. 14/15 (May 23, 1915), and Yangirov's biography of Thiemann in *Silent Witnesses*, pp. 588–90. What happened to Thiemann after he left Russia in 1918 is not known.

36. See, e.g., the reminiscences of A. A. Levitskii, *Rasskazy o kinematografe* (Moscow, 1964), p. 67.

37. Ginzburg, *Kinematografiia*, 161.

38. "Pavel Gustavovich Timan," *KZh* 3, no. 17 (September 8, 1912), pp. 33–34; "Aleksandr Aleksandrovich Khanzhonkov," *KZh* 3, no. 18 (September 23, 1912), pp. 28–29; "Iosif Nikolaevich Ermolev," *KZh* 3, no. 24 (December 23, 1912), p. 19.

39. "Iubilei," *KZh* 8, no. 17/24 (December 30, 1917), pp. 44–45. This was the journal's final issue.

40. See the Ermolev advertisements in *KZh* 5, nos. 3, 4, 8 (February 8 and 22 and April 19, 1914).

41. François Albera, "Cinéma russe, des primitifs aux futuristes," *Cahiers du cinéma*, no. 427 (January 1990), p. 50.

42. Vega, "Nado gotovitsia," *KZh* 6, no. 5/6 (March 20, 1915), pp. 112–17.

43. "Khronika," *KZh* 6, no. 9/10 (May 16, 1915), p. 79.

44. See the advertisements in *KZh* 6, no. 7/8 (April 18, 1915), pp. 6–7 and no. 9/10 (May 16, 1915), p. 8.

45. Ginzburg says it was a 12,000-ruble minimum (*Kinematografiia*, p. 162).

46. See advertisement in *Proektor*, no. 5 (March 1, 1916), p. v.

47. "Russkii amerikanets."

48. "Khronika," *KZh* 6, no. 17/18 (September 17, 1915), p. 94.

49. Ginzburg, *Kinematografiia*, 162.

50. Advertisement, *Proektor*, no. 5 (March 1, 1916), p. vii.

51. See François Albera's book on the company, *Albatros: des Russes à Paris,*

1919–1929 (Milan and Paris, 1995); in English, Richard Abel provides a brief description in his *French Cinema: The First Wave, 1915–1929* (Princeton, N.J., 1984), p. 19.

CHAPTER 2: AT THE MOVIES

1. See, e.g., the editorials in *KZh*, no. 7 (1911) and no. 17 (1913) for discussions of the success of the industry and various announcements related to theater openings and closings in *KZh*, no. 10 (1911).

2. Inimitably rendered in Russian words difficult to translate in their full intensity: *poshlost, erundistika, illiuzionshchina, kriklivost*; see S. M. Nikolskii, "Sinematografii pechat," *SF*, no. 8 (1911), pp. 6–7. (This was an article critical of those who disdained cinema.)

3. Aleksandr Andreevich Levitskii, *Rasskazy o kinematografe* (Moscow, 1964), p. 116.

4. See *RS* (February 11, 1909).

5. [Untitled], *Kinemo*, no. 12 (August 15, 1909), pp. 10–11.

6. [Editorial], *SF* 5, no. 7 (1912), p. 1.

7. *VK*, no. 6 (1913), [unpaginated advertising section].

8. *KZh*, no. 4 (1911), p. 32.

9. *KZh*, no. 20 (1910), p. 16.

10. For a detailed discussion of music in early Russian cinema, see Yuri Tsivian, *Early Cinema in Russia and Its Cultural Reception*, ed. Richard Taylor, trans. Alan Bodger (London, 1994), chap. 4.

11. See *KZh*, no. 21/22 (November 29, 1914), p. 108.

12. [Editorial], *SF* 4, no. 10 (February 15, 1911), pp. 5–6.

13. See Tsivian, *Early Cinema*, chap. 2, for a fascinating examination of "Projection technique as a factor in aesthetic perception."

14. "Stydno!" *VK*, no. 1 (1910), pp. 7–8; [editorial], *SF*, no. 5 (1910), p. 6.

15. Binom, "Reklamnye pustotsvetyi (Stranichka iz istorii russkoi kinematografii)," *VK*, no. 121 (1916), pp. 3–6.

16. *VK*, no. 6 (1911). In a later issue, interestingly enough, this picture was deemed "tasteless" and charged with provoking hysteria among the sensitive in the audience (presumably women); see I. Khudiakov, "Defektivy sovremennogo kinematografa," *VK*, no. 19 (1911), pp. 12–15.

17. *KZh*, no. 6 (1911), pp. 13–14.

18. "V odnom moskovskom elektro-teatre," *SF* 5, no. 24 (1912), p. 28.

19. See Lawrence Levine, *Highbrow/Lowbrow: The Emergence of Cultural Hierarchy in America* (Cambridge, Mass., 1988), p. 197.

20. "Skandal iz-za shliapy," *SF*, no. 3 (1910), p. 14.

21. [I. N. Khudiakov], "Doklad I. N. Khudiakova: Defektivy sovremennogo kinematografa s khudozhestvennoi storonyi," *VK* 1, no. 17 (August 20, 1911), pp. 16–19.

22. See the cartoon labeled "Universalnyi kinematograf," *KZh*, no. 18 (September 23, 1913), p. 41.

23. Vladimir Nabokov, *Speak, Memory: An Autobiography Revisited* (New York, 1967), p. 236.

24. N. Shulgovskii, "V kinematografe," *Niva*, no. 33 (1909), [unpaginated].

25. "Dvoistvennoe mnenie posviashchaetsia kritiku," *KZh*, no. 19 (1911), pp. 11–12. (Of course, this opprobrium undoubtedly has much to do with the fact that *Vestnik kinematografii* and *Kine-zhurnal* were rival publications.

26. "Katastrofa 'Grand Otel,'" *SF*, no. 3 (1910), p. 14.

27. Alexander Pasternak, *A Vanished Present: The Memoirs of Alexander Pasternak*, ed. and trans. Ann Pasternak Slater (Ithaca, N.Y., 1989), p. 95.

28. Konstantin Paustovsky, *The Story of a Life*, trans. Joseph Barnes (New York, 1965), p. 55.

29. "Katastrofa v Bologom," *SF*, no. 11 (1911), p. 6.

30. Ibid., pp. 6–7; for a detailed discussion of the evolution of cinema architecture, see Tsivian, *Early Cinema*, chap. 1.

31. [Untitled], *VK* 4, no. 90 (May 22, 1914), p. 30.

32. "Bologovskaia katastrofa," *Artist i stsena*, no. 4 (1911), p. 23.

33. Richard Abel, *The Ciné Goes to Town: French Cinema, 1896–1914* (Berkeley, Calif., 1994), p. 17.

34. D. Kumanov, "Pod svezhim vpechatleniem," *SF*, no. 11 (1911), p. 7.

35. See, e.g., in *SF*, no. 11 (1911), "Kto vinovat?" pp. 8–9, and "Kakiia posledstviia katastrofy mozhno zhdat?" pp. 9–10.

36. "Pozharnye deiateli o protivopozharnykh merakh" and "Administrativnoe zakrytie teatrov: Osmotr sinematografov," *SF*, no. 12 (1911), pp. 10–12; also "Proekt pravil razrabotannykh v Ministerstve vnutrennykh del dlia uvelicheniia bezopastnosti v sinematografakh," *SF*, no. 13 (1911), pp. 7–8.

37. For a brief discussion of the 1906–14 period, see Irina Paperno, *Suicide as a Cultural Institution in Dostoevsky's Russia* (Ithaca, N.Y., 1997), pp. 94–104.

38. "Dusha vremeni," *Niva*, no. 4 (1914), p. 67.

39. [Untitled] *VK*, no. 14 (1911), p. 18.

40. D. L., "Samoubiistvo mekhanikov," *SF*, no. 5 (1910), p. 6.

41. "Samoubiistvo pianista," *SF* 6, no. 16 (1913), p. 26. In *Suicide as a Cultural Institution*, Paperno offers an interesting chapter on the characteristics of the suicide letter (pp. 105–22).

42. "Samoubiistvo," *SF*, no. 22 (July 20, 1913), p. 25.

43. "Zagadochnoe samoubiistvo v teatre," *SF* 7, no. 21/22 (August 2, 1914), p. 39.

44. "Po kino-teatram," *KZh* 7, no. 1/2 (January 23, 1916), pp. 79–80.

45. "I. M. Timonin," *KZh* 7, no. 1/2 (January 23, 1916), p. 65.

46. "Samoubiistvo v sinematografe," *SF* 4, no. 8 (January 15, 1911), p. 1.

47. "Provintsiia," *VK* 1, no. 11 (May 16, 1911), p. 11.

48. "Reklama smerti," *VK* 3, no. 10 (May 18, 1913), p. 14.

49. "Teatr i kinematograf," *VK* 4, no. 87 (April 1, 1914), p. 19.

50. M. Brailovskii, "Dvenadtsat millionov," *SF* 7, no. 3 (November 9, 1913), pp. 21–22.

51. Z. Slezkinskaia, "Kinematograf i russkaia zhizn," *VK* 2, no. 47 (September 29, 1912), pp. 3–4.

52. "Agitatsiia v kinematograf," *VK* 2, no. 47 (September 29, 1912), p. 10.

53. "Guliganstvo," *KZh*, no. 13 (July 12, 1914), p. 75.

54. G. Tsyperovich, "Kinematograf," *Sovremennyi mir*, no. 1 (1912), pp. 181–210.

55. "Teatralnaia Moskva," *SF*, no. 13 (1911), pp. 15–16.

56. Obozrevatel, "Po gorodom i teatram," *SF*, no. 9 (1911), p. 18.

57. Shein-baum, "Promakhi rezhisserov i zriteli," *SF*, no. 18 (1911), pp. 9–10.

58. I. Mavrich, "S raznykh tochek zreniia," *SF*, no. 23 (August 3, 1913), pp. 20–22.

59. Pasternak, *Vanished Present*, pp. 95–96.

60. "Golos i pressy," *VK*, no. 22 (1911), p. 12; see also "Mneniia i fakty," *VK*, no. 51 (1912), p. 19.

61. "Nemonopolist *Oborona Sevastopolia*," *SF* 5, no. 5 (1911).

62. Pasternak, *Vanished Present*, p. 96.

63. Again on cinema architecture, see Tsivian, *Early Cinema*, chap. 1, and illustrations of theaters, pp. 66–77.

64. M. S-ev, "Muzyka v elektro-teatrakh," *VK* 4, no. 83 (February 1, 1914), pp. 11–12.

65. I. Pal, "Kinematografiia v Rossii," *KZh*, no. 11 (1912), pp. 10–13.

66. Levitskii, *Rasskazy*, p. 115.

67. See the advertisement from Thiemann, *KZh*, no. 7 (1914), p. 111.

68. "Anketa o dlinie lenty," *SF* 5, no. 5 (1911), pp. 15–16.

69. Pasternak, *Vanished Present*, p. 96.

70. I. Riaspov, "Kinematografy v Rossii," *VK*, no. 10 (1914), p. 10.

71. Arkasha, "Kinemo," *Teatr i kino*, no. 36 (September 3, 1916), p. 15.

72. "Novye teatry," *SF* 6, no. 23 (August 3, 1913), p. 34.

73. "Obozrenie teatrov," *Artist i stsena*, no. 16 (1911), p. 22.

74. "Otkrytie teatra," *Artist i stsena*, no. 18 (1911), p. 21.

75. "Po kinemo-teatram," *KZh* 6, no. 21/22 (1915), pp. 75–76.

76. "Nashi teatry," *KZh*, no. 15 (1913), pp. 46–47; advertisement in *VK*, no. 1 (1914), p. 10.

77. R. Erbus, "Po kinemo-teatram," *KZh*, no. 23/24 (1915), pp. 94–96.

78. Nero, "U ekrana," *KZh* 6, no. 13/14 (July 15, 1915), pp. 63–68.

79. Ibid.

80. Advertisement in *Kinematograf*, no. 2 (1915), [unpaginated].

81. See Huntly Carter's description of the condition of theaters after the revolution, quoted in Denise Youngblood, *Movies for the Masses: Popular Cinema and Soviet Society in the 1920s* (Cambridge, 1992), p. 15.

CHAPTER 3: SENSATION!

1. For two good examples, see *VK* 2, no. 39 (July 15, 1912) and *SF* 5, no. 10 (February 15, 1912), pp. 39–41, 44–45.

2. See photo caption, *SF* 5, no. 5 (December 1, 1911), p. 18, and the Tanagra advertisement, *SF* 5, no. 19 (July 1, 1912), p. 6.

3. Advertisement, *SF* 5, no. 19 (July 1, 1912), p. 56.

4. Advertisement, *SF* 5, no. 17 (June 1, 1912), [unpaginated].

5. See, e.g., Mintus advertisements in *KZh* 3, no. 11 (June 8, 1912).

6. Pathé Frères, *Ezhenedelnik novostei* 1, no. 20 (December 7, 1910).

7. "Maks Linder," *VK* 2, no. 54 (December 15, 1912), pp. 5–6.

8. Vladimir Nabokov, *Speak, Memory: An Autobiography Revisited* (New York, 1967), p. 158.

9. "Sharl Pate (otets kinematografii) v Moskve," *KZh* 3, no. 10 (May 23, 1912), pp. 18–20. An account of Linder's entire tour, as well as a full discussion of Linder's extensive career in French silent cinema, appears in Richard Abel, *The Ciné Goes to Town: French Cinema, 1896–1914* (Berkeley, Calif., 1994), p. 410 and passim.

10. I. Mavrich, "Maks v publike," *SF* 7, no. 5 (December 7, 1913), pp. 17–18.

11. Falstaff, "'Geroi' ekrana," *SF* 7, no. 4 (November 23, 1913), pp. 21–22.

12. See the cartoon showing Linder grabbed on all sides, *SF* 7, no. 5 (December 7, 1913), p. 34.

13. "Maks Linder v Peterburge," *KZh*, no. 23 (December 1, 1913), pp. 29–30.

14. Ibid., pp. 28–29.

15. [Editorial], *KZh*, no. 24 (December 14, 1913), pp. 19–20.

16. "Nedelia Maksa Lindera v Moskve," *KZh*, no. 24 (December 14, 1913), pp. 26–28.

17. W., "Banket v chest Maksa Lindera," *RS* (December 4, 1913).

18. "Maks Linder v Odesse," *SF* 7, no. 7 (January 4, 1914), p. 30. This article describes Linder's visit of December 17, 1913.

19. Vorwarts, "Maks," *KZh*, no. 24 (December 14, 1913), pp. 23–24. As Richard Taylor reminds me, *Vorwärts* was the name of the German SPD newspaper, thereby providing yet another "Marxist" pun.

20. B. S. Likhachev, *Kino v Rossii (1896–1926): Materialy k istorii russkogo kino*, vol. 1, 1896–1913 (Leningrad, 1927), p. 163.

21. Richard Abel, *French Cinema: The First Wave, 1915–1929* (Princeton, N.J., 1984), p. 222. Abel provides details on Linder's later career in this volume.

22. See, e.g., "Pamiati Maks Linder," *SF* 7, no. 23/24 (August 30, 1914), pp. 17–18; "Maks Linder," *VK* 4, no. 97 (September 1, 1914), pp. 9–10; "Maks Linder," *VK* 4, no. 98 (September 15, 1914), pp. 12–14; "Maks Linder zhiv!" *KZh*, no. 17/18 (September 20, 1914), pp. 30–31; [untitled, full page] *SF* 7, no. 25/26 (September 27, 1914), p. 25; "Maks Linder," *VK* 4, no. 99 (October 1, 1914), pp. 16–21. *Kine-zhurnal* readers were the first to get the happy news.

23. Ivan Perestiani, *75 let zhizn v iskusstve* (Moscow, 1962), p. 262; Fridrikh Ermler's entry in *Kak ia stal rezhisserom* (Moscow, 1946), p. 300.

24. Likhachev, *Kino*, 1:166–68.

25. Advertisements, *SF* 5, no. 20 (July 15, 1912), pp. 56–57, and *SF* 6, no. 24 (August 31, 1913), [unpaginated glossy insert].

26. *KZh* 4, no. 12 (June 23, 1913).

27. See, e.g., Perskii advertisements in *KZh* 4, no. 10 (May 23, 1913).

28. Perestiani, *75 let*, p. 261; Ermler, *Kak ia stal*, p. 300.

29. *VK* 1, no. 22 (November 2, 1911), [unpaginated]. The film was *Kashirskaia starina*.

30. [Editorial], *VK* 1, no. 24 (December 1, 1911), pp. 9–10.

31. "Drama i kinematograf," *KZh* 2, no. 14 (July 23, 1911), pp. 7–8.

32. Advertisement, *SF* 8, no. 6/7 (January 10, 1915), [unpaginated].

33. R. Mech, "Liubimtsy publiki," *SF* 2, no. 5 (December 1, 1908), pp. 4–5.

34. Vlad Maksimov, "Pobeditel," *Teatr i kino* 1, no. 1 (November 15, 1915), p. 16.

35. "Melochi," *VK*, no. 119 (August 1916), pp. 20–21.

36. Vega, "Kinematograf v Rossii i na Zapade (Beseda s V. V. Maksimovym), *KZh*, no. 23/24 (December 23, 1914); "Khronika," *KZh*, no. 7/8 (April 18, 1915); V. D. Khanzhonkova, comp., *Russkoe kino, 1908–1918* (Moscow, 1969), p. 33; Jay Leyda, *Kino: A History of the Russian and Soviet Film* (New York, 1960), p. 63.

37. B. Glovatskii, "Odin iz pervykh," *Iskusstvo kino*, no. 4 (1960), 160–62. The film was probably *Be Still, Sadness, Be Still*, discussed in chapter 5.

38. M. Dubrovskii, "Russkii kino-akter," *KZh* 6, no. 13/14 (July 15, 1915), pp. 72–74; Neia Zorkaia, "Les stars du muet," *Le cinéma russe avant la révolution* (Paris, 1989), pp. 44–46; R. Sobolev, *Liudi i filmy russkogo dorevoliutsionnogo kino* (Moscow, 1961), p. 139.

39. Nabokov, *Speak, Memory*, p. 237.

40. Aleksandr Sorin, "V. V. Maksimov and I. I. Mozzhukhin," *Teatr i kino* 2, no. 1 (January 1, 1916), p. 18.

41. See the Ermolev advertising insert in *SF* 8, no. 6/7 (January 10, 1915).

42. According to her niece, Marguerite Studemeister, Preobrazhenskaia was deliberately vague about her background, first to appease her family and then, in the Soviet period, to conceal her counterrevolutionary family connections. Preobrazhenskaia's brother Nikolai (Studemeister's father) was killed during the Civil War fighting for the White Army. M. Studemeister, letters to author, 1993.

43. See the announcement in *KhZ*, no. 11/12 (June 13, 1915), pp. 74–75.

44. Lir, "O. V. Gzovskaia," *Kulisy* 1, no. 7 (February 12, 1917), p. 15.

45. "*Voina i mir* na ekrane," *KZh*, no. 5/6 (March 20, 1915), pp. 131–35. See also the assessment in Dubrovskii, "Russkii kino-akter."

46. Raevskii, "Akts. O-vo Khanzhonkov," *Kulisy* 1, no. 8 (February 19, 1917), p. 15.

47. Likhachev, *Kino*, 1:136.

48. Sobolev, *Liudi i filmy*, p. 137.

49. V. R. Gardin, *Vospominaniia*, vol. 1, *1912–1921* (Moscow, 1949), pp. 68–69.

50. Perestiani, *75 let*, p. 263.

51. Ample pictorial evidence may be found in B. B. Ziukov, ed., *Vera Kholodnaia: K 100-letiiu so dnia rozhdeniia* (Moscow, 1995), a beautifully illustrated celebration of the actress's meteoric career.

52. R. Mech, "V. Kholodnaia," *KZh*, no. 18 (July 28, 1916): "Artistka prevoskhodnaia / Vot mnenie moskvicha / Familiia 'kholodnaia'- / Igra zhe goriacha."

53. See the advertisement in *KZh*, no. 11/12 (June 13, 1915), p. 82. The picture was *Pesna torzhestvuiushchei liubvy*. For the portrait see *KZh*, no. 19/20 (October 15, 1915), p. 77.

54. "Iubilei," *KZh*, no. 17/24 (December 30, 1917), pp. 44–45.

55. See Z. F. Bauer's photo in *Artist i stsena*, no. 12/13 (June 1910), p. 4.

56. Neia Zorkaia, "Evgenii Bauer," *Le cinéma russe*, p. 51; David Robinson, "Evgenii Bauer and the Cinema of Nikolai II," *Sight and Sound* (Winter 1989/90), p. 54.

57. Bauer died from complications, apparently blood poisoning and pneumonia, from a broken leg that he suffered after tumbling some thirty-five feet (five *sazhen*) down a cliff while shooting the film *To Happiness* in the Crimea.

58. "E. F. Bauer," *KZh*, no. 11/16 (August 30, 1917), p. 104.

59. "Iubilei," pp. 44–45.

60. See *VK* 1, no. 1 (December 18, 1910), p. 41.

61. Gardin, *Vospominaniia*, pp. 36–37, 46; Gardin (with T. D. Bulakh), *Zhizn i trud artista* (Moscow, 1960), pp. 116–18.

62. [A. Verbitskaia], "A. Verbitskaia o kartine *Kliuchi schastia* i o kinematografe: Otkrytoe pismo," *SF* 7, no. 1 (October 12, 1913), p. 28.

63. See the announcements from Gardin and Protazanov and the reply by Thiemann, *SF* 8, no. 11/12 (April 4, 1915), pp. 11–12.

64. Gardin and Bulakh, *Zhizn i trud artista*, pp. 5–12; Gardin, *Vospominaniia*, p. 33.

65. Gardin, *Vospominaniia*, pp. 89–91.

66. See the Vengerov & Gardin advertising section in *KZh*, no. 11/12 (June 13, 1915), pp. 5–12.

67. Protazanov's early life is covered in more detail in Denise Youngblood,

Movies for the Masses: Cinema and Soviet Society in the 1920s (Cambridge, 1992), pp. 106–8.

68. "Khronika," *KZh* 3, no. 20 (October 23, 1912), p. 20, and the advertisements in the same issue, pp. 42–43; although some scholars assert that *Passing of the Great Old Man* was only seen abroad, Boris Likhachev, author of the first history of early Russian history, says it had a limited release inside the country. See Likhachev, *Kino*, 1: 104–6.

69. "Tango . . . tango," *KZh* 5, no. 4 (February 22, 1914), p. 41.

70. Rashit Yangirov, "Vassili Gontcharov," *Le cinéma russe*, pp. 33–39.

71. See, e.g., the advertisements for *Zhenshchina zavtrashniago dnia*, starring Iureneva, and *Nemye svideteli*, directed by Bauer, in *KZh*, no. 7 (April 5, 1914), and *VK* 4, no. 87 (1914), p. 46.

72. "Postanovka *Sanina* zapreshchena," *SF*, no. 24 (August 31, 1913).

73. "A. Verbitskaia o kartine *Kliuchi schastia*," p. 28.

74. See, e.g., the advertisements for *Vavochka* and *Muzh* in *SF* 8, no. 1/2 (October 25, 1914).

75. See the advertisement in *SF* 8, no. 3 (November 15, 1915).

76. See advertisements in *SF* 8, no. 4/5 (December 13, 1914), pp. 84–85.

77. Aleksandra Tolstaia [letter to editor], *VK* 1, no. 19 (September 16, 1911), p. 22.

78. V. D., "Mutnaia voda — iz sluchainogo khlama," *Proektor* 1, no. 3 (November 1, 1915), p. 7. "Monopoly" in this case meant that a theater would have the exclusive right to show the film.

79. S. M. Nikolskii, "O nashikh 'shedevrakh,'" *SF* 6, no. 1 (October 1, 1912), pp. 18–19.

80. See Bernice Glatzer Rosenthal, Introduction, in Rosenthal, ed., *Nietzsche in Russia* (Princeton, N.J., 1986), p. 28.

81. "Chto trebuet publika ot kinematografa," *VK* 1, no. 16 (August 1, 1911), pp. 22–23; "Publika i kartiny s dlinnym metrazhem," ibid., p. 24.

82. See the Downey advertisement in *SF*, no. 14 (April 15, 1912), p. 37, and Ivan Perestiani's reminiscences about the film, *75 let*, p. 248.

83. Yuri Tsivian, *Early Cinema in Russia and Its Cultural Reception*, ed. Richard Taylor, trans. Alan Bodger (London, 1994), pp. 39–40.

84. See *KZh*, no. 19 (September 5, 1913), pp. 57–60.

85. See *KZh* 5, no. 1 (January 11, 1914), pp. 84–85.

86. See, e.g., *SF*, no. 23 (August 3, 1913), p. 31, and no. 27 (September 28, 1913), p. 89.

87. Gardin and Bulakh, *Zhizn i trud artista*, p. 121.

88. Gardin, *Vospominaniia*, p. 59.

89. Ibid., p. 60; Gardin and Bulakh, *Zhizn i trud artista*, pp. 115, 121.

90. Likhachev, *Kino*, 1: 121–23.

91. Gardin, *Vospominaniia*, p. 50.

92. "Sredi novinok," *KZh*, no. 19 (September 5, 1913), p. 40. Stills from the film appear on pp. 41 and 43.

93. "Sredi novinok," *SF*, no. 27 (September 28, 1913), p. 30.

94. Likhachev, *Kino*, 1:121–23.

95. "Khronika," *KZh* 4, no. 21 (November 2, 1913), p. 38.

96. See *KhZ*, no. 21 (November 2, 1916), pp. 61ff.

97. See *SF*, no. 27 (September 28, 1913), p. 89.

98. "Khronika," *KZh* 4, no. 21 (November 2, 1913), p. 38.

99. Z., "Russkoe proizvodstvo," *KZh* 5, no. 6 (March 22, 1914), p. 42.

100. See Thiemann advertisement, *KZh* 5, no. 7 (April 5, 1914), p. 111.

101. A. Verbitskaia, [letter to the editor], *KZh*, no. 15/16 (August 15, 1915), p. 135. Nonetheless, Perskii produced the film *Whose Guilt?* (*Chia vina?*), book and screenplay by Verbitskaia; see the advertisement, *KZh*, no. 3/4 (February 29, 1916), pp. 56–57.

102. See the announcement in *KZh*, no. 23/24 (December 25, 1916), pp. 82–83.

103. "Khronika," *KZh* 5, no. 5 (March 8, 1914), p. 45.

104. *RS* (January 10, 1915).

105. "Khronika," *KZh* 6, no. 1/2 (January 17, 1915), p. 76, and Vega, "Nado gotovitsia," *KZh* 6, no. 3/4 (February 14, 1915), pp. 64–67. See also the large advertisement in *Russkoe slovo* (January 10, 1915).

106. "Kinematograf—vrag rytsarei legkoi nazhivy," *VK*, no. 101 (November 1, 1914), p. 7. Keep in mind that *Vestnik kinematografii* was the organ of Drankov's archcompetitor, A. A. Khanzhonkov.

107. *RS* (February 15, 1915).

108. *KZh*, no. 10 (May 17, 1914), p. 114, and no. 23/24 (December 23, 1914), p. 4.

109. *RS* (January 3, 1915).

110. "Khronika kino," *Teatr i kino* 2, no. 21 (May 21, 1916), p. 12. See also the photo of Mozzhukhin, ibid., no. 19 (May 7, 1916), p. 19.

111. G., "*Pikovaia dama*," *KZh* 7, no. 7/8 (April 30, 1916), p. 52, and "Khronika," ibid.

112. See the advertisements in *RS*: *Revnost* (January 19, 1914), *Stenka Razin* (December 5, 1914), *Voina i mir* (February 15, 1915), *Muzh* (March 8, 1915).

113. "*Quo vadis?*—u nas i za granitsei," *VK* 3, no. 7 (April 6, 1913), pp. 4–5.

114. Nero, "U ekrana," *KZh* 6, no. 13/14 (July 15, 1915), pp. 63–64.

115. Tsivian, *Early Cinema in Russia*, pp. 40–41.

116. S. Um-skii, "Spravka o *Kabiri*," *VK*, no. 117 (May 6, 1916), pp. 5–8.

117. S. Um-skii, "Spravka o *Kabiri*," *Solntse Rossii*, no. 346 (October 1916).

CHAPTER 4: RESPECT AND RESPECTABILITY

1. "Sinematograf i gigena (K voprosu o vliianii sinematografa na glaza)," *SF* 2, no. 23 (September 1, 1908), pp. 6–7.

2. See Lawrence Levine, *Highbrow/Lowbrow: The Emergence of Cultural Hierarchy in America* (Cambridge, Mass., 1988).

3. Yuri Tsivian provides considerable detail on this subject in *Early Cinema in Russia and Its Cultural Reception*, ed. Richard Taylor, trans. Alan Bodger (London, 1994).

4. L. Dolinin, "Teatr i ekran," *VK*, no. 116 (October 1, 1915), pp. 49–50.

5. Nikesz, "Teatr i kinematograf (Mysli vslukh)," *SF*, no. 20 (October 19, 1913), pp. 25–26.

6. Vladimir Konenko, "'Russkiia' lenty na ekrane sinemo-teatrov," *SF* 3, no. 2 (October 15, 1909), pp. 5–6.

7. Pilot, "Frantsuzskaia illiustratsiia russkoi zhizni," *Kinemo*, no. 17 (November 1, 1909), pp. 7–9.

8. B. Dubinovskii, "Russifikatsiia kinematografii (Po povodu stati M. Domanskago 'Russkaia kinematografiia')," *SF*, no. 7 (April 5, 1914), pp. 43–46. Dubinovskii is reporting on and criticizing Domanskii's nationalist views.

9. B. S-on, "Kinematograf kak predovestnik mirovogo ideia," *SF*, no. 8 (April 19, 1914), pp. 38–39. This author favored internationalism over nationalism. Less sanguine was G. Iug, "Kinematograf, kak faktor mirovogo obedineniia," *SF*, no. 13 (July 12, 1914), pp. 55–57.

10. Armando, "Novaia era," *SF*, no. 9/10 (May 16, 1915), pp. 63–66.

11. See the advertisement for Miss Volta's show in *SF* 3, no. 8 (January 15, 1910); "Smert Kiki," *VK* 1, no. 22 (November 2, 1911), p. 18; Soubrette, "Diseuses," *Artist i stsena*, no. 4 (1911), p. 23; ad for Les Armands, *Artist i stsena*, no. 12 (1911), p. 8.

12. [I. N. Khudiakova], "Doklad I. N. Khudiakova: Defektivy sovremennogo kinematografa s khudozhestvennoi storonyi," *VK* 1, no. 17 (August 20, 1911), pp. 16–19. For an excellent discussion of Russian attitudes toward capitalism, see A. Walicki, *The Controversy over Capitalism: Studies in the Social Philosophy of the Russian Populists* (Oxford, 1969).

13. "Sinematograf v Iasnoi Poliane," *RS* (January 9, 1910).

14. [Editorial], *SF* 3, no. 19 (July 1, 1910), pp. 3–4; Sergei Iablonskii, "V kinematograf!" *RS* (November 29, 1915); for a detailed discussion of cinema aficionados from the Russian literary avant-garde, see Tsivian, *Early Cinema*, chap. 1 and passim.

15. "Sredi gazet i zhurnalov," *VK*, no. 119 (August 1916), pp. 18–20.

16. D. K., "*Sovremennyi mir* o kinematograf," *SF*, no. 13 (April 1, 1912), pp. 14–15.

17. See, e.g., "Doklad I. N. Khudiakova"; "Pishite gramotno!" *SF*, no. 23

(September 1, 1912), pp. 16–17; S. M. Nikolskii, "Budte gramotnyi!" *Proektor,* no. 6 (March 15, 1916), pp. 2–3.

18. Dubrovskii, "Russifikatsiia kinematografii."

19. Konstantin Paustovsky, *The Story of a Life,* trans. Joseph Barnes (New York, 1965), p. 55.

20. A. Kh., "Sinematograficheskii ekran," *SF,* no. 24 (September 15, 1912), p. 26.

21. Valentin Novus, "Kinematograf," *SF,* no. 27 (September 28, 1913), p. 38.

22. M. Brailovskii, "Kinemo-kultura," *SF* 7, no. 1 (October 12, 1913), pp. 16–17; A. Z. R., "Kinematograf," *Zritel* 1, no. 6 (July 17, 1905), pp. 5–7.

23. Alek, "V chem gore," *Pegas,* no. 1 (November 1915), p. 82.

24. [Editorial], *VK* 1, no. 5 (February 19, 1911); A. Shtokfish, "Kinematografiia — Nota bene," *Pegas,* no. 2 (December 1915), pp. 53–55.

25. Shtokfish, "Kinematografiia."

26. "V zhurnalakh i gazetakh," *Pegas,* no. 2 (December 1915), pp. 73–74.

27. Both quoted in "V zhurnalakh i gazetakh," pp. 76–78.

28. P. Chardynin, [untitled], *Pegas,* no. 2 (December 1915), p. 102.

29. E. Nagrodskaia, "Kinematograficheskiia goresti i radosti," *Kinematograf,* no. 1 (1915), pp. 5–7.

30. I. M. Vasilevskii, "(Ne bukva) Ego velichestvo — kinematograf," *Kinematograf,* no. 2 (1915), pp. 6–8.

31. B., "Teatr i kinemo," *SF* 5, no. 2 (January 25, 1914), pp. 31–33.

32. S. Shimanskii, "Podmostki i ekran," *Kinematograf,* no. 1 (1915), p. 15.

33. N. Vilde, "Kinovlechenie i kinopaseniia," *VK,* no. 116 (October 1, 1915), pp. 42–44.

34. "V zhurnalakh i gazetakh," 72–73.

35. "Iskusstvo vcheriashnogo dnia (Beseda s K. S. Stanislavskim)," *SF,* no. 8 (April 19, 1914), pp. 34–35.

36. Stephen Bottomore, comp. and ed., *I Want to See This Annie Mattygraph: A Cartoon History of the Coming of the Movies* (Gemona, 1995), p. 143.

37. Some of their writings on this subject have been translated in Richard Taylor and Ian Christie, eds., *The Film Factory: Russian and Soviet Cinema in Documents, 1896–1939,* trans. Richard Taylor (Cambridge, Mass., 1988), docs. 2–6.

38. Iu. Volin, "Svoim putem," *Kinematograf,* no. 1 (1915), pp. 14–15.

39. Vasilevskii, "(Ne bukva) Ego velichestvo."

40. Ibid.

41. S. Letopolnyi, "Iskusstvo ili balagan?" *Kinemo,* no. 14 (September 15, 1909), pp. 1–2. Presumably the author didn't know there were nine muses.

42. See, e.g., A. Voznesenskii, "Futurizm na ekrane," *VK,* no. 116 (October 1, 1915), pp. 38–40; I. G., "Futurizm i kinematograf," *SF,* no. 13/14 (July 15, 1915), pp. 74–77.

43. S., "Novoe v zhizni," *VK* 2, no. 32 (April 1, 1912), pp. 23–24.

44. Drug ekrana, "Velikii [sic] kinemo, kak istoricheskii dokument," SF, no. 11/12 (June 13, 1915), pp. 90–94.

45. I. Khudiakov, "'Detskiia' kartiny," VK 2, no. 45 (September 15, 1912), pp. 5–6.

46. For the view that cinema is merely childish entertainment, see, e.g., Ada Chumachenko, "V kinematografe," Russkoe bogatstvo, no. 1 (1911), 53–54; Sergei Radlov, "Ugroza kinematografa," Apollon, no. 8/10 (1917), p. 46.

47. See the Thiemann studio advertising insert, VK 2, no. 52 (November 17, 1912).

48. Paustovsky, Story of a Life, p. 55.

49. A. I. Zak, "Kinematograf, kniga, i deti," Vestnik Evropy, no. 9 (1914), pp. 276–95.

50. Joan Neuberger, Hooliganism: Crime, Culture, and Power in St. Petersburg, 1900–1914 (Berkeley, Calif., 1993), p. 183.

51. Alexander Pasternak, A Vanished Present: The Memoirs of Alexander Pasternak, ed. and trans. Ann Pasternak Slater (Ithaca, N.Y., 1989), p. 96.

52. [Editorial], Ekran Rossii, no. 1 (1916), pp. 1–2.

53. "Voennyi nalog na bilety," Proektor, no. 7/8 (April 10, 1916), pp. 8–9.

54. Fedor Mashkov, "Russkii kinematograf," Proektor 2, no. 4 (February 15, 1916), pp. 3–4.

55. L. Ia., "Demokratizatsii iskusstva," Proektor, no. 13/14 (July 15, 1916), pp. 3–4.

56. Boris Martov, "Iz knigi ekrana," Proektor, no. 15 (August 1, 1916), pp. 5–6.

57. [Editorial], Proektor, no. 24 (December 25, 1916), p. 1.

58. P. Valov, "Puti nemogo," Proektor, no. 13/14 (July 15, 1916), pp. 6–7.

59. [Editorial] and S. N., "Kinematograf osvobozhdennoi Rossii," Proektor, no. 7/8 (April 1, 1917), pp. 1–4; [editorial] ibid., no. 9/10 (May 1, 1917), pp. 1–2; [editorial], ibid., no. 17/18 (November 1917), pp. 1–2.

60. "Kinematograf i revoliutsii," Proektor, no. 17/18 (November 1917), pp. 3–6.

61. See the announcement in Proektor, no. 19/20 (December 1917). This was the journal's last issue before the Ermolev studio decamped to Yalta.

CHAPTER 5: SEX AND SUICIDE

1. See Bram Dijkstra, Idols of Perversity: Fantasies of Feminine Evil in Fin-de-Siècle Culture (New York and Oxford, 1986), pp. 333–34, for a brief contextualization of the rusalki.

2. Because of the variability of projection speeds, running times are to a certain extent artificial but are noted so that the reader will get a sense of surviving length.

3. "Khronika," *SF*, no. 26 (September 14, 1913), p. 34.

4. Kristin Thompson, "The International Exploration of Cinematic Expressivity," in *Film and the First World War*, ed. Karel Dibbets and Bert Hogenkamp (Amsterdam, 1995), pp. 65–85.

5. Olga Preobrazhenskaia's 1926 film *Peasant Women of Riazan* (*Baby riazanskie*) is a brilliant example of the Soviet campaign against *snokhachestvo*.

6. This term is appropriated from Thomas Kuhn, who coined it (in *The Structure of Scientific Revolutions* [Chicago, 1962]) to describe the transformation of science during the Scientific Revolution.

7. Yuri Tsivian, *Silent Witnesses: Russian Films, 1908–1919*, ed. Paolo Cherchi Usai, Lorenzo Codelli, Carlo Montanaro, David Robinson (London and Pordenone, 1989), p. 218. *Silent Witnesses* is an invaluable resource for everyone interested in early Russian cinema. It is an illustrated catalogue of the extant titles and includes translated excerpts from memoirs and trade journals.

8. B. S. Likhachev, "Materialy k istorii kino v Rossii (1914–1916), *Iz istorii kino*, vol. 3 (Moscow, 1960), p. 41.

9. Bram Dijkstra, *Evil Sisters: The Threat of Female Sexuality and the Cult of Manhood* (New York, 1996). My thanks to Lois Becker for bringing this work to my attention.

10. The description of this film's plot in *Silent Witnesses* is slightly different, ascribing Lebedev's role to the husband's boss; this is not, however, what happens in the print held by the Library of Congress.

11. Neia Zorkaia, "Les stars du muet," in *Le cinéma russe avant la révolution* (Paris, 1989), p. 41.

12. The title does appear in a Mozzhukhin filmography. See O. A. Iakubovich, *Ivan Mozzhukhin: Rasskaz o pervom russkom kinoaktere* (Moscow, 1975), p. 11. Iakubovich says the story is an adaptation of a novella by Guy de Maupassant.

13. Tsivian, *Silent Witnesses*, pp. 466–70.

14. Scholarly literature over the past quarter century is replete with analyses of this issue. In addition to Dijsktra's *Idols of Perversity* and *Evil Sisters*, already cited, see, e.g., H. R. Hays, *Dangerous Sex: The Myth of Feminine Evil* (New York, 1969), and Peter Gay, *The Bourgeois Experience: Victoria to Freud*, vol. 1, *The Education of the Senses* (New York and Oxford, 1984), especially his chapter "Offensive Women and Defensive Men."

CHAPTER 6: MURDER AND MAYHEM

1. See the ad in *KZh*, no. 16 (August 23, 1913), p. 104.

2. Yuri Tsivian, *Silent Witnesses: Russian Films, 1908–1919*, ed. Paolo Cherchi Usai, Lorenzo Codelli, Carlo Montanaro, David Robinson (London and Pordenone, 1989), p. 182. Tsivian says, however, that recent evidence indicates the

story was based on a nineteenth-century play—making the sensationalized publicity even more interesting in my view (letter to author, 1998).

3. On the popularity of this opera in Russia, see Kristi A. Groberg, "'The Shade of Lucifer's Dark Wing': Satanism in Silver Age Russia," in *The Occult in Russian and Soviet Culture*, ed. Bernice Glatzer Rosenthal (Ithaca, N.Y., 1997), pp. 115–16. Fedor Chaliapin's appearance as Bertram no doubt enhanced its appeal.

4. Ibid.

5. In their introduction to their anthology *Cinema and the Invention of Modern Life* (Berkeley, Calif., 1995), p. 5, Leo Charney and Vanessa Schwartz quote Janet Wolff on the supposed impossibility of "inventing" the *flâneur*. The female version of the *flâneur* is, however, discussed in Anne Friedberg, *Window-Shopping: Cinema and the Postmodern* (Berkeley, Calif., 1993), p. 36.

6. Again, a discussion of women as entrepreneurs may be found in Muriel Joffe and Adele Lindenmeyr, "Daughters, Wives, and Partners: Women of the Moscow Merchant Elite," in *Merchant Moscow: Images of Russia's Vanished Bourgeoisie*, ed. James L. West and Iurii A. Petrov (Princeton, N.J., 1998), pp. 95–108.

7. "Sredi novinok," *KZh*, no. 9/10 (May 29, 1916), p. 52. An excerpt from this review appears in *Silent Witnesses*, pp. 326–28.

8. "*Zhizn za zhizn*," *VK*, no. 118 (June 1916), pp. 19–21.

9. *Silent Witnesses*, p. 328.

10. Bram Dijkstra, *Idols of Perversity: Fantasies of Feminine Evil in Fin-de-Siècle Culture* (New York and Oxford, 1986).

11. See, e.g., the full-page announcement for the film in *VK*, no. 121 (November 1916), p. 48.

12. The screenplay was published in *Pegasus*; see Zoia Barantsevich, "Umi-raiiushchii lebed," *Pegas*, no. 8 (August 1916), pp. 21–36.

13. See, e.g., *VK*, no. 123 (January 1917), cover and pp. 25–26.

14. For a complete discussion of this see Groberg, "The Shade of Lucifer's Dark Wing," pp. 99–134.

15. Tsivian, *Silent Witnesses*, pp. 422–26. This review includes a very nuanced and intelligent discussion of the acting in the film.

16. See Judith N. Goldberg, *Laughter through Tears: The Yiddish Cinema* (Rutherford, N.J., 1983), pp. 29–30, and Eric A. Goldman, *Visions, Images, and Dreams: Yiddish Film Past and Present* (Ann Arbor, Mich., 1983), pp. 1–2.

17. M. S. S., [letter to editor], *KZh*, no. 4 (February 23, 1911), pp. 11–12.

18. Tsivian, *Silent Witnesses*, pp. 102–04.

19. Ibid., p. 26.

20. According to *Silent Witnesses*, the name is "Chamberaud"; the title on the Library of Congress print gives it as "Champierre."

21. Bauer asked Kuleshov to replace Vladimir Strizhevskii at the last minute, since Strizhevskii had become ill. Kuleshov humorously recalled the humiliation

of his not-very-good performance as Enrico in his memoirs, excerpted in Tsivian, *Silent Witnesses*, p. 390.

INTERMISSION: FUN AND FOOLERY

1. Yuri Tsivian, *Silent Witnesses: Russian Films, 1908–1919*, ed. Paolo Cherchi Usai, Lorenzo Codelli, Carlo Montanaro, David Robinson (London and Pordenone, 1989), p. 140.

2. Ibid., pp. 180–82. These are the recollections of Sofia Goslavskaia.

3. See the full-page ad for Galinskii's act, *Artist i stsena*, no. 10 (1911), inside back cover, and cover of no. 11.

4. A contemporary reviewer described it as "vividly hilarious" (Tsivian, *Silent Witnesses*, p. 246).

5. My thanks to Josephine Woll for this observation.

6. Lenny Boger, "Ladislav Starewitch: Le magicien de Kovno," *Le cinéma russe avant la révolution* (Paris, 1989), pp. 73–85.

7. Tsivian, *Silent Witnesses*, pp. 200–202, the recollections of Boris Mikhin.

8. Ibid., p. 152. Of course we must keep in mind that this comment appeared in the *Cinematographic Courier*, the organ of the film's producer.

CHAPTER 7: HISTORY AND LITERATURE

1. A subject covered in detail in Denise Youngblood, *Soviet Cinema in the Silent Era, 1918–1935* (Ann Arbor, Mich., 1985 and Austin, Tex., 1991), and Youngblood, *Movies for the Masses: Popular Cinema and Soviet Society in the 1920s* (Cambridge, 1992), chap. 2.

2. As quoted in Yuri Tsivian, *Silent Witnesses: Russian Films, 1908–1919*, ed. Paolo Cherchi Usai, Lorenzo Codelli, Carlo Montanaro, David Robinson (London and Pordenone, 1989), p. 96.

3. As quoted in Ibid., p. 92. V. Akhramovich's diatribe appeared in St. Petersburg's *Teatralnye vedomosti* in 1910.

4. See Richard Taylor, *The Politics of the Soviet Cinema, 1917–1929* (Cambridge, 1979), and my *Soviet Cinema in the Silent Era, 1918–1935*.

5. Tsivian, *Silent Witnesses*, pp. 420–22.

6. E. Nagrodskaia, "Kinematograficheskiia goresti i radosti," *Kinematograf*, no. 1 (1915), pp. 5–7.

7. Tsivian, *Silent Witnesses*, p. 110.

8. B. S. Likhachev says the picture was not actually banned, but that it was little seen owing to fears of angering the Tolstoi family, *Kino v Rossii (1896–1926): Materialy k istorii russkogo kino*, vol. 1, *1896–1913* (Leningrad, 1927), pp. 104–6.

9. Tsivian, *Silent Witnesses*, p. 162.

10. V. R. Gardin, *Vospominaniia*, vol. 1, *1912–1921* (Moscow, 1949), pp. 121–22.

11. Veronin, "*Pikovaia dama*," *Pegas*, no. 4 (April 1916), pp. 91–97. The quotation appears on p. 96.

12. See, e.g., Tsivian, *Silent Witnesses*, pp. 256–58, for a sarcastic *Projector* review of *Children of the Age*.

13. G., "*Pikovaia dama*," *KZh* 7, no. 7/8 (April 30, 1916), p. 52, and on the same page, "Khronika."

14. This should not be confused with Iurii Zheliabuzhskii's 1925 version of the story, *The Collegiate Registrar*, also quite interesting; see Youngblood, *Movies for the Masses*, pp. 86–87.

CHAPTER 8: THE GUIDE TO LIFE

1. Discussed in Denise Youngblood, *Movies for the Masses: Popular Cinema and Soviet Society in the 1920s* (Cambridge, 1992), pp. 75–76.

2. See the discussion of the interior design aesthetics of the bourgeoisie in Rémy G. Saisselin, *The Bourgeois and the Bibelot* (New Brunswick, N.J., 1984), p. 29.

3. This phrase is borrowed from a chapter title in Rosalind H. Williams, *Dream Worlds: Mass Consumption in Late Nineteenth Century France* (Berkeley, Calif., 1982).

4. See, e.g., Williams, *Dream Worlds*, and Anne Friedberg, *Window-Shopping: Cinema and the Post-Modern* (Berkeley, Calif., 1993).

5. Even the "thick" intellectual journals like *Vestnik Evropy* carried car ads; see, e.g., no. 1 (1913), p. 460.

6. Saisselin, *Bourgeois and the Bibelot*, p. 63.

7. See the lively advertisements for beauty aids featured in 1914 issues of *Rodina*, an "illustrated journal for family reading."

8. See, e.g., advertisements in *Russkoe slovo* (December 4, 1913).

9. Katia, "Ta-Tao," *Sovremennaia zhenshchina*, no. 5 (June 10, 1914), p. 115.

10. See the feature on the tango in the tony *Stolitsa i usadba*, no. 1 (December 15, 1913), and the photograph of a couple dancing the tango in the illustrated magazine *Solntse Rossii*, no. 221 (May 1914), to give but two of many examples.

11. "Tango . . . tango," *KZh* 5, no. 4 (February 22, 1914), p. 41.

12. Yuri Tsivian offers an excellent discussion of the tango phenomenon in his "Russia, 1913: Cinema and the Cultural Landscape," in *Silent Film*, ed. Richard Abel (New Brunswick, N.J., 1996), pp. 203–8.

13. Bram Dijkstra, *Evil Sisters: The Threat of Female Sexuality and the Cult of Manhood* (New York, 1996), pp. 80–81 and passim.

14. Eric Naiman, *Sex in Public: The Incarnation of Early Soviet Ideology* (Princeton, N.J., 1997), p. 18. Naiman draws on Gasparov's ideas as expressed in the introduction to Alexander D. Nakhimovsky and Alice Stone Nakhimovsky, eds., *The Semiotics of Russian Cultural History* (Ithaca, N.Y., 1985).

CONCLUSION: MOVIES, MIRRORS, AND MODERNITY

1. Alek, "V chem gore," *Pegas*, no. 1 (November 1915), p. 81.

2. Jeffrey Brooks, *When Russia Learned to Read: Literacy and Popular Literature, 1861–1917* (Princeton, N.J., 1985); Louise McReynolds, *The News under Russia's Old Regime: The Development of a Mass-Circulation Press* (Princeton, N.J., 1991); Richard Stites, *Russian Popular Culture: Entertainment and Society since 1900* (Cambridge, 1992).

3. Referring again to Valentin T. Bill's *The Forgotten Class: The Russian Bourgeoisie from the Earliest Beginnings to 1900* (New York, 1959).

4. Irving Howe, ed. and intro., *The Idea of the Modern in Literature and the Arts* (New York, 1967).

5. Ibid., p. 12.

6. Ibid., pp. 14–15.

7. Ibid., p. 30.

8. Ibid., p. 13.

9. Ibid., p. 15.

10. Denise Youngblood, *Soviet Cinema in the Silent Era, 1918–1935* (Ann Arbor, Mich., 1985 and Austin, Tex., 1991), chap. 1 and passim.

11. Denise Youngblood, *Movies for the Masses: Popular Cinema and Soviet Society in the 1920s* (Cambridge, 1992), table 5, p. 40.

12. Ibid., table 7, p. 92.

13. Youngblood, *Soviet Cinema*, chap. 1; *Movies for the Masses*, chap. 2.

14. This suggestion is not original to this work, although it provides new evidence with which to support it. See, e.g., Richard Taylor, *The Politics of the Soviet Cinema, 1917–1929* (Cambridge, 1979).

SELECTED FILMOGRAPHY

Antosha Ruined by a Corset (*Antosha korset pogubil*), dir. Eduard Puchalski, prod. Lucifer, 1916.

Be Still, Sadness, Be Still (*Molchi, grust, molchi*), dir. Petr Chardynin, prod. Kharitonov, 1918.

Behind the Drawing Room Doors (*Za gostinoi dveriami*), dir. Ivan Lazarev and Petr Chardynin, prod. Khanzhonkov, 1913.

The Bourgeois, Enemy of the People (*Burzhui—vrag naroda*), dir. Petr Chardynin, prod. [unknown], 1917.

The Brigand Brothers (*Bratia razboiniki*), dir. Vasilii Goncharov, prod. Khanzhonkov, 1912.

The Cameraman's Revenge (*Mest kinematograficheskoe operatora*), dir. Wladyslaw Starewicz, prod. Khanzhonkov, 1912.

Child of the Big City (*Ditia bolshogo goroda*), dir. Evgenii Bauer, prod. Khanzhonkov, 1914.

Children of the Age (*Deti veka*), dir. Evgenii Bauer, prod. Khanzhonkov, 1915.

Christmas Eve (*Noch pered Rozhdestvom*), dir. Wladyslaw Starewicz, prod. Khanzhonkov, 1913.

Cold Showers (*Kholodnye dushi*), dir. Evgenii Bauer, prod. Khanzhonkov, 1914.

The Daughter-in-Law's Lover (*Snokhach*), dir. Aleksandr Ivanov-Gai, prod. Khanzhonkov, 1912.

Daydreams (*Grezy*), dir. Evgenii Bauer, prod. Khanzhonkov, 1915.

Dead Souls (*Mertvye dushi*), dir. Petr Chardynin, prod. Khanzhonkov, 1909.

The Defense of Sevastopol (*Oborona Sevastopolia*), dir. Vasilii Goncharov, prod. Khanzhonkov, 1912.

The Diligent Batman (*Userdnyi denshchik*), dir. N. Filippov, prod. Drankov, 1908.

The Dragonfly and the Ant (*Strekoza i muravei*), dir. Wladyslaw Starewicz, prod. Khanzhonkov, 1913.

Drama in a Gypsy Camp near Moscow (*Drama v tabore podmoskovnykh tsigan*), dir. Vladimir Siversen, prod. Khanzhonkov, 1908.

The Dying Swan (*Umiraiushchii lebed*), dir. Evgenii Bauer, prod. Khanzhonkov, 1916.

Father Sergius (*Otets Sergii*), dir. Iakov Protazanov, prod. Ermolev, 1917.

Granny of the Russian Revolution (*Babushka russkoi revoliutsii*), dir. Boris Svetlov, prod. Drankov, 1917.

The Idiot, dir. Petr Chardynin, prod. Khanzhonkov, 1910.

In a Busy Place (*Na boikom meste*), dir. Petr Chardynin, prod. Khanzhonkov, 1911.

Iurii Nagornyi, dir. Evgenii Bauer, prod. Khanzhonkov, 1916.

The Keys to Happiness (*Kliuchi schastia*), dir. Vladimir Gardin and Iakov Protazanov, prod. Thiemann & Reinhardt, 1913.

The King of Paris (*Korol Parizha*), dir. Evgenii Bauer and Olga Rakhmanova, prod. Khanzhonkov, 1917.

The Lady Orsha (*Boiarina Orsha*), dir. Petr Chardynin, prod. Khanzhonkov, 1910.

The Life and Death of Pushkin (*Zhizn i smert Pushkina*), dir. Vasilii Goncharov, prod. Gaumont-Moscow, 1910.

A Life for a Life (*Zhizn za zhizn*), dir. Evgenii Bauer, prod. Khanzhonkov, 1916.

The Lily of Belgium (*Liliia Belgii*), dir. Wladyslaw Starewicz, prod. Skobelev Committee, 1915.

Little Ellie (*Maliutka Elli*), dir. Iakov Protazanov, prod. Ermolev, 1918.

The Little House in Kolomna (*Domik v Kolomne*), dir. Petr Chardynin, prod. Khanzhonkov, 1913.

The Maidservant Jenny (*Gornichnaia Dzhenni*), dir. Iakov Protazanov, prod. Ermolev, 1917 or 1918.

Merchant Bashkirov's Daughter (*Doch kuptsa Bashkirova*), dir. Nikolai Larin, prod. Libken, 1913.

Merry Scenes from the Lives of Animals (*Veselye stsenki iz zhizni zhivotnykh*), dir. Wladyslaw Starewicz, prod. Khanzhonkov, 1912.

The One Thousand and Second Ruse (*Tysiacha vtoraia khitrost*), dir. Evgenii Bauer, prod. Khanzhonkov, 1915.

The Passing of the Great Old Man (*Ukhod velikogo startsa*), dir. Iakov Protazanov and Elizaveta Thiemann, prod. Thiemann & Reinhardt, 1912.

The Peasants' Lot (*Krestianskaia dolia*), dir. Vasilii Goncharov, prod. Khanzhonkov, 1912.

The Peddlers (*Korobeiniki*), dir. Vasilii Goncharov, prod. Khanzhonkov, 1910.

Play on Words (*Igra slov*), dir. [unknown], prod. Khanzhonkov, 1909.

Prince Serebrianyi (*Kniaz Serebrianyi*), dir. [unknown], prod. Khanzhonkov, 1914.

Princess Tarakanova (*Kniazhna Tarakanova*), dir. Kai Hansen and André Maître, prod. Pathé-Moscow, 1910.

The Queen of Spades (*Pikovaia dama*), dir. Petr Chardynin, prod. Khanzhonkov, 1910.

The Queen of Spades (*Pikovaia dama*), dir. Iakov Protazanov, prod. Ermolev, 1916.

The Revolutionary (*Revoliutsioner*), dir. Evgenii Bauer, prod. Khanzhonkov, 1917.

The Robber Vaska Churkin (*Razboinik Vaska Churkin*), dir. E. Petrov-Kraevskii, prod. Drankov, 1915.

Romance with Double Bass (*Roman s kontrabasom*), dir. Kai Hansen, prod. Pathé-Moscow, 1911.

Rusalka, dir. Vasilii Goncharov and Vladimir Siversen, prod. Khanzhonkov, 1910.

Sashka the Seminary Student (*Sashka seminarist*), dir. Czeslaw Sabinski, prod. Ermolev, 1914.

Satan Triumphant (*Satana likuiushchii*), dir. Iakov Protazanov, prod. Ermolev, 1917.

The Secret of House No. 5 (*Taina dom no. 5*), dir. Kai Hansen, prod. Pathé-Moscow, 1912.

Silent Witnesses (*Nemye svideteli*), dir. Evgenii Bauer, prod. Khanzhonkov, 1914.

A Sixteenth-Century Russian Wedding (*Russkaia svadba XVI stoletiia*), dir. Vasilii Goncharov, prod. Khanzhonkov, 1908.

Sonka the "Golden Hand" (*Sonka zolotaia ruchka*), dir. Iurii Iurevskii and Vladimir Kasianov, prod. Drankov, 1915.

The Sons of Peter Smirnov (*Petra Smirnova synovia*), dir. Zygmunt Wiesielowski and Grigorii Libken, prod. Libken, 1916.

The Sorrows of Sara (*Gore Sarry*), dir. Aleksandr Arkatov, prod. Khanzhonkov, 1913.

The Stationmaster (*Stantsionnyi smotritel*), dir. Aleksandr Ivanovskii, prod. Ermolev, 1918.

Stenka Razin, dir. V. Romashkov, prod. Drankov, 1908.

To Happiness (*K schastiu*), dir. Evgenii Bauer, prod. Khanzhonkov, 1917.

To Life (*L'Khaim*), dir. André Maître and Kai Hansen, prod. Pathé-Moscow, 1910.

Twilight of a Woman's Soul (*Sumerki zhenskoi dushi*), dir. Evgenii Bauer, prod. Khanzhonkov & Pathé-Moscow, 1913.

Vadim, dir. Petr Chardyinin, prod. Khanzhonkov, 1910.

The Wedding Day (*Den venchaniia*), dir. Evgenii Slavinskii, prod. Mintus, 1912.

The Wet Nurse (*Kormlitsa*), dir. Petr Chardynin, prod. Khanzhonkov, 1914.

SELECTED BIBLIOGRAPHY

PRIMARY SOURCES

Books

Bek-Nazarov, A. *Zapiski aktera i kinorezhissera*. Moscow, 1965.

Bottomore, Stephen, comp. *I Want to See This Annie Mattygraph: A Cartoon History of the Coming of the Movies*. Gemona, 1995.

Gardin, V. R. *Vospominaniia*. Vol. 1: *1912–1921*. Moscow, 1949.

Gardin, V. R., with T. D. Bulakh. *Zhizn i trud artista*. Moscow, 1960.

Kak ia stal rezhisserom. Moscow, 1946.

Khanzhonkova, V. D., comp. *Russkoe kino, 1908–1918*. Moscow, 1969.

Levitskii, A. A. *Rasskazy o kinematografe*. Moscow, 1964.

Listov, V. S., and E. S. Khokhlova. *Istoriia otechestvennogo kino: Dokumenty, memuary, pisma*. Vol. 1. Moscow, 1996.

Nabokov, Vladimir. *Speak, Memory: An Autobiography Revisited*. New York, 1967.

Pasternak, Alexander. *A Vanished Present: The Memoirs of Alexander Pasternak*. Ed. and trans. Ann Pasternak Slater. Ithaca, N.Y., 1989.

Paustovsky, Konstantin. *The Story of a Life*. Trans. Joseph Barnes. New York, 1965.

Perestiani, Ivan. *75 let zhizn v iskusstve*. Moscow, 1962.

Taylor, Richard, and Ian Christie, eds. *The Film Factory: Russian and Soviet Cinema in Documents, 1896–1939*. Trans. Richard Taylor. Cambridge, Mass., 1988.

Tsivian, Yuri. *Silent Witnesses: Russian Films, 1908–1919*. Ed. Paolo Cherchi Usai, Lorenzo Codelli, Carlo Montanaro, David Robinson. London and Pordenone, 1989.

Vishnevskii, Veniamin. *Khudozhestvennye filmy dorevoliutsionnoi Rossii: Filmograficheskoe opisanie*. Moscow, 1945.

Journals and Newspapers

Apollon
Artist i stsena
Ekran Rossii
Gazeta kopeika
Kinematograf
Kinemo
Kine-zhurnal (KZh)
Kulisy
Niva
Pegas
Proektor
Russkoe bogatstvo
Russkoe slovo (RS)
Sine-fono (SF)
Solntse Rossii
Sovremenny mir
Stolitsa i usadba
Teatr i kino
Vestnik Evropy
Vestnik kinematografii (VK)
Zritel

Articles

A. Kh. "Sinematograficheskii ekran." *SF*, no. 24 (September 15, 1912), p. 26.

A. Z. R. "Kinematograf." *Zritel* 1, no. 6 (July 17, 1905), pp. 5–7.

"Administrativnoe zakrytie teatrov: Osmotr sinematografov." *SF*, no. 12 (1911), pp. 10–12.

"Agitatsiia v kinematograf." *VK* 2, no. 47 (September 29, 1912), p. 10.

Alek. "V chem gore." *Pegas*, no. 1 (November 1915), pp. 81–82.

"Aleksandr Aleksandrovich Khanzhonkov." *KZh* 3, no. 18 (September 23, 1912), pp. 28–29.

"Anketa o dlinie lenty." *SF* 5, no. 5 (1911), pp. 15–16.

Arkasha. "Kinemo." *Teatr i kino*, no. 36 (September 3, 1916), p. 15.

Armando. "Novaia era." *SF*, no. 9/10 (May 16, 1915), pp. 63–66.

B. "Teatr i kinemo." *SF* 5, no. 2 (January 25, 1914), pp. 31–33.

Barantsevich, Zoia. "Umiraiiushchii lebed." *Pegas*, no. 8 (August 1916), pp. 21–36.

Binom. "Reklamnye pustotsvetyi (Stranichka iz istorii russkoi kinematografii)." *VK*, no. 121 (1916), pp. 3–6.

"Bologovskaia katastrofa." *Artist i stsena*, no. 4 (1911), p. 23.

Brailovskii, M. "Dvenadtsat millionov." *SF* 7, no. 3 (November 9, 1913), pp. 21–22.

Brailovskii, M. "Kinemo-kultura." *SF* 7, no. 1 (October 12, 1913), pp. 16–17.

Chardynin, P. [Untitled]. *Pegas*, no. 2 (December 1915), p. 102.

"Chto trebuet publika ot kinematografa." *VK* 1, no. 16 (August 1, 1911), pp. 22–23.

Chumachenko, Ada. "V kinematografe." *Russkoe bogatstvo*, no. 1 (1911), pp. 53–54.

D. K. "*Sovremennyi mir* o kinematografe." *SF*, no. 13 (April 1, 1912), pp. 14–15.

D. L. "Samoubiistvo mekhanikov." *SF*, no. 5 (1910), p. 6.

"Dmitrii Ivanovich Kharitonov." *KZh*, no. 20 (October 19, 1913).

Dolinin, L. "Teatr i ekran." *VK*, no. 116 (October 1, 1915), pp. 49–50.

"Drama i kinematograf." *KZh* 2, no. 14 (July 23, 1911), pp. 7–8.

Drug ekrana. "Velikii [*sic*] kinemo, kak istoricheskii dokument." *SF*, no. 11/12 (June 13, 1915), pp. 90–94.

Dubinovskii, B. "Russifikatsiia kinematografii (Po povodu stati M. Domanskago 'Russkaia kinematografiia')." *SF*, no. 7 (April 5, 1914), pp. 43–46.

Dubrovskii, M. "Russkii kino-akter." *KZh* 6, no. 13/14 (July 15, 1915), pp. 72–74.

"Dusha vremeni." *Niva*, no. 4 (1914), p. 67.

"Dvoistvennoe mnenie posviashchaetsia kritiku." *KZh*, no. 19 (1911), pp. 11–12.

"E. F. Bauer." *KZh*, no. 11/16 (August 30, 1917), p. 104.

[Editorial]. *Ekran Rossii*, no. 1 (1916), pp. 1–2.

[Editorial]. *Kinemo*, no. 12 (August 15, 1909), pp. 10–11.

[Editorial]. *KZh*, no. 24 (December 14, 1913), pp. 19–20.

[Editorial]. *Proektor*, no. 24 (December 25, 1916), p. 1.

[Editorial]. *Proektor*, no. 9/10 (May 1, 1917), pp. 1–2.

[Editorial]. *Proektor*, no. 17/18 (November 1917), pp. 1–2.

[Editorial]. *SF*, no. 5 (1910), p. 6.

[Editorial]. *SF* 3, no. 19 (July 1, 1910), pp. 3–4.

[Editorial]. *SF* 4, no. 10 (February 15, 1911), pp. 5–6.

[Editorial]. *SF* 5, no. 7 (1912), p. 1.

[Editorial]. *VK*, no. 14 (1911), p. 18.

[Editorial]. *VK* 1, no. 5 (February 19, 1911).

[Editorial]. *VK* 1, no. 24 (December 1, 1911), pp. 9–10.

[Editorial]. *VK* 4, no. 90 (May 22, 1914), p. 30.

Erbus, R. "Po kinemo-teatram." *KZh*, no. 23/24 (1915), pp. 94–96.

Falstaff. "'Geroi' ekrana." *SF* 7, no. 4 (November 23, 1913), pp. 21–22.

G. "*Pikovaia dama*." *KZh* 7, no. 7/8 (April 30, 1916), p. 52.

"G. I. Libken." *KZh*, no. 20 (October 19, 1913), p. 32.

"Golos i pressy." *VK*, no. 22 (1911), p. 12.

"Guliganstvo." *KZh*, no. 13 (July 12, 1914), p. 75.

I. G. "Futurizm i kinematograf." *SF*, no. 13/14 (July 15, 1915), pp. 74–77.

"I. M. Timonin." *KZh* 7, no. 1/2 (January 23, 1916), p. 65.

Iablonskii, Sergei. "V kinematograf!" *RS* (November 29, 1915).

"Iosif Nikolaevich Ermolev." *KZh* 3, no. 24 (December 23, 1912), p. 19.

"Iskusstvo vcherashnogo dnia (Beseda s K. S. Stanislavskim)." *SF*, no. 8 (April 19, 1914), pp. 34–35.

"Italianskaia fabrika Gloria." *KZh* 4, no. 6 (March 23, 1913), p. 20.

"Iubilei." *KZh* 8, no. 17/24 (December 30, 1917), pp. 44–45.

Iug, G. "Kinematograf, kak faktor mirovogo obedineniia." *SF*, no. 13 (July 12, 1914), pp. 55–57.

"Kakiia posledstviia katastrofy mozhno zhdat?" *SF*, no. 11 (1911), pp. 9–10.

"Katastrofa 'Grand Otel.'" *SF*, no. 3 (1910), p. 14.

"Katastrofa v Bologom." *SF*, no. 11 (1911), pp. 6–7.

Katia. "Ta-tao." *Sovremennaia zhenshchina*, no. 5 (June 10, 1914), p. 115.

"Khronika." *KZh* 3, no. 20 (October 23, 1912), p. 20.

"Khronika." *KZh* 4, no. 21 (November 2, 1913), p. 38.

"Khronika." *KZh* 5, no. 5 (March 8, 1914), p. 45.

"Khronika." *KZh* 6, no. 1/2 (January 17, 1915), p. 76.

"Khronika." *KZh* 6, no. 7/8 (April 18, 1915).

"Khronika." *KZh* 6, no. 9/10 (May 16, 1915), p. 79.

"Khronika." *KZh* 6, no. 17/18 (September 17, 1915), p. 94.

"Khronika." *KZh* 7, no. 7/8 (April 30, 1916), p. 52.

"Khronika." *SF* 7, no. 25/26 (September 27, 1914), p. 23.

"Khronika kino." *Teatr i kino* 2, no. 21 (May 21, 1916), p. 12.

Khudiakov, I. N. "'Detskiia' kartiny." *VK* 2, no. 45 (September 15, 1912), pp. 5–6.

[Khudiakov, I. N.] "Doklad I. N. Khudiakova: Defektivy sovremennogo kinematografa s khudozhestvennoi storonyi." *VK* 1, no. 17 (August 20, 1911), pp. 16–19.

"Kinematograf i revoliutsii." *Proektor*, no. 17/18 (November 1917), pp. 3–6.

"Kinematograf—vrag rysarei legkoi nazhivy." *VK*, no. 101 (November 1, 1914), p. 7.

Konenko, Vladimir. "'Russkiia' lenty na ekrane sinemo-teatrov." *SF* 3, no. 2 (October 15, 1909), pp. 5–6.

"Kto vinovat?" *SF*, no. 11 (1911), pp. 8–9.

Kumanov, D. "Pod svezhim vpechatleniem." *SF*, no. 11 (1911), p. 7.

L. Ia. "Demokratizatsii iskusstva." *Proektor*, no. 13/14 (July 15, 1916), pp. 3–4.

Letopolnyi, S. "Iskusstvo ili balagan?" *Kinemo*, no. 14 (September 15, 1909), pp. 1–2.

Lir. "O. V. Gzovskaia." *Kulisy* 1, no. 7 (February 12, 1917), p. 15.

M. S-ev. "Muzyka v elektro-teatrakh." *VK* 4, no. 83 (February 1, 1914), pp. 11–12.

M. S. S. [Letter to editor]. *KZh*, no. 4 (February 23, 1911), pp. 11–12.

"Maks Linder." *VK* 2, no. 54 (December 15, 1912), pp. 5–6.

"Maks Linder." *VK* 4, no. 98 (September 15, 1914), pp. 12–14.

"Maks Linder." *VK* 4, no. 99 (October 1, 1914), pp. 16–21.

"Maks Linder v Odesse." *SF* 7, no. 7 (January 4, 1914), p. 30.

"Maks Linder v Peterburge." *KZh*, no. 23 (December 1, 1913), pp. 28–30.

"Maks Linder zhiv!" *KZh*, no. 17/18 (September 20, 1914), pp. 30–31.

Maksimov, Vlad. "Pobeditel." *Teatr i kino* 1, no. 1 (November 15, 1915), p. 16.

Mars. "Na fabrikakh Akts. O-va A. Khanzhonkov i Ko." *KZh* 6, no. 9/10 (May 16, 1915), pp. 76–77.

Martov, Boris. "Iz knigi ekrana." *Proektor* 2, no. 15 (August 1, 1916), pp. 5–6.

Mashkov, Fedor. "Russkii kinematograf." *Proektor* 2, no. 4 (July 15, 1916), pp. 3–4.

Mavrich, I. "Maks v publike." *SF* 7, no. 5 (December 7, 1913), pp. 17–18.

Mavrich, I. "Ob universalnosti kino." *SF* 7, no. 8 (January 18, 1914), p. 17.

Mavrich, I. "S raznykh tochek zreniia." *SF*, no. 23 (August 3, 1913), pp. 20–22.

Mech, R. "Liubimtsy publiki." *SF* 2, no. 5 (December 1, 1908), pp. 4–5.

Mech, R. "V. Kholodnaia." *KZh*, no. 18 (July 28, 1916).

"Melochi." *VK*, no. 119 (August 1916), pp. 20–21.

Mikan. "A. O. Drankovu." *KZh* 6, no. 23/24 (December 19, 1915).

"Mneniia i fakty." *VK*, no. 51 (1912), p. 19.

Nagrodskaia, E. "Kinematograficheskiia goresti i radosti." *Kinematograf*, no. 1 (1915), pp. 5–7.

"Nashi teatry." *KZh*, no. 15 (1913), pp. 46–47.

"Nedelia Maksa Lindera v Moskve." *KZh*, no. 24 (December 14, 1913), pp. 26–28.

"Nemonopolist *Oborona Sevastopolia*," *SF* 5, no. 5 (1911).

Nero. "U ekrana." *KZh* 6, no. 13/14 (July 15, 1915), pp. 63–68.

Nikesz. "Teatr i kinematograf (Mysli vslukh)." *SF*, no. 20 (October 19, 1913), pp. 25–26.

Nikolskii, S. M. "Budte gramotnyi!" *Proektor*, no. 6 (March 15, 1916), pp. 2–3.

Nikolskii, S. M. "O nashikh 'shedevrakh.'" *SF* 6, no. 1 (October 1, 1912), pp. 18–19.

Nikolskii, S. M. "Sinematografii pechat." *SF*, no. 8 (1911), pp. 6–7.

Novus, Valentin. "Kinematograf." *SF*, no. 27 (September 28, 1913), p. 38.

"Novye teatry." *SF* 6, no. 23 (August 23, 1913), p. 34.

"Obozrenie teatrov." *Artist i stsena*, no. 16 (1911), p. 22.

Obozrevatel. "Po gorodom i teatram." *SF*, no. 9 (1911), p. 18.

"Odessa i kinematograf." *Teatr i kino*, no. 28 (January 9, 1916), p. 12.

"Otkrytie teatra." *Artist i stsena*, no. 18 (1911), p. 21.

Pal, I. "Kinematografiia v Rossii." *KZh*, no. 11 (1912), pp. 10–13.

"Pamiati Maks Linder." *SF* 7, no. 23/24 (August 23, 1914), pp. 17–18.

Pathé Frères. *Ezhenedelnik novostei* 1, no. 20 (December 7, 1910).

"Pavel Gustavovich Timan." *KZh* 3, no. 17. (September 8, 1912), pp. 33–34.

Pilot. "Frantsuzskaia illiustratsiia russkoi zhizni." *Kinemo*, no. 17 (November 1, 1909), pp. 7–9.

"Pishite gramotno!" *SF*, no. 23 (September 1, 1912), pp. 16–17.

"Po kinemo-teatram." *KZh* 6, no. 21/22 (1915), pp. 75–76.

"Po kino-teatram." *KZh* 7, no. 1/2 (January 23, 1916), pp. 79–80.

"Postanovka *Sanina* zapreshchena." *SF*, no. 24 (August 31, 1913).

"Pozharnye deiateli o protivopozharnykh merakh." *SF*, no. 12 (1911), pp. 10–12.

"Proekt pravil razrabotannykh v Ministerstve vnutrennykh del dlia uvelicheniia bezopasnosti v sinematografakh." *SF*, no. 13 (1911), pp. 7–8.

"Provintsiia." *VK* 1, no. 11 (May 16, 1911), p. 11.

"Publika i kartiny s dlinnym metrazhem." *VK* 1, no. 16 (August 1, 1911), p. 24.

"*Quo vadis?* — u nas i za granitsei." *VK* 3, no. 7 (April 6, 1913), pp. 4–5.

Radlov, Sergei. "Ugroza kinematografa." *Apollon*, no. 8/10 (1917), p. 46.

Raevskii. "Akts. O-vo Khanzhonkov." *Kulisy* 1, no. 8 (February 19, 1917), p. 15.

"Reklama smerti." *VK* 3, no. 10 (May 18, 1913), p. 14.

Riaspov, I. "Kinematografy v Rossii." *VK*, no. 10 (1914), p. 10.

"Russkii amerikanets." *Teatr i kino*, no. 41 (October 8, 1916).

S. "Novoe v zhizni." *VK* 2, no. 32 (April 1, 1912), pp. 23–24.

S. N. "Kinematograf osvobozhdennoi Rossii." *Proektor*, no. 7/8 (April 1, 1917), pp. 1–4.

S-on, B. "Kinematograf kak predovestnik mirovogo ideia." *SF*, no. 8 (April 19, 1914), pp. 38–39.

"Samoubiistvo." *SF*, no. 22 (July 20, 1913), p. 25.

"Samoubiistvo pianista." *SF* 6, no. 16 (1913), p. 26.

"Samoubiistvo v sinematografe." *SF* 4, no. 8 (January 15, 1911), p. 1.

"Sharl Pate (otets kinematografii) v Moskve." *KZh* 3, no. 10 (May 23, 1912), pp. 18–20.

Shein-baum. "Promakhi rezhisserov i zriteli." *SF*, no. 18 (1911), pp. 9–10.

Shimanskii, S. "Podmostki i ekran." *Kinematograf*, no. 1 (1915), p. 15.

Shtokfish, A. "Kinematografiia—Nota bene." *Pegas*, no. 2 (December 1915), pp. 53–55.

Shulgovskii, N. "V kinematografe." *Niva*, no. 33 (1909).

"Sinematograf i gigena (K voprosu o vliianii sinematografa na glaza." *SF* 2, no. 23 (September 1, 1908), pp. 6–7.

"Sinematograf v Iasnoi Poliane." *RS* (January 9, 1910), p. xx.

"Skandal iz-za shliapy." *SF*, no. 3 (1910), p. 14.

Slezkinskaia, Z. "Kinematograf i russkaia zhizn." *VK* 2, no. 47 (September 29, 1912), pp. 3–4.

"Smert Kiki." *VK* 1, no. 22 (November 2, 1911), p. 18.

Sorin, Aleksandr. "V. V. Maksimov and I. I. Mozzhukhin." *Teatr i kino* 2, no. 1 (January 1, 1916), p. 18.

Sorskii. "Khronika." *SF* 4, no. 16 (May 15, 1911), p. 9.

Soubrette. "Diseuses." *Artist i stsena*, no. 4 (1911), p. 23.

"Sredi gazet i zhurnalov." *VK*, no. 119 (August 1916), pp. 18–20.

"Sredi novinok," *KZh*, no. 19 (September 5, 1913), p. 40.

"Sredi novinok." *KZh*, no. 9/10 (May 29, 1916), p. 52.

"Stydno!" *VK*, no. 1 (1910), pp. 7–8.

"Tango . . . tango." *KZh* 5, no. 4 (February 22, 1914), p. 41.

"Teatr i kinematograf." *VK* 4, no. 87 (April 1, 1914), p. 19.

"Teatralnaia Moskva." *SF*, no. 13 (1911), pp. 15–16.

Tolstaia, Aleksandra. [Letter to editor]. *VK* 1, no. 19 (September 16, 1911), p. 22.

Tsyperovich, G. "Kinematograf." *Sovremennyi mir*, no. 1 (1912), pp. 181–210.

Turkin, Nikandr. "Zapisnaia knizhka Pegasa." *Pegas*, no. 11 ([November 1916]?), p. 84.

Turkin, Valentin. *See* Veronin.

Um-skii, S. "Spravka o *Kabiri*." *Solntse Rossii*, no. 346 (October 1916).

Um-skii, S. "Spravka o *Kabiri*." *VK*, no. 117 (May 6, 1916), pp. 5–8.

"Universalnyi kinematograf." *KZh*, no. 18 (September 23, 1913), p. 41.

V. D. "Mutnaia voda — iz sluchainogo khlama." *Proektor* 1, no. 3 (November 1, 1915), p. 7.

"V odnom moskovskom elektro-teatre." *SF* 5, no. 24 (1912), p. 28.

"V zhurnalakh i gazetakh." *Pegas*, no. 2 (December 1915), pp. 73–74.

Valov, P. "Puti nemogo." *Proektor*, no. 13/14 (July 15, 1916), pp. 6–7.

Vasilevskii, I. M. "(Ne bukva) Ego velichestvo — kinematograf." *Kinematograf*, no. 2 (1915), pp. 6–8.

Vega. "Kinematograf v Rossii i na Zapade (Beseda s V. V. Maksimovym). *KZh*, no. 23/24 (December 23, 1914).

Vega. "Nado gotovitsia." *KZh* 6, no. 3/4 (February 14, 1915), pp. 64–67.

Vega. "Nado gotovitsia." *KZh* 6, no. 5/6 (March 20, 1915), pp. 112–17.

Vega. "Trezvaia Rossiia i kinematograf." *KZh* 6, nos. 1–2 (January 17, 1915), p. 59.

[Verbitskaia, A.]. "A. Verbitskaia o kartine *Kliuchi schastia* i o kinematografe: Otkrytoe pismo." *SF* 7, no. 1 (October 12, 1913), p. 28.

Verbitskaia, A.. [Letter to editor]. *KZh*, no. 15/16 (August 15, 1915), p. 135.

Veronin [Valentin Turkin]. "*Pikovaia dama*." *Pegas*, no. 4 (April 1916), pp. 91–97.

Vilde, N. "Kinovlechenie i kinopaseniia." *VK*, no. 116 (October 1, 1915), pp. 42–44.

"Voennyi nalog na bilety." *Proektor*, no. 7/8 (April 10, 1916), pp. 8–9.

"*Voina i mir* na ekrane." *KZh*, no. 5/6 (March 20, 1915), pp. 131–35.

Volin, Iu. "Svoim putem." *Kinematograf*, no. 1 (1915), pp. 14–15.

Vorwarts. "Maks." *KZh*, no. 24 (December 14, 1913), pp. 23–24.

Voznesenskii, A. "Futurizm na ekrane." *VK*, no. 116 (October 1, 1915), pp. 38–40.

W. "Banket v chest Maksa Lindera." *RS* (December 4, 1913).

Z. "Russkoe proizvodstvo." *KZh* 5, no. 6 (March 22, 1914), p. 42.

"Za piat let." *SF* 6, no. 1 (October 1, 1912), pp. 14–15.

"Zagodochnoe samoubiistvo v teatre." *SF* 7, no. 21/22 (August 2, 1914), p. 39.

Zak, A. I. "Kinematograf, kniga, i deti." *Vestnik evropy*, no. 9 (1914), pp. 276–95.

"Zhizn za zhizn." *VK*, no. 118 (June 1916), pp. 19–21.

SECONDARY SOURCES
Books

Abel, Richard. *The Cine Goes to Town: French Cinema, 1896–1914*. Berkeley, Calif., 1994.

Abel, Richard. *French Cinema: The First Wave, 1915–1929*. Princeton, N.J., 1984.

Albera, François. *Albatros: des Russes à Paris, 1919–1929*. Milan and Paris, 1995.

Bater, James. *St. Petersburg: Industrialization and Change*. Montreal, 1976.

Bill, Valentin T. *The Forgotten Class: The Russian Bourgeoisie from the Earliest Beginnings to 1900*. New York, 1959.

Bradley, Joseph. *Muzhik and Muscovite: Urbanization in Late Imperial Russia*. Berkeley, Calif., 1985.

Brooks, Jeffrey. *When Russia Learned to Read: Literacy and Popular Literature, 1861–1917*. Princeton, N.J., 1985.

Brower, Daniel. *The Russian City between Tradition and Modernity, 1850–1900*. Berkeley, Calif., 1990.

Charney, Leo, and Vanessa R. Schwartz, eds. *Cinema and the Invention of Modern Life*. Berkeley, Calif., 1995.

Clowes, Edith W., Samuel D. Kassow, and James L. West. *Between Tsar and People: Educated Society and the Quest for Public Identity in Late Imperial Russia*. Princeton, N.J., 1991.

DeBauche, Leslie Midkiff. *Reel Patriotism: The Movies and World War I*. Madison, Wisc., 1997.

Dijkstra, Bram. *Evil Sisters: The Threat of Female Sexuality and the Cult of Manhood*. New York, 1996.

Dijkstra, Bram. *Idols of Perversity: Fantasies of Feminine Evil in Fin-de-Siècle Culture*. New York and Oxford, 1986.

Engelstein, Laura. *The Keys to Happiness: Sex and the Search for Modernity in Fin-de-Siècle Russia*. Ithaca, N.Y., 1992.

Friedberg, Anne. *Window-Shopping: Cinema and the Post-Modern*. Berkeley, Calif., 1993.

Gay, Peter. *The Bourgeois Experience: Victoria to Freud*. Vol. 1: *The Education of the Senses*. New York and Oxford, 1984.

Ginzburg, S. *Kinematografiia dorevoliutsionnoi Rossii*. Moscow, 1963.

Goldberg, Judith N. *Laughter through Tears: The Yiddish Cinema*. Rutherford, N.J., 1983.

Goldman, Eric A. *Visions, Images, and Dreams: Yiddish Film Past and Present.* Ann Arbor, Mich., 1983.

Hamm, Michael F. *The City in Late Imperial Russia.* Bloomington, Ind., 1986.

Hays, H. R. *Dangerous Sex: The Myth of Feminine Evil.* New York, 1969.

Howe, Irving, ed. and intro. *The Idea of the Modern in Literature and the Arts.* New York, 1967.

Iakubovich, O. A. *Ivan Mozzhukhin: Rasskaz o pervom russkom kinoaktere.* Moscow, 1975.

Jahn, Hubertus F. *Patriotic Culture in Russia during World War I.* Ithaca, N.Y., 1995.

Kuhn, Thomas S. *The Structure of Scientific Revolutions.* Chicago, 1962.

Lebedev, N. A. *Ocherk istorii kino SSSR.* Vol. 1: *Nemoe kino.* Moscow, 1947.

Lenin, V. I. *The Development of Capitalism in Russia.* Moscow, 1974.

Levine, Lawrence. *Highbrow/Lowbrow: The Emergence of Cultural Hierarchy in America.* Cambridge, Mass., 1988.

Leyda, Jay. *Kino: A History of the Russian and Soviet Film.* New York, 1960.

Likhachev, B. S. *Kino v Rossii (1896–1926): Materialy k istorii russkogo kino.* Vol. 1: *1896–1913.* Leningrad, 1927.

Lincoln, W. Bruce. *Between Heaven and Hell: The Story of a Thousand Years of Artistic Life in Russia.* New York, 1998.

McReynolds, Louise. *The News under Russia's Old Regime: The Development of a Mass-Circulation Press.* Princeton, N.J., 1991.

Naiman, Eric. *Sex in Public: The Incarnation of Early Soviet Ideology.* Princeton, N.J., 1997.

Neuberger, Joan. *Hooliganism: Crime, Culture, and Power in St. Petersburg, 1900– 1914.* Berkeley, Calif., 1993.

Paperno, Irina. *Suicide as a Cultural Institution in Dostoevsky's Russia.* Ithaca, N.Y., 1997.

Rosenthal, Bernice Glatzer, ed. *Nietzsche in Russia.* Princeton, N.J., 1986.

Saisselin, Rémy G. *The Bourgeois and the Bibelot.* New Brunswick, N.J., 1984.

Sobolev, R. *Liudi i filmy russkogo dorevoliutsionnogo kino.* Moscow, 1961.

Stites, Richard. *Russian Popular Culture: Entertainment and Society since 1900.* Cambridge, 1992.

Taylor, Richard. *The Politics of the Soviet Cinema, 1917–1929.* Cambridge, 1979.

Thompson, Kristin. *Exporting Entertainment: America in the World Film Market, 1907–34.* London, 1985.

Tsivian, Yuri. *Early Cinema in Russia and Its Cultural Reception.* Ed. Richard Taylor. Trans. Alan Bodger. London, 1994.

Walicki, A. *The Controversy over Capitalism: Studies in the Social Philosophy of the Russian Populists.* Oxford, 1969.

West, James L., and Iurii A. Petrov. *Merchant Moscow: Images of Russia's Vanished Bourgeoisie.* Princeton, N.J., 1998.

Williams, Rosalind H. *Dream Worlds: Mass Consumption in Late Nineteenth Century France.* Berkeley, Calif., 1982.

Wirtschafter, Elise Kimerling. *Social Identity in Imperial Russia.* De Kalb, Ill., 1997.

Youngblood, Denise J. *Movies for the Masses: Popular Cinema and Soviet Society in the 1920s.* Cambridge, 1992.

Youngblood, Denise J. *Soviet Cinema in the Silent Era, 1918–1935.* Ann Arbor, Mich., 1985; Austin, Tex., 1991.

Ziukov, B. B., ed. *Vera Kholodnaia: K 100-letiiu so dnia rozhdeniia.* Moscow, 1995.

Articles

Albera, François. "Cinéma russe, des primitifs aux futuristes." *Cahiers du cinéma*, no. 427 (January 1990).

Boger, Lenny. "Ladislav Starewitch: Le magicien de Kovno." In *Le cinéma russe avant la révolution.* Paris, 1989.

Carlson, Maria. "Fashionable Occultism: Spiritualism, Theosophy, Freemasonry, and Hermeticism in Fin-de-Siècle Russia." In *The Occult in Russian and Soviet Culture*, ed. Bernice Glatzer Rosenthal. Ithaca, N.Y., 1997.

Corrsin, Stephen D. "Warsaw: Poles and Jews in a Conquered City." In *The City in Late Imperial Russia*, ed. Michael F. Hamm. Bloomington, Ind., 1986.

Glovatskii, B. "Odin iz pervykh." *Iskusstvo kino*, no. 4 (1960).

Groberg, Kristi A. "'The Shade of Lucifer's Dark Wing': Satanism in Silver Age Russia." In *The Occult in Russian and Soviet Culture*, ed. Bernice Glatzer Rosenthal. Ithaca, N.Y., 1997.

Hamm, Michael F. "Continuity and Change in Late Imperial Kiev." In *The City in Late Imperial Russia*, ed. Michael F. Hamm. Bloomington, Ind., 1986.

Joffe, Muriel, and Adele Lindenmeyr. "Daughters, Wives, and Partners: Women of the Moscow Merchant Elite." In *Merchant Moscow: Images of Russia's Vanished Bourgeoisie*, ed. James L. West and Iurii A. Petrov. Princeton, N.J., 1998.

Kenez, Peter. "Russian Patriotic Films." In *Film and the First World War*, ed. Karel Dibbets and Bert Hogenkamp. Amsterdam, 1995.

Likhachev, B. S. "Materialy k istorii kino v Rossii (1914–1916)." *Iz istorii kino.* Vol. 3. Moscow, 1960.

Orlovsky, Daniel. "The Lower Middle Strata in Revolutionary Russia." In *Between Tsar and People: Educated Society and the Quest for Public Identity in Late Imperial Russia*, ed. Edith W. Clowes, Samuel D. Kassow, and James L. West. Princeton, N.J., 1991.

Robinson, David. "Evgenii Bauer and the Cinema of Nikolai II." *Sight and Sound* (Winter 1989/80), p. 54.

Singer, Ben. "Modernity, Hyperstimulus, and the Rise of Popular Sensational-ism." In *Cinema and the Invention of Modern Life*, ed. Leo Charney and Vanessa R. Schwartz. Berkeley, Calif., 1995.

Skinner, Frederick W. "Odessa and the Problem of Urban Modernization." In *The City in Late Imperial Russia*, ed. Michael F. Hamm. Bloomington, Ind., 1986.

Thompson, Kristin. "The International Exploration of Cinematic Expressivity." In *Film and the First World War*, ed. Karel Dibbets and Bert Hogenkamp. Amsterdam, 1995.

Tsivian, Yuri. "Russia, 1913: Cinema and the Cultural Landscape." In *Silent Film*, ed. Richard Abel. New Brunswick, N.J., 1996.

Yangirov, Rashit. "Vassili Gontcharov." In *Le cinéma russe avant la révolution*. Paris, 1989.

Zorkaia, Neia. "Les stars du muet." In *Le cinéma russe avant la révolution*. Paris, 1989.

INDEX